Good War, Great Men.

313th Machine Gun Battalion

of

World War I

Andrew J. Capets

313

MACHINE GUN BATTALION

Good War, Great Men. The 313th Machine Gun Battalion. 1st edition.

Front Cover: A portion of a larger photo taken of the 313th Machine Gun Battalion at Camp Lee, Virginia, 1918, (courtesy Lewis McComb).

Published with CreateSpace, On-Demand Publishing, LLC.

For photos, maps, and other items related to the history of the 313th Machine Gun Battalion, please visit
goodwargreatmen.com

ISBN-10: 0692951024

ISBN-13: 978-0692951026

This book is dedicated to
Grandpap
and the men of the
313th Machine Gun Battalion
who served in the Great War.

The sun came up and shone down on us through the trees and we turned lazily in our blankets and looked up at the blue sky and said it was a good war.

Minard Hamilton
September 3, 1918

CONTENTS

ACKNOWLEDGMENTS

The completion of this project would not have been possible without the generosity of the following people who shared their letters, journals, documents, photographs and stories about the members of the 313th Machine Gun Battalion: Jim Agostine, Dr. Lee S. Anthony, John H. Armstrong III, Michael E. Bigelow, Amber Brown, John Bryne, John Capets, Victor Capets, Roger Carter, Christopher S. Condlin, Jon Corklin, Ariel Dougherty, Mary C. Farach-Carson, Linda Galmish, Geoff Gentilini, Rachael Goldberg, Francis Grandinetti, Kristin Grandinetti, Mina Hamilton, Dr. Richard Hamilton, Marilyn Holland, John Kean, Mark J. Leinhauser, Otto P. Leinhauser III, Molly Lundquist, Alexander D. MacWilliam Jr., Lewis McComb, Leonard Pokriva, Carol Ray Porch, Jan Pringle, Bill Schroh Jr., Bruce & Cecelia Smith, Andy Specht, Dr. Chris Thomas, Joyce Clarkson-Veilleux, and Page Wilson; you have my heartfelt thanks. And to Sandra Ruttan and Pretti Singh for help with book arrangement and editing.

Most importantly, I wish to thank my loving wife, Mariann, and our two boys, Joshua and Jacob. You've provided me with constant support and encouragement throughout this project. I am truly blessed.

GLOSSARY AND ABBREVIATIONS

Archie Anti-aircraft fire or artillery piece

A.E.F. American Expeditionary Forces

Battery Organization of artillery pieces

Billet Living quarters usually with a roof overhead

Blighty Injury or wound

Bivvy Short for bivouac, a temporary outside encampment

Boche A derisive term referring to a German soldier

C'est la guerre French meaning "it's the war" or "such is war"

Cooties Slang term used by the troops referring to lice

Corps Organization consisting of two or more Divisions

D Day The day an attack or an operation is to begin

Digger Slang term for the Austrailian troops

Dirigible An air ship or balloon that can be steered

Fritz Nickname for King Frederick II of Prussia and Frederick III, German Emperor; also German soldier

F.O.P. Forward Observation Post

H Hour The time of day for an attack to begin

Hardtack Biscuit or cracker

Hub hub Artillery pieces lined up wheel hub to wheel hub

Hun derogatory nickname to describe the German Army

Jerry Slang name for a German soldier

Limbers Wheeled cart for carrying machine guns/ammunition

Lorry Motor vehicle for transporting troops or supplies

N.C.O. Non-Commissioned Officer

Non-com Non-Commissioned Officer

P.C. Post of Command

Pas bon French for "not good"

Platoon subdivision of a Company forming a tactical unit typically commanded by a lieutenant

Polack a person from Poland or of Polish descent

Poilu Slang term for French infantryman

Puttee Cloth worn tightly around the leg below the knee

R.O.T.C. Reserve Officers Training Corps

Sam Browne Leather belt supported with a strap passing diagonally over the shoulder; part of an officer's uniform

Striker Naval slang for crew, non-rate, or on the job training

Sturmtruppen German *Stoßtruppen* assault troops; Storm Troops

Tres bein   French for "very good"

Tout de suite   French for "immediate or happening now"

Tommy   Slang term for British soldier

Turcos   Algerian light infantry serving in the French Army

W.A.A.C.   Women's Army Auxiliary Corps

Whiz Bang   High speed shell heard as it flies through the air

Wops   Racial slur; reference an Italian or southern European; without passport paper, working on pavement

Zero Hour   The time an attack would commence

5.9 and 4.2   German artillery shells; sizes 5.9 and 4.2 inch.

Examples of the unit sizes:

80th Division comprised of 28,105 men on November 11, 1918:
(991 officers and 27,114 enlisted)

159th Infantry Brigade comprised these 3 units on July 31, 1918:
317th Infantry Regiment had 3,399 men
318th Infantry Regiment had 3,256 men
313th Machine Gun Battalion had 698 men

313th Machine Gun Battalion onboard the *USS Mercury* May 1918:

Headquarters Company	50
A Company	175
B Company	169
C Company	176
D Company	177
Medical Detachment	17
Total men	764

INTRODUCTION

A small crowd gathered in a community park for an annual Memorial Day observation. Neighbors were milling around, shaking hands and exchanging pleasantries with one another. A gentleman stood near a podium making last minute notes on his index cards. Members of the American Legion were arranging folding wooden chairs to accommodate the growing size of the crowd. An eight-year-old boy worked his way from the back of the crowd up to the front of the gathering where four monuments stood at the center of the arranged chairs. An older couple stood in front of the World War I monument looking at the names, occasionally pointing when they recognized a name on the list. The monument was a massive, rough chiseled granite stone standing about 5 feet tall and about 4 feet wide. It held a bronze plaque with an American eagle stretching its wings over top of a list of about 120 names arranged in three columns and listed in alphabetical order. In the right column, two names stood out from the others. These two names were not cast with the original bronze but were later added to the plaque using rectangular plates and fastened with screws. The boy gently rubbed his fingers across one of these names. He used his thumb to trace the individual letters of the name that was familiar to him. A voice came across the PA system, "Please take your seats."

The American Legion Commander adjusted the microphone as the crowd settled into their places. The boy left the front of the monument and joined his family near the back of the crowd. He leaned against a large tree, only occasionally paying attention to the gentleman behind the podium. As his attention drifted, he spotted a large black ant working its way across the bark of the tree. The boy was now more interested in the travels of this creature than what was being said at the podium. As he followed the path of the ant he heard, "Oh, Andy Capets." The boy looked up, thinking he was caught not paying attention. "Andy, we almost forgot you again." The boy then realized that the man was not talking about him, but was looking at his grandfather.

All eyes in the crowd were now turned on an older gentleman, a World War I veteran, sitting comfortably in his wooden chair. The veteran politely nodded at the Legion Commander and remained stoic while momentarily becoming the center of attention. The Legion commander was acknowledging the presence of all the World War I veterans who were in attendance at this gathering. The veteran remained humbly silent when his name was initially not mentioned in the roll call. Someone in the crowd recognized that the Commander forgot to mention this veteran by name. The error was corrected, but it underscored a mistake that was made many years earlier.

The young boy instinctively recognized the meaning behind the Commander's statement, "we almost forgot you again." He knew that statement was referring to the fact that his grandfather's name was not cast on the original 1919 plaque, requiring the name to be added later. The boy realized that his grandfather was nearly forgotten again during the ceremony, and yet he was sitting right there, among all the other veterans.

That minor episode was brief, but it made a significant impression on that young boy in 1975. I know this because I can remember that ceremony as if it happened only months ago. I was named after my grandfather, Andrew Capets, who everyone called Andy. I can't explain why that one moment has been etched in my memory for so many years. Perhaps it was simply a brief incident of recognition, magnified in the eyes of an eight-year-old boy, watching the family patriarch recognized by others in the community.

I do remember being delighted to go into that park and see 'my name' cast in bronze, even though I knew it wasn't 'my name.' It gave me a little more attention when my classmates and I walked from our school to the park for a mini fieldtrip. My peers were familiar with the name, and it didn't hurt that it stood out from the other ones on the memorial. While I enjoyed the ego boost, I still wondered why my grandfather's name was forgotten in the first place.

When I ponder the reasons why I put this book together, I am drawn back to that moment as a young boy in the park. I've carried that brief incident with me for many years. No one wants to be forgotten, and I doubt my grandfather even gave that brief moment in the park a second thought. However, as a child, impressions can be carried for years, and it was something about that feeling of exclusion that stuck with me. I wanted my grandfather to feel included and acknowledged for his actions.

Many years later, I never imagined that my journey into the history of my grandfather's Battalion would lead me to cross paths with so many other people that shared a similar interest, a desire to ensure that the service of their relatives would not be forgotten. I met individuals who also wanted to know more about their own family member's service, and through their generosity, gave me the privilege of sharing their family history, and the history of this Battalion through this book.

My journey into the background of this Battalion actually started when I stood in the Soldiers and Sailors Hall in Pittsburgh, Pennsylvania, staring into a display case of World War I relics. Behind the glass were faded khaki uniforms, the familiar Doughboy helmet, and a variety of old military items on display arranged to give the visitor a snapshot of what the men of the Great War used in their daily life. Prominently displayed in one section was a 1917 type machine gun, tripod, and water hose that led to the gun's water jacket. My father, Victor Capets said, "That's the kind of machine gun my father shot when he was in France." I repeated those words in my head because I had never pondered this before. It was a story unfamiliar to me. Of course I knew that my grandfather was in the Army, but I never considered what he did during his service, or the details of his foreign service. It seemed so obvious at the time that I should have made the connection, but admittedly, I never contemplated the thoughts of my grandfather fighting on a battlefield. The notion of him as a young man fighting a war, let alone his using that style of machine gun, was far from my thoughts. I just stood there staring at this weapon.

One of my first thoughts was fixated on the fact that this object was principally designed to inflict multiple casualties quickly. Plain and simple, it was a device made to kill. The idea of my grandfather turning this machine onto another human was extremely hard to grasp.

I was at the Memorial Hall that evening for a fundraiser to support the building of the National Museum of the Marine Corps in Virginia. The topic of our military service and the need to honor our history was in my immediate conscience, but for some unknown reason, the subject now seemed so foreign and the questions unexpected.

The few questions I initially asked came with few answers. We walked away from the display case, but my thoughts were still on the images of that machine gun. The gun looked heavy and my grandfather was a slender man and short in stature. What did he do in France? Where did he go? A family figure from my childhood that everyone adored and spoke so highly of, was suddenly a mysterious person that I knew little about.

I thought about the familiar military photograph that hung on my grandfather's wall for as long as I can remember. It was a Battalion photo of nearly two hundred men taken while the unit was in France. The background reveals a French hotel with the name *Hotel De Le Place Bordeau* painted on the outside of the building. As young children running around our grandparent's house, my cousins and I could easily stop and point out our Grandpap in the photo. He looked nothing like the old man we knew, which is probably why the thoughts to connect him with those events were so difficult. However, his service in the war was an important part of his life that caused him to keep that daily reminder hanging in his home. He often attended the Battalion reunions in Erie, Pennsylvania, and was a member of the local American Legion Post. He was undoubtedly proud to let people know that he served, all while revealing very little to his family about that year spent in France.

I asked those who knew my grandfather if they were ever told stories about his service. My Uncle Edward Capets remembered his father being so cold one night in France that he slept on a pile of manure just to keep warm. My Uncle Leonard Pokriva recalled a story of my grandfather being gassed during the war, but the details he was given were few, and he could only reiterate that his father-in-law rarely discussed the war with anyone. My Uncle John Capets told me that his father was running to take cover during a battle and jumped into a hole; he landed on top of the body of a dead solider. I've tried to imagine that scene. He was running and leaping to keep himself alive, and came face to face with the absolute horrors of war. What triggered that memory to cause him to share a singular event with his son? How often were those memories recalled, and how was he able to suppress his thoughts for years without feeling the need to share more with his family?

A portrait of my grandfather in his uniform hangs on the wall of my parents' home and reveals the shoulder patch of the 80th Division (see the back cover of this book). One of the first books I read to learn more about his service was written by Private Rush Stephenson Young (1894-1969), called *Over the top with the 80th: 1917-1919*. Private Young, a member of the 318th Infantry, was in the same Division as my grandfather and wrote these words, "The woods were strewn with dead and wounded. The ones who had been shell shocked were screaming like maniacs, and the wounded, groaning in pain. Further back in the woods could be heard the horses and mules that had been hit, nickering and groaning. If this had lasted much longer we would all have been crazy; it was getting on my nerves" (Young).

Young described some of the hardest days of fighting experienced in the Meuse-Argonne, and my grandfather's Battalion was on that same battlefield supporting Young's regiment. The descriptions written by Young answered some of my questions about wanting to know what my grandfather may have witnessed in France, but I wanted more firsthand accounts specifically taken from the men attached to his Battalion.

My research led to the discovery of several unpublished works written by different members of the 313th Machine Gun Battalion. The bulk of these writings came from Wallace Ben Holland (1894-1918), William George Thomas (1899-1942), Minard Hamilton (1890-1976), Otto Paul Leinhauser (1891-1954), and John Kean (1888-1949).

The correspondence of these men, unless otherwise noted, is dated and can be referenced in the bibliography. One of my primary goals for writing this book was to share my findings with other people who had family members who also served in this Battalion. The amount of material was overwhelming, and I found it necessary to scale the content down to a manageable amount of correspondence that did not take away the core message of their history, or his-story.

This book does not reiterate every word written in the hundreds of pages of letters and journal correspondence. For ease of reading, their spelling and/or punctuation was corrected. It is important to note that the letters of these men were censored, and research was necessary to place the men in locations throughout France based on the recorded troop movements found in multiple unit histories.

As I read their correspondences, I would often come across the name of a person mentioned in a letter, and I would do additional research on the background of that individual. This often led to finding the draft card of the individual or locating a copy of the person's death certificate. On a few occasions I discovered that the soldier I was researching returned home from the war, but sadly ended his own life. I could not help but draw my own conclusions, right or wrong, that some of these men likely suffered from PTSD (Post-Traumatic Stress Disorder), and suffered during an era when help was not as readily available as we see today.

When the veterans of World War I returned home from the war, they were not provided with the resources we have available today to help identify and treat the effects of post-traumatic stress. The use of the term 'shell shock' may have described a soldier's condition, but there were few services available, by today's comparison, to help these veterans return to the routines of everyday life or provide them with methods they could use to help cope with the horrific memories from their brutal days in France.

The repression of emotions and memories was likely a common method of survival for the returning Doughboys. We often hear family members state that their father or grandfather never really talked about his experiences in the war. Who could blame a man for not wanting to recall an image seared into his psyche or to relive an episode that we would find grotesque or inhumane? The horrors of the battlefield were hardly the topic of polite conversation. How could anyone expect a veteran of World War I to casually talk about watching their friends obliterated by incoming mortar rounds, or verbalize what it felt like to have mustard gas burn through the surface of their skin?

For anyone who had a family member survive the battlefields in France, it would be natural to question what their soldier may have witnessed and ask how he was able to survive the mental trauma. I've considered these questions about my own grandfather's life and discussed the topic with my family, as well as other descendants of his Battalion. What did these men witness during the war?

My interest in the subject truly took off when I was given the writings of Minard Hamilton, an officer in the 313th Machine Gun Battalion. It peaked my interest because Hamilton happened to be my grandfather's Platoon and Company Commander. Hamilton wrote letters home to his family during his training at Camp Lee, but the majority of his archived correspondence from the war started with letters dated about three months after his arrival in France. His purpose for documenting his experiences in

France was to keep the family informed of his wellbeing. He also expressed an interest in eventually pulling his stories together for possible publication. His complete writings were never fully published, but he did allow his sister, Amy Gordon Hamilton Grant (1892-1967), to use some of his war stories in her book, *Letters from Armageddon*. She only used a few pages from his journal, but curiously, the letters in her book did not identify Minard Hamilton as the author. Instead, the writings only reference; 'Extracts from an American Officer's Diary' (Grant 193).

Fortunately, the papers of Hamilton, and these other men in the Battalion, have been preserved by family members or archived by institutions for future generations to study.

Researching the ranks, I found many relatives willing to share the stories of their soldiers who served in the Battalion. Stephen Fredrick Filicky (1895-1986) was drafted into the 313th Machine Gun Battalion as a 22-year-old machinist apprentice from Johnstown, Pennsylvania. He survived the war, but was haunted by the memories of the Argonne. He shared stories with his family who remembered how he would gaze off into the distance as he recalled his days in France. His family witnessed him shaking as he recalled his war experiences. Filicky's grandson, Francis Grandinetti, reiterated the stories told by his grandfather, "It was very bad. It was cold, wet and dark. The men were issued gloves to handle the hot guns. The gun barrels had to be cooled by filling a water jacket. At one point the men had no water to cool them and had to urinate into containers to keep the guns firing. While feeding the belt into the machine gun, two of his friends were killed" (Francis Grandinetti interview February 2016).

This book will primarily focus on the personal experiences these men wrote about during the war, and how the war impacted their lives. Unlike Mr. Grandinetti, I never heard my grandfather's firsthand accounts of his experiences in France. Therefore, I had to gather the correspondence of multiple men and piece together a story while trying to imagine what these men witnessed. Using their stories, I now feel I have a better understanding of where my grandfather traveled, where he slept, where he fought, and what he witnessed as a young soldier at war.

The collected works of this Battalion provide an historic account that I believe can be appreciated by anyone interested in better understanding the service of the men who served in the Great War.

Andrew Albert Capets (1895-1976) was born in Tyrone, Pennsylvania, to Slavic immigrant parents Andrej Kapec (1863-1937) and Anna Petrovic (1865-1938). Acknowledging the immigrant experience is significant to understanding the background of a large portion of foreign born men that made up the ranks of the United States Army and this Battalion. Capets himself was born in the United States, but for his parents, English was not their native language. Andrej Kapec worked in the quarries of Tyrone for the American Lime & Stone Company to provide for his family. As a first generation immigrant, a labor intensive livelihood gave his son Andy, the primer to making his own hard-earned wage. The opportunity for a university education was not likely an endeavor Andrej Kapec would have encouraged his son to pursue while being raised in Blair County, Pennsylvania.

When examining the ranks of the 313th Machine Gun Battalion, there is a clear contrast in the education of the enlisted versus that of its officers. The majority of the officers of the Battalion had deep roots already established in the United States. For many in the enlisted ranks, English may not have been the primary language spoken in the household.

My grandfather left his family and friends to work as a laborer in a small town just outside of Pittsburgh, Pennsylvania; a town then called Trafford City. He moved into a boarding house situated along the Turtle Creek rail line, across the creek from his new employer, the Wynn & Starr Brick Company. Trafford City was a relatively new community organized and chiefly financed by industrialist George Westinghouse. The industrial age of the time drew thousands of immigrant families to Pittsburgh and its surrounding communities, giving able bodied men an opportunity for work. The Nation eventually drew upon these men to fill the ranks of its Army.

On April 6, 1917, the United States declared war on Germany. The Selective Service Act was passed and over the next 15 months, twenty four million men between the ages of 18 and 45 registered. The first registration took place on June 5, 1917, requiring all men between the ages of 21 and 31 to register for the draft. When the Nation committed itself to entering the war, it was incumbent upon the local draft boards to supply Washington with the names of those men living in their district.

A lottery was held in Washington D.C. on July 20, 1917, using all the names collected in the June registration. The lottery called for 10,500 capsules with small pieces of paper inside to be drawn. The numbers drawn were telegraphed to newspapers all over the country. The newspapers then published the names of the men from their districts. The New Castle News headline read "First Lucky or Unlucky Number is 258 – Drawn by Secretary Baker" ("Draft Begun This Morning" 1).

In McKean County, Pennsylvania, registrant number 258 was Alfred Julius Swanson (1892-1960) from Ludlow, Pennsylvania. He was a 24-year-old foreman in a hide house. Swanson was drafted into the 80th Division and eventually fought in France with Private Young's 318th Infantry.

In Titusville, Pennsylvania, an Associated Press operator named Kathryn Welsch posted the first list of draftees on the Titusville Herald's bulletin board. The numbers were read aloud, "Number one is 258, number two is 2522, 9613, 4532..." ("City Tensely Interested" 1).

Lloyd Edwin Roche (1894-1960) of Cochranton, Pennsylvania, was registrant number 258 and was the first man drawn from Crawford County's men. He was a single, 23-year-old laborer in a saw mill. In time, Roche would find himself in the Argonne Forest fighting with Company A of the 313th Machine Gun Battalion.

My grandfather was assigned draft registration number 1,010 in Westmoreland County. The Army had its list of draftees, but it still had a tremendous amount of work that needed to be done before it could call all of these men for service. My grandfather waited eight months before he was officially inducted into the Army, receiving instructions to report to Irwin's City Hall on April 5, 1918 at 2:00 PM. He took his oath and was sworn into the Army before a large crowd at City Hall. Various dignitaries gave speeches before the crowd, but because the train was soon approaching, the induction ceremony was cut short. A parade marched the men down the Main Street of Irwin to the train station.

Capets and sixty-four other local draftees boarded the 4:20 PM train headed to Camp Lee, Petersburg, Virginia. He was assigned to the 80th Division, known as the "Blue Ridge Division," and served his entire military service with the 313th Machine Gun Battalion, Company C.

The following chapters tell the story of the men of this Battalion from the time they reached Camp Lee, throughout their service in France, and the return of most of the Battalion members who were lucky enough to survive the war. The final chapter provides a few comments on some of the men from the Battalion post-war.

Note: This book is comprised of letters and journals written by various men of the Battalion. Due to the abundance of letters, this book does not attempt to reproduce the writings in their entirety, and in many cases have omitted subject matters relating strictly to the followings of family happenings back home, tracking the arrival of letters and boxes, or repeated salutations that often appeared in nearly every letter. In some cases the letters were reproduced word for word to allow the reader an insight into better understanding what was happening around the men, and how they were dealing with being away from home. While letters were dictated to correct spellings as often as possible, an effort was made to allow their text to be read without interpretation.

The correspondence does not always identify the intended recipient of their letter. The correspondence has been arranged in chronological order and each entry begins with the date the document was written, followed by the author's last name in CAPITAL letters.

For example, a letter written home from Wallace Ben Holland to his mother may appear as follows:

August 21, 1918 - HOLLAND

Holland's text will follow his name and a clear separation has been given for a different item of correspondence. Words that appear in [blocked parenthesis] have been added by the author to give additional detail to the story or identify a person being written about in the correspondence.

CHAPTER 1
BUILDING THE BATTALION

Believing it would eventually enter the war; the United States undertook a national effort to strengthen its military. Part of the effort included the Preparedness Movement which, during the summers of 1915 and 1916, set up civilian-military camps to train college and professional men as potential Army officers. One such future officer of the 313th Machine Gun Battalion was William George Thomas. In the summer of 1916, Thomas joined a camp in Plattsburg, New York, where he spent six weeks learning to march, shoot and perform military maneuvers.

The following year, in May 1917, Thomas arrived at his Reserve Officers Training Camp held in Fort Myers, Virginia. In a letter to his mother dated July 8, 1917, Thomas wrote, "I know you realize what a wonderful opportunity I have had. I wouldn't take anything for having gone to Plattsburg. It is a whole lot of a help, and must have its influence later on. Things are very bright for me now. The draft will take a bunch, won't it? I'm glad I'm not going to be in the ranks" (Thomas).

THOMAS

As an officer, Thomas provided a contrast to a large contingent of the ranks that made up the 313th Machine Gun Battalion. To his men, he would have likely been viewed as privileged, based on his upbringing and background. Thomas was educated at the University of North Carolina at Chapel Hill. He was the captain of the varsity football team, president of the Mecklenburg Country Club, and a member of one of the University's secret societies, the Order of the Gorgon's Head. After graduating from college,

Thomas worked for the German American Insurance Company of New York with an office in Richmond, Virginia.

By the time Thomas was ready to be promoted to the rank of Captain, his initial military preparedness and training as a junior officer was in a sense over. It was now time for him to focus on preparing to lead troops. On August 9, 1917, just before leaving his R.O.T.C. training in Fort Myers, Thomas wrote to his mother, "I am certain of my Captaincy now, I am glad to say, but sometimes I feel like the responsibility is too much. I'm going to do my best though and feel sure I can come through. I was fifth on the list in the Company as I am informed and I think that is pretty good. Don't say anything about this to anyone 'til the commissions actually come out" (Thomas).

Great Britain and France were providing the United States officers assistance in training the United States military. The machine gun battalions were instructed at Camp Lee on Hotchkiss and Vickers machine guns provided by French and British instructors. In addition to this training, the need for more specialized training of the machine gun units required that officers be sent to the Infantry School of Arms at Fort Sill, Oklahoma. Thomas was one of these officers and was selected for a special assignment. He left Camp Lee, Virginia for training at Fort Sill.

In a letter to his father dated August 9, 1917, Thomas wrote, "I was the only man to get an appointment for special instruction out of the whole company and one of the ten from the camp" (Thomas).

Once Thomas arrived at Fort Sill, and received his orientation, he was not pleased with the situation. He wrote, "In a sense I think I have picked a lemon. That is, I am afraid I won't be able to go across with the crowd I trained with, as I am supposed to be turned out here as a bayonet expert, to have charge of a whole division, and may have to keep up this work" (Thomas).

Thomas displayed a high aptitude as a leader of men while in these specialized courses. The school was broken down into training with bayonets, grenades, automatic rifles, musketry, and field fortifications. Training on machine guns was expected to last about two months. Thomas continued, "I think if I come through this thing, I'll be a better man. It is curious how very much alike 250 men from every State in the Union, and originally from every walk in life are. I believe though, I know as much as a bunch of regulars and am better off than darn near all the militia. This is inside dope though, between you and me. The men from the Training Camps are good though and I've got standing here with my two bars" (Thomas).

On August 27, 1917 the officers of the newly formed 80th Division were instructed to report to Camp Lee, Virginia. These officers were largely drawn from Pennsylvania, Virginia, and New Jersey and this compilation of writings reflects the same. Kean and Hamilton were from New Jersey, Leinhauser was from Pennsylvania, and Thomas was from Virginia.

Camp Lee was the largest of the National Army cantonments designed to hold just over 60,000 men. The barracks could each hold about 150 men. When the National Army was being organized, the divisions were organized by geographical boundaries with the 80th Division being comprised of men from Western Pennsylvania, West Virginia, and Virginia. The men of the 313th Machine Gun Battalion were predominantly from Western Pennsylvania, with most men mustering from the Erie County region.

One of the first Battalion members to arrive at Camp Lee was Wallace Ben Holland, a handsome, 23-year-old single draftee from Union City, Pennsylvania, a small borough in Erie County. Everyone knew him as Ben. He registered for the draft while working as a moulder for the Ajax Iron Works in Corry, Pennsylvania. He was born in Geneva, Pennsylvania to parents George Washington Holland (1866-1944) and Mary Alphoretta Culver (1871-1939). Holland's father worked for the railroad, and his mother was a homemaker. She raised a total of twelve children and her youngest daughter Zada Holland (1915-1972) was just two years old when Holland was drafted into the Army.

Because Holland was one of the Battalion's early arrivals to reach Camp Lee in September 1917, he provided insights into what was happening to the enlisted men at that time. While at training camp, he wrote letters nearly every day to either his mother, other family members, or also to one of his several girlfriends back home. The letters that have survived were mostly written to his mother, and the majority of these writings were completed before he arrived in France. Once he

HOLLAND

25

was overseas, the letters became less frequent. As the letters written by the officers of the Battalion during training camp are sporadic, Holland provides ample material on the subject of camp life, as well as his personal feelings about his upcoming deployment. His letters provide a great resource for learning about daily routines and general tasks that were happening at Camp Lee.

September 21, 1917 – HOLLAND

[Postcard] Feeling fine and will write more when I get time. Address: Company C, 313th Machine Gun Battalion Camp Lee, Petersburg Virginia. Be good.

September 22, 1917 - HOLLAND

Just come up to the YMCA to write a few letters. We was examined yesterday. We got examined and inoculated for typhoid fever and also have a lot more of them coming. I haven't got my uniform yet but will soon. We are just 75 miles from the Atlantic Coast and the sun goes down at 6 o'clock. The nights are cool and days quite warm. It is quite a good place and a few arrangements. They have barbershops and grocery stores. One can buy most everything he wants in the line of tobacco and edibles. We also have moving pictures, boxing, wrestling, singing, and many other things every night all free. The boys are playing the Victrola and piano now. We get up at 5:45 and go to drill at 7:30, and off at 11:30, and then four more hours in the afternoon. It beats working. I had a headache this afternoon so I reported and did not drill. The officers are awful good and all the rest of the boys are.

You know there's thousands just like a city and they are from all around home Greenville, Erie and every other town that one can think of, someone doesn't feel as though he was a way down here alone when he knows lots and always meets a friend he knows. We have Wednesday afternoons off and Saturday we can leave camp and don't have to come back until 11:00 at night, that is, we can leave at noon and go to Petersburg or any other town near. I saw the Capital from the train about three in the morning. We came through Harrisburg, Philadelphia, Washington and many other cities that was interesting, but believe me, we was tired when we got here.

We each have a cot and everyone washes his own canteen, that's a knife, fork, cup and two plates, they are aluminum. We have good feeds, meat, bread and potatoes and desserts three times a day. Well, I will ring off to go out to see the sights. Here's hoping you are all well as I. Bye, answer soon and be sure to get the address right. I have wrote a million cards and letters, some of the boys get some mail today for the first time.

September 25, 1917- HOLLAND

I had eight hours drill today and feel good tonight. It's cold down here today everybody shivers. We haven't our uniform yet. There's hundreds of men coming every day, five or six trains come every day. There's going to be 60,000 here. It's just like a city. I can tell interesting stories when I get home and write a book of advice.

I am going down to Petersburg on payday, that will be a month I guess, then I will get some pictures. They fed us twice on the way down. That box you packed come in handy and with all the feed I had, I was 15 hours without feed. I wish you would send that suitcase of mine and put a small size pillow in it and then I can send my clothes back in it. They furnished underwear and everything one wears. I have been in the hospital once with a headache and rheumatism, just had it in my knee, ha ha, that's kind of natural. Bye-bye, don't worry, I don't.

September 28, 1917 - HOLLAND

I am feeling pretty good tonight, having drilled only a day and a half since I been here. Anyone can pass the exams down here, fools and everything, but when they take the one for France, everyone must be perfect, and the rest will stay in the US.

I had very bad eyes and a hospital record since I have been here, rheumatism. The doctor asked me the other day if I had passed the exams, and I said yes, and he laughed and said, 'Go back to the Battalion and stay there until you get shoes,' and he also told me more to tell the Captain, so I will never see France.

I don't see what makes you so bugs about me being down here. I am alright and will be home for sure before one year, that's not long. This week has been short to me. This is someplace for one. We have a fool thinking he is Captain and everybody does as he says.

Thanks for the stamps, they are very scarce down here, sometimes we can't buy them. I haven't got my uniform yet, and don't give a damn if I never get one. Over half of the boys can come home Christmas. It will cost $30 car fare. I don't believe I will go, it's an awful long trip. The ones they figure on going to France, they will let go home, and the rest can't go home. I think the war will be over by spring.

∽

The next letter was written by Captain Thomas to his mother from Camp Lee shortly after the officers received their unit assignments. The letter gives a glimpse of Thomas' impression about the background and makeup of some of the men who were first being mustered into the ranks of the newly formed 313th Machine Gun Battalion.

September, 1917 - THOMAS

I was assigned a company in the Depot Brigade in a crowd with my bunch from Fort Myer. Was in the same barracks with Spig [Gladden Hunt Spigener 1888-1957] and was getting along fine.

After staying there a day I was given a Company in the Division Machine Gun Battalion and had to pack up and move all over again. I have a bunch of draft from Erie, PA and 32 of the 172 can't speak English. I have a Polish interpreter, a Romanian interpreter, an Italian interpreter, and a Greek interpreter. My First Sergeant gives his orders in English and then in Polish. I have everything in my company from insurance agents to bellboys. Chiefly miners and ironworkers. It's the roughest crowd you ever saw. I also have a racetrack bookmaker and a merchant tailor. I have two First Lieutenants and three Second Lieutenants to help me, and we are kept busy. It is usually very interesting, but all the glamour of military life is gone. It is work. It shows how funny the government is, but it's a question of not kicking.

We have nice quarters, and the food is good, but I don't see day light ahead for three months anyway. It's a fine chance however, and I hope they don't jerk me away to teach bayonet until I have this Company in shape. I am with a peach of a bunch though and know I will get along O.K.

October 2, 1917 - HOLLAND

I received the suitcase today, and the pillow is fine. I have two blankets and a straw thick on a cot. We have butter once a day and enough to eat, but it's not cooked right. The oranges were good and I am chewing candy now.

I got two pair of shoes today, one for good and one pair of calf hides with big nails in Hunky shoes. Four pairs of socks, three suits underclothes, and the uniform hasn't come yet. It's not so bad down here, just about the same as when father lives in the car, only one has lots of bosses and doesn't say a word back and can't drink on the job, or quit, that's all I don't like.

I will have to drill now that I have shoes. I don't believe I will send my clothes home as they are worthless, holes in the pants, and otherwise, I need the suitcase to put things in. Company A down in Georgia has a disease, smallpox or something. There's one company here about 3 miles from us that has smallpox. I feel good now, I just have one small shot yet and it don't amount to much.

October 3, 1917 – HOLLAND

I wouldn't mind it a bit if we don't have to go to battle, and yet there's no fun down here, and if we do go to battle, the machine gun company don't do anything, as long as the Army don't lose, and if the Army does begin to lose, then comes us and we fire on the heavy artillery, that's the big guns. And if the machine gun company gets the heavy artillery before they get them, all right, and if they don't, goodbye in three or four minutes.

It's not often we fight, and when we do, it don't last long either way, whichever way it may be, don't very often get into trenches, it's the emergency company or the last hopes for a victory.

I had a good sleep last night on my pillow. Hell, I can sleep anywhere now on the floor and there's not noise enough to wake me but the bugle, I wake right up then. We get up at 5:45, and on Sundays we can sleep all day if we don't want any breakfast, it's at 7:00 AM Sunday, and at 6:30 other times.

I don't know why you worry, hell I am good for it, and let nature take its course. There's only one man gets killed out of a hundred, and if I do, it will save funeral expenses, there's no big loss without some small gain.

There's better weather down here, nice summer days now like July. Where we drill is a big peanut field and we tramp hundreds of bushels under our feet, awful sandy, it's an old battlefield.

Well it's time for mess, supper at 5:15, its 10 minutes to 5:00 now. Mess, that's what we call our feeds. Well, cheer up, and when I come home we will celebrate. Bye-bye, answer soon a big long letter.

October 9, 1917 – HOLLAND

As it is raining and cold we haven't gone out to drill yet. It's now 2:30 PM. We got paid last night $13 and then I went up to see the boys, they came from home, so I didn't have time to write much last night. They all felt pretty blue, the same as we did. I worked in the kitchen yesterday. I hear they are going to send all married men home, that looks good. The boys have their overcoats on, we haven't any fire but they have big stoves. I don't think Germany can last much longer. When I get the rest of my uniform I will go to Petersburg and get some pictures taken. The boys shot craps all night and some are broke this morning. One guy had so much money he couldn't get it in his pockets and an arm full too.

October 12, 1917 – HOLLAND

Things are getting better down here now. We got a quilt today and that makes two blankets and one quilt and I put my overcoat over me, but at first it was pretty tough. The guys that come here now have things nice, besides what we did. We got here a little after noon and had to get things ready so we could have a place to sleep. I haven't gotten a uniform and don't know when I will. We didn't drill this afternoon on account of rain. We run now five minutes and walk two and then run again, they roughen one up. Ha ha. We are going to march at the Petersburg Fair Wednesday and next, that will be fun if we get close.

October 16, 1917 – HOLLAND

I received your box today. All O.K. and the butter tasted good, I had some for dinner. It's awful hot today, just like the hottest days in summer up there. I am crumb boss today so I have little time to write. I am going to try to go down to the Petersburg Fair tomorrow. I haven't been to Petersburg yet.

It will be four weeks tomorrow since I left and it hasn't been very long. A week goes fast down here. We are not drilling very much, just cleaning up rubbish and puttering around, and it doesn't seem as though they was in a very big hurry to get trained men. I think the most of it is a bluff, but I think we will go to France, and it will be a real nice trip and that will be all.

The American men are easily trained six months and will make good soldiers out of us. They train the man with wooden guns and old sticks. We haven't any real guns yet, we get pistols, not guns.

October 17, 1917 - HOLLAND

This is Wednesday afternoon off, and 40 of the boys have gone to the Fair. I did not go. 40 are going tonight. Most of them got pants, but they didn't have any that would fit me. I have an old pair, and a full uniform, but I am not going to get any pictures taken until I get good clothes and look decent.

I don't have it hard down here, easier than working and we get better feeds now. I have bought a little and if I was to go home I would never be sorry that I had to come down here. I would like to go to France if I knew I would come back safe, and enjoy it, and would like more traveling, but I don't like the idea of the battle part.

It is a nice day down here. I sent some views of the camp last night and it is just what it looks like. We are either going to Texas or Georgia, or move over to the other side of this camp so we can practice the machine gun work, and I think it will be in the next month. Yes, I got my last shot two weeks ago and it didn't bother me much, and my vaccination was a good one, but the scab never came off and the doctor said it wouldn't leave much of a scar, but it's just about the size of a quarter now, but not sore.

≪⑥

The earlier letter written by Captain Thomas revealed a bit about the ethnic makeup of a portion of the Battalion. In October 1917, Camp Lee had a field day competition to celebrate the War Department's Second

Liberty Loan drive. Eleven units came together to compete in various events throughout the day. Some men were allowed to return home to help boost Liberty Bonds sales in their home district. On the day of the celebration, General Adelbert Cronkhite (1861-1937) offered a $2,000 Liberty Bond credit to the one unit that provided the most entertaining presentation of the day. The 313th Machine Gun Battalion won first place by organizing five squads, each man carrying flags of a nation represented in the war. The Battalion recruited men for the presentation who were native to Russia, Belgium, Ireland, Italy, and the United States. As the squads entered the parade field, the bugler played the national anthem of their county. The squad leader then called out orders in his native language as the men performed various military formations. The finale involved all the squads coming together in front of the judges to group the flags "showing that liberty is the bond in which all of the nations have entered the war" ("Soldiers at Camp Lee").

October 19, 1917 – HOLLAND

It's been hotter than hell down here today and they ran the dickens out of us today. It's raining now just since 6 o'clock. There's five of the boys going to Georgia. Some have gone away, and one can sign up to go if they want to, but I don't care about going, its hot enough here. The guys are playing the violin and clogging. We have one guy that can clog to perfection, have a square dance every night.

I bought a cake of Fels-Naptha soap $0.10 and everything just the same. I bought a chicken dinner down to Hopewell last Sunday, $1.00 and the chicken was rotten and everything was just as bad and didn't eat. Everything is booming around these towns, so many soldiers, and a soldier just takes what he gets, and he pays a double price for it. I have a uniform, but it doesn't look just as good as it might. One has to take what clothes they can get, everything is rushed.

They had a Liberty Loan Bond field celebration yesterday and every company put on an exercise. There was only 30,000 in the field, and our Company got the first prize. When anyone gets ahead of the northern people, they have to hurry. It was our own get up. We divided our Company into different nationalities, and of course, I was in with the Irish. We each carried a flag of their countries and marched, and in the end, the Liberty Loan flag, we had it fixed up, and the American flag marched in and was victorious. See, it represented all the countries in war, and in the end, the American was victorious with the aid of the Liberty Loan Bond. It was the greatest doings I ever saw. It was the meaning of the parade that took the prize. There was moving pictures taken, and that's the second time I have been taken in the movies. When we was drilling for the parade, the Irish bunch got into a fight and had an awful mix-up. The Irish is ahead of the world. All they know is to slur and fight.

October 27, 1917 – HOLLAND

Well this is Saturday and a half day off. We didn't drill this afternoon either, just fooled around all forenoon. We have some easy days, and altogether it beats working in a good place for one who has no home. I feel good today and happy. It's pretty hot today. I have a washing to do today, one suit of underwear, socks, handkerchief, shirt and one pair of khaki pants. I could get it done at the laundry, but I don't bother, there's a laundry here in camp and they do it cheap about $0.20 a week.

We get together every evening and box and wrestle. One gets pretty tough and not afraid of anyone. You have no idea what a change it makes in the guys. One guy, when he comes down here, we could make him believe anything, and get him to box, and he would cry if he got a knock, and now he is a man, and a hard nut, just as gamy as anyone. It's the best thing there is for a man.

I don't mind it now, only France, and I don't really believe we will ever go over there. We have prize fighters, wrestlers, artists, singers and everything. We went to Hopewell the other night and Manuel [Samuel Manuel 1895-1970] from our Company boxed the guy from Washington, 10 rounds, and it was bloody. We just owned the town.

October 1917 - THOMAS

Work is still getting on fine. I think we are really doing something with the Company, although still laboring under difficulties. You get so used to being busy all the time that it doesn't make any difference. I always have a thousand things to do, but get so I don't mind it. I have just about got my exemptions. I had a stenographer on them alone for a solid week. I am sending you a letter of the kind that I have got about fifty of.

They just railroaded a bunch down here on us and we had all the work to do. A whole bunch were sent from here to Atlanta Georgia to fill out the draft down there. I don't know what kind of success they are going to make out of it mixing the crowds. I am perfectly satisfied with my Wops. They are so childish and eager. I'm going to start an English school for them pretty soon. I have ordered some charts for them and will have it four nights a week. I am getting along fine and have so much to do, it keeps me busy all the time and therefore very happy.

I haven't had a chance to leave camp much, and don't care about it especially. Anytime you and daddy care to come now, why come ahead. I'm living under a continual bugaboo that I'm going to be taken away and made an instructor. The Major has promised to do all he can for me, and I am so well satisfied at present.

My battalion took first prize in the whole Division at a Liberty Bond celebration today, and I got up the idea. Pretty lucky I think. Don't read this enclosed letter out of the family.

❧

Captain Thomas referenced the following letter he received from Mrs. Natalia Okoniewski Koscielniak, a woman who was then residing in Erie, Pennsylvania, and pleading for her husband John Joseph Koscielniak (1892-1960) to be returned home. Mrs. Koscielniak had someone write the follow message to Captain Thomas on October 14, 1917, "I am writing you a few lines from Miss Effie Koscielniak to Mr. Captain Thomas. If you so kind sent John Koscielniak home because I got two children, I am sick and I have little baby, so I can go to work, please do this for me, I never forget you so you is good for me because I have thirty dollars my pay a month. I can live a month because every think is so dear and I have to pay ten dollars rent. And please would be so good and sent him beg please help me because I ant got nobody to help me here, I am one and I ant got no mother nor father, and I am from old country. Its hard for me because I can talk English so good, if you not help me so I ant got nobody else to help me out"(Company Records).

Captain Thomas wrote to his father on December 10, 1917 that he was going to get rid of a bunch of men, "as I have about 30 who will never make machine gunners, I don't think" (Thomas).

Private Holland's letters indicated that a number of men continued to be transferred out of the machine gun battalion frequently. It is unknown if Koscielniak was ever given the opportunity to seek an exemption before the draft board. Despite the pleas of his wife, Koscielniak was not returned back to Erie. Instead, he was transferred out of the machine gun battalion into placed into the Medical Corps and served overseas for one year and did not take part in any battle engagements.

Thomas wrote that he received multiple letters like the one written for Mrs. Koscielniak, and he referenced his stenographer being busy for a solid week addressing these issues. Other draftees and their families asked for exemptions on various grounds.

Captain John Kean of C Company interviewed Francis Xavier Scherrer (1894-1971) of Erie, and stated in a memoranda that he believed Mrs. Scherrer was unable to support herself. The memo included a statement by Private Scherrer, who wrote under oath, that he should be granted an exemption due to his wife's poor health. He expressed that his wife had been under a doctor's care since his marriage, and although they did not have children, she was unable to work to support herself. The request was submitted through the chain of command, but his exemption was denied. Scherrer remained with the 313th Machine Gun Battalion throughout the war (Company Records).

In another case, Pietro Giammarco (1894-1985) of Erie also applied for exemption on the grounds that he was not a citizen of the United States, could not read English, and could only speak the language a little. He claimed he did not know his right to claim an exemption when he appeared before the board. Ultimately his request was denied because the local board stated that they provided him with an interpreter at the time of the registration and he did not file an exemption in a timely manner. He was eventually transferred out the 313th Machine Gun Battalion and later served with the 5th Machine Gun Battalion for the duration of the war. (Company Records).

❧

November 5, 1917 - HOLLAND

We had it easy today, just lectures and a lot of junk. We have to go out in the woods, a dozen or so of us, and some from another company, at night to scout around and see who can discover each other first, just for practice. They even have one walk so far to count steps to see how far he steps, and have us guess distances, ask us how far it is from one tree to another, or something like that, just to see how good one is on such stuff, and his judgment. That's the way they will choose their gunners.

The weather is like fall up home, frosty nights and nice sunny days. This is easier than work, but it don't sound good when they tell one all of that battle junk and have you crawl half a mile on his belly. One guy said today if we was ever out on a scout, and had a message, even if we did lose a man, to be sure to get the message back for it was more valuable than a man.

I guess I will go up to the YMCA tonight to see the movies, they are free. I kind of like it now. I am not afraid. Here's hoping you are as well as I am. If you need any money I will send some. I will have $25 after a settle up.

November 9, 1917 – HOLLAND

We got our heavy underclothes tonight. Fleece lined ones, drawers and shirts. The guys were gambling, and a lieutenant came up and got their names just now, and all the guys that were watching the game too. I wasn't in it. They will get a month in the kitchen or pick and shovel for a week. I will tell you what they give them in my next letter. Someone gets pinched every day around here. Two guys have been shipped, perhaps they will come back in a week. One can be gone 10 days before it is a desertion, but if they were gone over 10 days, then they are a deserter. If they come back in a week they will get a $10 fine and 10 days in the guardhouse.

We had an easy day today, just jimmying and sneaking around in the woods and scouting around on each other, about the same as hiding-seek, only when we find them, they are supposed to be captured or shot. It's all practice and we learn to sneak up on the enemy and hide from the enemy also.

November 11, 1917 - HOLLAND

I didn't go to town today, there's nothing down there. I still have $25, but I will have to spend one for pictures, if they ever come. The guys that got pinched for gambling got a week in the kitchen and can't leave camp for a month, and they are doing the same thing this minute, they don't care.

Two of the guys from this company are in Erie Jail now. They skipped last payday. Their names are Mike Cardon and Samuel Manuel both Hunkys, perhaps you will see it in the paper.

November 12-17, 1917 - HOLLAND

We are going for a hike all day tomorrow and take our dinner, figuring on about 30 miles. I heard today that we might not go to France until about June, can't tell, we may never go. We don't march much anymore, have it soft every day now and yet they keep us exercised. Maybe we are just used to it and it seems easier. I won't write a letter to be put in the paper, for if I did, it would disgrace the U.S.

They announced tonight that they would issue passes five days or more. No, you don't want to come down here, it's an awful trip. You can't imagine what it is like, but it would be alright for father to come and stay a couple days and I could show him around and go home with him.

We are digging trenches and I am going to get my picture taken in a trench. We all wear overalls and jackets now. The weather is hot down here.

I heard that the US would pay half the fare if father could come down and stay a day or two, perhaps, and I could get five days, but could not tell the week ahead. It is doubtful if he could carry a soldier on a pass or not. I will send a picture I had taken yesterday. I don't know who that guy is. All soldiers are just like brothers, he is not a Wop but looks like one. I weighed 141 pounds just the way I am in the picture, so I have gained a little.

I heard today that we were going to take a hike to the Atlantic coast and it will take a week or more to make the trip. It's 80 miles to the coast so that will be a 160 mile walk. We got our tents today. Each man carried one half of a tent and it's about the size of a bed sheet. Also other tent equipment, two blankets, mess equipment, and a lot of other junk. That will be fun seeing all the country and we have a good time on a hike. Everyone look us over as we go by that we don't flirt, but we are a gamy bunch and make all kinds of remarks and fun.

I think it will be a long time before we ever go to France. I am not excited, but I do think that the US will train all the men to get prepared. We have it easier now and get good eats. They just put green guys in the kitchen to learn to cook, and of course, we had to stand the bad cooking, but now they cook pretty good. I have five more letters to write so I will be busy a few minutes spreading the bull. One of the guys I had my picture taken with today is comical. He was talking about how the US would soon be dry and he said, 'By Gosh, they can't stop cider from getting hard.' He always says something comical. Red Kelly likes it, there's lots that does.

November 18 - 19, 1917 – HOLLAND

I read your letters and always ready to get them. I keep paper, pencil, and much junk in my suitcase and we have a big bag like a mail pouch made out of overalls to keep our clothes in and lots of things. Every Saturday morning we have to red up for the officers to come and inspect everything. There can't even be a piece of paper on the floor and everyone has to be shaved and shoes shined and all dressed up. That is at 9:00 AM in the morning, every Saturday, and then we go for a walk until noon. One doesn't leave camp until they look him over to see if he looks right, and if he doesn't, he stays home. We are just like a lot of kids having to go ask Papa everything, and if he says no, that means no. Saturday is an easy day, we only have four full days to drill.

November 21, 1917 – HOLLAND

Each soldier has to make an allotment if he has to support someone, and if he doesn't support anyone, he fills out a blank to say so. They haven't any blanks to fit my cause, and I won't sign and say I haven't any, when I have. If I give $15 they will give $5 dollars. That would make $20 you would get. I told them that $5 dollars wasn't any object for me to sign my right of support away. The blanks read grandmother, grandfather, mother or father, wife or child, wholly support. Of course it doesn't say brother or sister, which is just as close, and needs support just as much as any other relation. If I sign a blank, the blank of course will settle the whole case. I will sign when they come across with the money, and as much as I give home, which was more than $40 monthly, and the right kind of a blank, I can't sign a blank that reads that way. Of course, if they take ones support and kill them, and they are paying an allotment, they have to continue to do so. They will send a man home first. If I give $15 and they give $25, that would make $40 and then that is yours, and you can do as you please with it. Send it back to me if you want, it's nobody's business. But don't worry, I won't sign for nothing, and it's got to be straight, for such things often come up when one's an old man. See, in the other war, some of the papers weren't right and the soldiers got nothing when they were old. Continue your correspondence with the Adjutant General and don't be afraid. Someone's got to do business. They tried to doubt my word and I showed them some of your letters. Their face dropped and I said I would wait a few days. These things have to be straight. One can't let this his people go to the dogs. They can't scare me. They had three guys that wouldn't sign anything, not even the payroll. They wouldn't put on a uniform, they just read the Bible all the time. They put them in the guardhouse and fed them bread and water and they never gave up. I guess they are home now. When I wants buck they can shoot if they like, one might as well die for his friends in this country as in France for someones money. I am a soldier and I will fight for my home rights first.

November 22, 1917 – HOLLAND

They brought them two guys back that skipped and went to Erie. They are in the guardhouse, and I don't know what will be the results.

I have been down here nine weeks yesterday, that's not very long. They was just after me for an allotment and I said no, and told them the case. I showed your letter and he said if that was the case, it was an exception, 11 brothers and sisters, and he would take it up with the congressman. If I give $20 a month, they will give $20, so that would be $40 a month. Of course they might make other arrangements for help. They just called me down again and asked a lot of questions. The men that have to support will be the ones that will go home first.

◈

Michael Cardon (1894-1980) was transferred out of the Battalion and served with 153th Depot Brigade until he was honorably discharged from the Army in December 1918. Samuel Manuel (1895-1970) was also transferred out of the Battalion but served with the 126th Infantry for the remainder of the war. Manuel was wounded in November 1918, while fighting for Company D during the Meuse-Argonne offensive (*Pennsylvania, WWI Veterans Service and Compensation Files*).

November 30, 1917 - HOLLAND

We sure had some feed. Turkey, celery, cake, pie, bread, tea and coffee, oysters, boiled onions, nuts, apples, oranges, candy, cigars and cigarettes, cranberries, and many other things. It sure was some feed. I think I will come home, but if they take $15 out of my pay I will be short car fare, and I sure will have to come back, and no delay either. I don't know whether I can be home for Christmas or not, but I don't care when it is Christmas it is not a good time anyway, there's too many people going and coming in every train and would be late and crowded. Tell Will to save that money, for if I get home and haven't enough to go back, it would mean the guardhouse for me.

December 5-11, 1917 - HOLLAND

This has been a busy week for me haven't had much time to write. I was on guard Sunday and Monday. Tuesday drill all day. Had a parade before the Secretary of War this afternoon. Every man in the camp marched and it took me half a day to pass. Just imagine 40,000 men, some string.

There is a lawyer in Richmond taking up our case with the Adjutant General. I put up a good spiel with the lieutenant, and his father is a lawyer, so he has his father see to it. But you keep after them and if you had a lawyer write for you, it would be better.

The Major went today to see about getting a special train for us. The train will cost about $6,000 both ways, that's three up and three back, and there will be two trains, so it will cost $12,000 for the whole Battalion, or 600 men. That's some car fare.

We will come by way of Pittsburgh and come over the Bessiemer from there, so we will go through Greeneville and Adamsville to Erie. It won't go through Union. We have to go back to Erie to get the train back. If I stay in Erie Friday night the 28th, then I can be home Saturday, but I will have to go to Erie Monday in the morning to get the troop train back, which will leave about noon. I am not going to drink a bit while I am home, for one would wouldn't realize they had been home. I might take a little on the way back, ha ha. There's no danger of me catching cold when I come home for this is like sleeping in a barn.

December 12-13, 1917 - HOLLAND

I received your letter and sure was sorry to hear father had his wrist broke. All I can say is you are out of luck. That is what they tell us down here. Get a letter fixed up by a lawyer and signed by the doctor stating that he is crippled and disabled to work. Don't make it too plain you understand, and that the US has your only support, and you will get some money, and make more than money, you know bluffing sometimes works. Every dollar helps nowadays and get the dollar anyway one can.

We took a little hike this morning and practiced gun sitting and wearing the gas masks this afternoon. They take pretty good care of us and we are careful not to get sick. We all have to take out an insurance in February if we ever get a pension or any damage. See, that is a scheme. The men pay their own pension and the men that haven't any dependents, and don't make an allotment, the US takes so much out of their pay and saves it for them. So I might as well have it go home, as let them have the use of it when it is needed at home.

The lieutenant was asking me if I had heard anything from home and I told him nothing, only that father had gotten his arm broken and he said that's good concerning your case. Just keep writing and they will come across. See they can't look up every little case, they are rushed, and if it is approved or signed by a doctor, that's as far as they will go. What do you care if people knows you are not rich, and anyway, get the money and keep it in the pocket, don't never put a cent in the bank if you ever get a full. See, the lieutenant is a lawyer, and his father is a lawyer in Richmond. They never speak to a private like me, only when they give instructions, but he is a sort of a decent common guy and somehow likes to help a guy, and I make the case so strong that I have to converse with him. See, he knows just about what can be done, so the best thing you can do is get a lawyer to do your writing and signed by the doctor.

December 14, 1917 - HOLLAND

I work in the kitchen today and didn't get done until 8 o'clock. Tomorrow I have to help haul coal all day. That's the way we get half days off on Saturday, always have some detail work for us to do. They are sorting out the men now. There's 28 leaving this company tomorrow, fools and sick ones, they are going to North Carolina and I think about 20 more soon. I hope I go, them guys will never go to France. Red Kelly is going. I passed the examination good mentally, but physically I don't know, and the nuts or foolish exam was rather a stiff one, but I have a little education yet, and believe me, if I go to take it next time, I will be a nut.

They are making room fast for the next call. The machine-gun company has to have good men, and it's the best branch of service. We keep hidden and they never know where the machine gun is located, and if they find out, they cut loose with the heavy artillery and its goodbye. These guns shoot 400 shots a minute and are not much bigger than a shotgun.

December 16, 1917 - HOLLAND

There is a great scattering down here. They are sending them every direction to make room for the next call. All the German and Austrian men that haven't citizen papers are going as prisoners of war and went from this company yesterday. They are just keeping the good men here. Kelly and Pitt are going to Camp Green North Carolina and expect to go any minute, there are about 20 going with them. I start to school tomorrow afternoon from 1:00 until 4:30 every day. Study guns and pistols. We have to know them well, every little piece.

December 22, 1917- HOLLAND

Some of the boys went home today, and some will go the 27th. Then there will be two leaves each day all next month, and February also, so I no doubt will be home in January. There's 25 more men going to leave this company soon, going to Philadelphia PA, and if I should be one, I won't be home. I don't think I will be one, but I hope I will. They will be second-class men, and the other bunch that went was third class, and the ones that stay here will be first class. I think I am first class and will stay here until June, that's the calculation now. About half of the men that come in the draft are physically fit to go to France. The call ups will be sent to the Philippines Islands, Panama Canal, and to forts and harbors and border guard duty is all they will do.

I bought a new suitcase today, one dollar, just like the old one. I done a big washing this afternoon and it kept me busy getting it dry. I also took a bath and dolled up but didn't do any pressing, flat irons are scarce down here. Don't forget to keep things stirred up. When one gets anything they have to fight for it.

December 27, 1917 - HOLLAND

Just came off guard at four this afternoon. I walked the post from 5 to 7 last night and then from 11 to 1, and from 5 to 7 this morning, and from 11 to 1 this afternoon. Two hours on, and two hours off for rest. There's 28 more men going to leave this company soon, and if I should be one, it will be all off for a while getting home. They are either going to North Carolina or Philadelphia.

I am room orderly tomorrow, or rather crumb boss. Each man sweeps under his own bunk, and makes it up every morning, and all the crumb boss does is sweep the halls, carry the coal, clean the ashes, and empty the spit boxes and so on.

There's lots of men deserting this camp. Some from West Virginia, out of the mountains, just left and said, 'If you want to know where we are going, just follow our footsteps.' They will get them just the same. I think I will be home Tuesday the 1st, New Year's Day, and if I am not, I will be in a few days later, so don't be surprised.

❧

Private Holland was granted a furlough and travelled back to Union City to stay with his family for a few days. His letters resumed once again when he returned to Camp Lee.

January 6-9, 1918 - HOLLAND

I got here all safe at 4:30 Saturday afternoon and was awfully tired and dirty. I am on guard tomorrow. There's only about 25 men here now, just enough to do the detail work. Most all have gone home. There's 28 more going to be transferred soon. I am not in this bunch. There will be just enough left here to break in the new bunch when they come. There will be more transferred after this bunch and I may be in it. If I am not transferred I will be corporal when the new drafts comes. I got here Saturday, about dark, just three or four hours late, but there was nothing said. They are inspecting every camp and the best ones will go, and the poorest all separated and sent everyplace.

I am going to get two teeth pulled. I passed the feet and lung examinations all O.K. There are lots dying with pneumonia, and they examined our lungs.

January 12, 1917 - HOLLAND

I think I will be transferred. The Captain told me today that he had a special job for me. I signed up as a molder. Maybe I will go to a shell plant, molding shells, or on the railroad. One thing for sure, it will not be carrying a gun in the trenches. Maybe breaking or firing on a munitions train in France. There were 28 transferred today, and just three when I get it. One of us is an officer, going as a Polish instructor, and I don't know who the other one is, or what I am going to do.

January 20, 1918 - HOLLAND

We are going to move tomorrow. Each company will have four barracks, room for 260 men easy. There's 23 that sleep in my room now, where there used to be about 65. Nearly everyone has been transferred. It looks to me as they intend to fill our companies with the next draft, and if that is the case, we will be here three or four months longer. The men in the machine gun companies are sorted very close, and have to be good physically and mentally, and be a man that is not yellow, and will stick when the rest fall back. All we need to do is tell the Captain we are a quitter, and he will soon transfer us. That's why we are called the suicide companies, because we never retreat, and when we could save ourselves, we don't do it, we stick and save others, but we have to have a wicked little weapon. It shoots from 400 to 600 times a minute. Hell, we will die with old age here in Camp Lee.

Julia [Julia Anna Gibeaut] proposed to me in her last letter, and told me how her father and mother said she could never get a better man, but hell, they will have to bait the hook with different meat. I have about a dozen already, waiting to have the word said. A soldier is the man of today, and can get just what he wants, but one has to be so damn tough to be a soldier that when he spits it bounces.

January 26 1918 - HOLLAND

I just took out insurance for $10,000, it costs $6.50 a month. If one don't get insured, he has to sign all his rights away and wouldn't ever get a cent. But if I get crippled I will get $66 a month for my lifetime, and if I get killed you will get $66 until the $10,000 is paid, and if you die, someone else will get it. If I get out of the Army I can drop it.

Any monthly pay will be $8.50 a month now. Some of the guys are only getting one or two dollars a month now. We haven't drilled much in the last two weeks. It takes most of us to guard the prisoners. The way the papers read, the war won't last long. I am going on guard today at one, and will be on until tomorrow, Sunday.

Taft [Former President William Howard Taft] is speaking here in camp today. I could have gone, but what do I care to hear all the junk he is peddling, always someone telling us to be good. The Captain asked me today if you had got the allotment yet, and I told him you haven't.

February 17, 1918 – HOLLAND

We have some new men in our company now and they seem like nice guys. I was up and saw the Crawford, Mercer, and Erie County men and did not see Vern, John or Carl Sloan. I guess there wasn't any of the three come. I saw J. Bennett [Jay Henry Bennett 1889-1969] that used to work in the Union City chair factory.

There's a lot of the boys going to France from this camp now. I guess there will be a lot more go before the 28th of this month. I don't think we will go and only had men enough for half a company before the new fellers came. See the machine gun men has to have brains, so they

45

sorted us pretty close and it takes a long time to get a bunch of the right kind of men.

The bunch that first come down, they split them all up and scattered them all over the camp. I mean the Erie and Erie County bunch. Our Major was the cause of it. He said he had saw wild men, but we was the wildest he ever saw, and so they separated the last bunch. There's only been 76 court martials since we been here.

We had spinach for dinner one day and the Lieutenant asked the Mess Sergeant why he didn't put some vinegar on the table. The Mess Sergeant said he did, but they drinked it. The Lieutenant said, 'Jesus Christ, drink vinegar, what kind of men are they?'

They stole $8 worth of lemon extract out of the kitchen and had a good drunk one night. The Captain said he was going to Erie and see what kind of damned place it was.

February 19, 1918 - HOLLAND

Five months ago this time I was on the train coming to camp and pretty well hooked up. Well, the boys that came down when I did, and were transferred, have started for France last Sunday. I felt as though I wanted to go with them when I saw them get on the train. Two trainloads, they looked nice with their packs on their backs. I guess they are going to stop offering another camp for a while, but one can't tell. No doubt they will stop when they get across. The rookies are pretty quiet and so sore they can't walk. If this pen writes crooked it's not my fault for a Polack borrows it, so it's hard to make it write in two languages.

March 9, 1918 - HOLLAND

Next week we get the gas and sham battles. We are going to have it days and night sessions all week. The gas is deadly poison and almost sudden death if one breathed of it. It comes in a cloud of smoke and is used in shells. Also, 35 percent of the shells used abroad are gas shells. One of our Lieutenants has gone over to France already. I think the whole of us will go, new men and all. We will get training over there. It will be a nice trip if we go, but hell, we don't know one thing about it.

Private Holland mentioned one of the Lieutenants being sent over to France. There is record that Second Lieutenant Randolph F. Mason (1878-1918) was sent overseas early to receive additional training. Lieutenant Mason, a graduate of the University of Virginia, and a former professor of English and French at the U.S. Revenue Cutter School in Baltimore, Maryland received his commission at Fort Myers and joined the Machine Gun Battalion in August 1917. He was sent to France in March 1918, and after receiving six weeks of training he was transferred to the 103rd Infantry, 26th Division. He was killed in action on July 20, 1918. While official records show him as a member of the 103rd Infantry, Mason spent the majority of his military days with the 313th Machine Gun Battalion ("Lieutenant Mason Is Killed In France").

As new draftees arrived at camp, they had to be quarantined in their own barracks for two weeks in the event that they were ill. The new arrivals still received training while being quarantined, for it was expected that the entire Division would sail to France together. The Battalion officers selected the men that they wanted to keep as potential machine gunners while others were moved into less specialized infantry ranks.

Private Holland mentioned that men were dying from pneumonia while at camp. There were at least three men who died prematurely while serving with the Battalion while stationed at Camp Lee. John Bernard Crook (1894-1918) from Waterford, Pennsylvania, died of lobar pneumonia. John Wasielewski (1895-1918) from Erie, Pennsylvania, died of spinal meningitis. Harry Kelley (1888-1918) was a draftee from Titusville, Pennsylvania, and died prematurely in the Richmond Memorial Hospital after an unfortunate accident that occurred on the *Seaboard Air Line* Railroad. While returning from leave, Kelley reportedly boarded a passenger train that was heading back to Camp Lee, but he fell ill and had to get off the train. Later, he attempted to board a freight train heading toward Camp Lee, but as he was climbing aboard up between two freight cars, he fell. Both of his legs were amputated below the knees. Ironically, Kelley's older brother, Joseph Kelley, died less than a year earlier in Corry, Pennsylvania when he, too, fell from a freight train and died after having his right foot amputated ("Harry Kelley Is Killed").

March 18, 1918 - HOLLAND

We are going to be examined Wednesday for overseas duty. Company A was examined today and seven did not pass. I suppose there will be six or seven in each company that won't pass. I'll pass alright, there's nothing wrong with me, other than a little squackie eyed.

March 29, 1918 - HOLLAND

You needn't worry about me coming home, for it don't matter much anyway. Yes, the papers get off a big spiel to advertise Liberty Loan Bonds. I guess Erie is going to pay for the fare for two squads out of each company. That would be 64 men out of about 700, and 636 would have to pay their own fare. They are going to march in Erie to advertise Liberty Bonds. I am going to see the Captain about the allotment, you will get it sooner or later. We have inspection tomorrow to march in review before the General, and believe me, it takes some work.

Always put return on your letters, for it's hard to tell what day we might change, and if I did know, I wouldn't tell you, for you know the movement of any troops is kept a secret. I don't know, nor have any idea, when we will move. I don't think it will be any sooner than a month.

I wish you could see us parade once, some outfit. Each squad has a wagon, a squad is eight men, to haul the gun and ammunition. It's a two wheeled wagon, and on a long march we have a mule to haul it, and then we wear a pack of course. It contains two blankets, half tent, tent poles, stakes, rope, one raincoat, two pairs of socks, one suit of underwear, towel, soap, comb, glass, toothbrush and paste, three days ration, all on our back. And then on our belt is a pistol, water bottle, cup, shovel, wire pliers and a first aid box that contains bandages, safety pins and so on. In the pack we have our mess kit with knife, fork, spoon, and so on. We carry all the junk when we drill every day and sometimes sweat under the harness, ha ha. And of course we carry a gas mask. I might have forgotten a few articles, but one or two little things don't matter when one has a load and is used to carrying it. If I should come home, I have lots of little stories that would make you laugh.

April 6, 1918 - HOLLAND

I was up and saw the boys from Union. I saw three I knew. Dan Layden [Daniel John Layden 1895-1985] and a couple others, they feel pretty blue. Also saw George Pierson [George Anthony Pierson 1894-1963] I haven't saw him for a couple of months, he is a cook now and looks good. We are getting 50 new men in our company, rookies. I don't think we will go across for some time yet. I don't see how we can when we have a bunch of rookies, and then we have lots to learn.

April 10, 1918 - HOLLAND

The weather is rainy. It has rained for two days and two nights. Last night I had to get up at 2 o'clock and go out and dig trench in the rain until seven in the morning. We have raincoats and good shoes. They make us get used to everything. I am sending a picture of my sweetheart in Erie. She sent me a pin and other Catholic dope to wear around my neck. She thinks I am a Catholic. I have had experience with them girls before.

❧

Few letters in this compilation were written by the officers of the Battalion about their daily experiences while at Camp Lee. From the few that were written by Captain Thomas, it is apparent that the officers had little free time. In April, the Battalion received a period of 12 to 24 hours of fighting simulation that attempted to closely duplicate the muddy conditions in France. It can be implied from Private Holland's letter that the officers had waited for the weather conditions to turn poor to allow the men to experience the sloppy conditions they would find in France. In addition to the sham battles that took place, the training included multiple hours of range fire and gas instruction given by the officers. While training and drill took up most of the day, the officers were expected to continue to work into the evening. Such was the case for Thomas who was teaching language classes to the non-English speaking draftees in the evening.

April 21, 1918 - THOMAS

There is no definite news of our leaving. Don't think it will be before May 15 anyway, so take your own sweet time, and please don't worry on that account. My company is about full now, and we haven't had too much time to whip this crowd into shape. I got a peach of a bunch of men in this last time, and am going to have a good company right away.

We had a Division inspection by the General yesterday, and I got by fine. They were very complementary about my Company, but the Company certainly did work for it.

I will let you know as much as possible, but our orders are exceedingly strict as you know on the subject. Spig is going to Fort Sill next Saturday to be gone a month. I don't suppose the Depot Brigade is going with us.

April 21, 1918 - HOLLAND

We had inspection by General Cronkite Saturday. He is commanding general. He said we didn't look like soldiers, our clothes don't fit and so on. You can write the U.S. about the money if you know who to write to. There's no use of writing to the Captain, he can do nothing. His name is Captain John Kean Company C.

Company Order No. 13. "Starting May 12 at retreat, this company is placed in quarantine. No one will be allowed to leave the battalion area except men acting as orderlies or when marched out in detachments. Men will not go to the YMCA. By order of John Kean, Captain" (Company Records).

May 12, 1918 - HOLLAND

I have been expecting to move for over a week and haven't moved yet. We are going over there. I won't be home on a furlough, so there's no use on you expecting me. You can answer, but I might not get it. I won't bother sending it back the watch. Bye-bye. And hi, this is Mother's Day.

May 12, 1918 - THOMAS

You're very much appreciated letter reached me in exactly the same fix you left me in. That is, completely packed and ready to go. It may be six hours and it may be six days, but all the Company stuff has gone with some exceptions. I am writing this of course in strictest confidence. I have my hands busy with getting recruits whipped into some kind of shape and keeping the Company more or less keyed up, which is some job as you can realize.

There is something else that I wanted to write you about. Both times you and Mama have been here, I'm afraid I have seemed a little unappreciative of your presence. It is not that I have not wanted to see you both and be with you, but here in the camp there is always something to do and there is no place to be alone. With you somewhere else it would be fine. I know you understand this. But I'm always busy at one thing or another here.

I wasn't much disappointed about not going over ahead of the Company. I've had one experience with this school thing and it is rotten. There is no service like service with troops, and I want to stay with mine.

I've been in the Army one year tomorrow, and all things considered, I think it is the best year I have ever spent. From all outlooks, this is a long war, and there will be a plenty of chance for all of us, so I try not to be impatient. It's a matter of a few days now, but I do wish we could get started.

Just got my little overseas cap today. It is very funny, and not especially adapted to my peculiar type of beauty. Another one of my lieutenants got married yesterday, but none for me.

May 1918 - THOMAS

Just as things go, after keeping us waiting for three days, and order came out last night calling the whole thing off, so we leave with the Division, which will be in a few days, I think.

I've got Mr. Jimmy Ferraro [1896-1983] my Striker now and he keeps my belt and puttees immaculate. He is going to be fine I think. We are still in a desperate rush. You can never tell how things are going. I'm trying to get all clothes issued out as soon as possible.

May 14, 1918 - HOLLAND

I will write a few lines just to let you know I am still alive. We are under guard and can't leave our Battalion grounds. Believe me, we raise hell every night. We had a parade tonight, tin pan drums and every old thing we could find, sing and holler, and now there's a square dance in the kitchen. I don't believe there will be anything left of the place by the time we leave, we sure have lots of fun, just like a lot of kids.

I guess I will send this down town with a guy's wife that is here tonight. You can write, I may be here a month yet, one can't tell. The weather is rainy down here for a day or so. I am well and happy. I wish we would move anytime. I am in a hurry to go.

P.S. don't worry about me, I am alright. It will take about 15 or 18 days for us to cross. You will get a card as soon as I get over.

May 18, 1918 - HOLLAND

Just a short letter to let you know I am all O.K. Eight months since I've been here, and it seems like a short time doesn't it? Everything is quiet at the present, we may be here for some time, one can't tell. It is quite warm and I have a letter to write to Marie [Marie Frazier 1897-2001] yet tonight. I won a watch last night in a raffle. It cost me $0.35 and they offered me $10 for it back. I guess I should have taken the money. It's an Elgin 17 jewel, I will raffle it off sometime after a payday when everything quiets down. It doesn't take long to sell 75 or 80 chances when they have a little money.

I am sending a picture of the gun we will use abroad, and the boys in my squad. Three of us not in the picture, Holleran, Terry [Lonnie Lee Terry 1894-1924] and Holland are absent, down working in the stables. We had to send this picture to Washington before they were made to see if they would allow the gun in a picture, so they printed them left-handed on purpose. Just hold it in the front of a looking glass and it will look alright in the glass. It is cooled by water and the hose running to the box condenses the steam so the enemy can't see steam and locate the gun.

May 21, 1918 - HOLLAND

I will write to let you know I am here, but don't expect to be very long, perhaps 15 minutes or maybe a week. The weather is warm and the sun is hot. I have my pack already made for the big trip. Believe me, I have a lot of junk. I haven't any news, only I got my forehead skimmed last night boxing. We have some time. 'We have all gone to war, and we don't know what it's for, but we will raise hell while we are here.' That's the chorus of a song we sing while we are marching.

May 22, 1918 - THOMAS

I appreciate you calling me last night very much. I rode over to Richmond after dinner with Captain Cox [Robert Hill Cox 1882-1961] and we went out to the country club last night. It was quite thrilling to have you call me there.

Things here are just the same. First it is one thing and then another. We may be here a day or two or an hour or two. Everybody's girl or wife seems to be around and it is hard to make things move. I wish we could get on out of here. It will be ever so much easier. The dust has been horrible, but we had a nice shower this afternoon.

All of the Battalion is confined to the area on account of measles. I think there are a few cases only and it will all be over by morning. This letter is of course really confidential and I hope you won't let it get out of the family. I am feeling fine. My tonsils are not bothering me. I will try my best to phone you before leaving, but can't promise.

CHAPTER 2
ARRIVAL IN FRANCE

The Battalion left Camp Lee in the early morning hours of May 23, 1918, and hiked to City Point, Virginia, about eight miles north of camp. At this port they boarded the *USS Pocahontas* and headed down the James River to the Newport News Naval Base. At Newport News, they disembarked from the *Pocahontas* and waited around for several hours before they were permitted to board their ship destined for France.

The historian of the 314th Machine Gun Battalion described falling in behind the 313th on their march from Camp Lee. "It was a dark march, but a lively one. The pace was brisk, and the men sang nearly all the way; the long expected adventure overseas had begun. At Hopewell and City Point, the singing column brought many inhabitants to their windows and doors, and soon they began to appear on the sidewalk, many very scantily attired. It was very early, scarcely daylight, when the battalion arrived, but the word spread around quickly that part of the Blue Ridge Division was leaving for Europe by way of the James River. Presently, a large crowd had gathered to bid goodbye to the troops. Many of the officers and men recognized friends in the crowd, as no attempt was made by the military authorities to keep the people from gathering on the wharf. So they stood at the gang planks and along beside the steamers, as the troops marched on board, bidding them a sincere God-speed and good luck" (Furr 16).

When the 313th Machine Gun Battalion boarded the *USS Mercury* on May 24, 1918, the unit consisted of 29 officers and 735 enlisted men. The Battalion was under the command of Major Oscar Foley (1878-1953), a seasoned machine gun officer. Foley's three years of past experience leading a machine gun troop made him a suitable choice to lead the men of this Battalion. A descendant of English and Irish parents, Foley spent his youth on a family farm in northwestern Missouri. He was commissioned a Second Lieutenant in 1898 at the age of 20. After graduating from West Point Military Academy in 1902, he was assigned to the United States Army Sixth Cavalry and stationed in the Philippine Islands. Foley worked his way up through the ranks until August 1914, when he was given command of a machine gun troop with the 3rd Calvary in Brownsville, Texas. Although the leadership assignments changed often during the war, the men of the 313th Machine Gun Battalion had Foley at the helm to take them from training to fighting. But, a new leader would return the men back home after the war. The concerns expressed by many of the men during this time was who in their ranks would not return home.

Over the next two days, other American troops converged on Newport News, but the *Mercury* remained docked until the afternoon of May 26. The ship set sail across the Atlantic with a convoy of 12 other ships. As the boats crossed the sea, the convoy scattered in the vast ocean so that only one or two ships were visible to the others.

During the day, the men were required to go on watch, looking out to the sea in search of enemy submarines. At night they travelled without lights to avoid detection. When the men were not on watch, they were entertained with motion pictures, or had music and singing during their meals. The Atlantic crossing also gave many of the men their first taste of sea sickness, particularly during bouts of rough weather.

&

Among the officers aboard the *Mercury* was a 27-year-old Second Lieutenant from Sharon Hill, Pennsylvania, named Otto Paul Leinhauser. He was born in Philadelphia, Pennsylvania to German immigrants Christian Leinhauser (1866-1946) and Margaret Gehring Leinhauser (1860-1955).

Christian Leinhauser emigrated to the United States in 1883 and became a naturalized citizen within a few short years. While he was one of 11 children born in Germany, most of his siblings remained in the old country. In the years leading up to the United States entry into the Great War, anti-German sentiment was building across the country, leading to many prejudices against German-Americans. Despite the bigotry, no one needed to question the loyalty of Christian, the "father of this intensely patriotic family" ("Leinhauser Quartet"). In addition to son Otto enlisting,

Christian's other son Frank also served in the United States Army.

Christian was an iron worker for the majority of his life, and son Otto followed in his footsteps. Otto Leinhauser first learned the trade working at the Baldwin Locomotive Works in Eddystone, Pennsylvania. In 1916, he went to work for the Wetherill Company in Chester, Pennsylvania, the same company that had employed his father since 1898. Wetherill was purchased by the Sun Shipbuilding and Dry Dock Company in 1916, and after about a year at the plant, Otto Leinhauser enlisted in the Army. He was sent to Fort Myer, Virginia, where in August 1917, he was commissioned a Second Lieutenant in the Infantry, Officer Reserve Corps. His first assignment was being attached to the 80th Division and sent to Camp Lee, Virginia to prepare the troops of the 313th Machine Gun Battalion. He was one of the most admired men among both the officers and the enlisted men in the ranks of the Battalion.

In January 1918, Leinhauser was granted leave while serving at Camp Lee and returned to Philadelphia where he married Elizabeth Simmer (1887-1978). Leinhauser frequently wrote letters home to his wife, but the majority of his military writings were recorded in a journal that he wrote while overseas. Because this journal was not censored by any of the other officers, his notations stating the names of towns and villages in France complement the censored writings of the other officers in the Battalion. He started journaling **LEINHAUSER** shortly after the Battalion left Virginia.

May 28-29, 1918 - LEINHAUSER

Came off watch at 6:00 instead of 7:30 a sick man. I went under. Was sick all day, went on watch again at 7:00 PM until 1:00 felt fine. Felt good this morning. On watch 11:00 to 3:00. We are having some rough weather just now, not so awful bad. Blowing pretty lively. Spray is coming over the side and wetting the boys who are foolish enough to stay out.

June 1, 1918 - LEINHAUSER

Starting a new month with a clean slate. Our transports had target practice this morning. One boat tows a target about four feet high and from 700 to 2400 yards. Each gun shoots 5 times. We had some good shots. Am writing a letter today, someone said mail goes back today. It is now 11:30 but it counts for 12:00 as the clock is set ahead about 25 minutes each day. 13 boats in our convoy – Barbarossa, Huron, Fredrick Der Grosse, Siboney, Kaiserin, Von Steuben, section of the Etel Frederick at Philadelphia, Amerika, Mongolia, Tenadores. All the boats are scattered now, can't see but two or three.

June 2, 1918 - THOMAS

This is written on board ship and will be mailed as soon as we land. I suppose we will land in about a week but I haven't the slightest idea where we are going and won't know until we arrive.

I am very proud of myself as a sailor. We started off with beautiful weather then for two days we had rather rough going. I haven't been sick a bit, but got really close once. A bunch of men got sick, but we are up in a state room and there is no reason why we should be uncomfortable at all.

We were supplied with plenty of those cards (I HAVE ARRIVED SAFELY OVERSEAS) and I sent you one. I hope you will receive it. I also wrote you this day before we pulled out.

This was all very interesting on account of the change, but we have been out a week now and I am about ready to go on to land. The food is fine though and you are Uncle Sam's guest all of the time you are aboard, so that makes it quite nice. We have a vaudeville performance and moving-pictures every night in the dining room and then turn in about ten o'clock. There are no lights in any state rooms and all are our matches have been taken away from us. It is all very interesting and rather hard to believe that there is any danger. I don't think there is much. Everybody says our Navy has accomplished wonders in the war zone and I'll admit that they are certainly efficient.

They had the usual joke yesterday of getting mail out for a mailbouy, sending men to the Captain of the boat for rubber envelopes and all that kind of thing, but of course they didn't catch me. You know me all.

After all the mystery about sailing it was all quite simple. I'll tell you all about it sometime. A lot of my friends are on board and I'm having quite a pleasant time. Am of course tickled to death not to be sick. It was certainly a pleasant surprise. I will write some more to this before landing, and then get it off immediately. Today is wonderful. Not a ripple on the ocean.

∽

While Captain Thomas presided over D Company as the senior officer, the enlisted men of C Company also had a commanding officer far different in social class than their own. Captain John Kean, pronounced 'Kane' by the family, was a 28-year-old Harvard graduate from Elizabeth, New Jersey. He led the men of C Company through most of their time in France.

Kean's different social class was evident in the letters he sent home and in his family pedigree. John Kean was born in New York in 1888 to former United States Senator Hamilton Fish Kean (1862-1941), and Katharine Winthrop Kean (1866-1943). He was raised at the family estate then known as *Ursino*, now called *Liberty Hall*, that is currently owned by Kean University of Union, New Jersey. His mother was a direct descendant of John Winthrop, the first governor of the Massachusetts Bay Colony. On his mother's side,

KEAN

the Winthrop ancestors passed down a sizable fortune to the family.

His father's side of the family boasted of a prominent place in American politics and history. Hamilton Fish Kean was a member of the Republican National Committee before running for a seat in the United States Senate. Captain Kean's uncle, John Kean (1852-1914), was also a United States Senator and served two terms in the United States House of Representatives.

Captain Kean's second great-grandfather, also named John Kean (1756-1795), was a delegate for South Carolina in the Continental Congress and was appointed by George Washington to be the Cashier of the Bank of the United States. His stature in the family was legendary, as the story of

Patriot John Kean was passed down through the generations. John Kean the Patriot died at the age of 39 from a respiratory disease contracted as a prisoner of war at sea during the American Revolution. Members of the Kean family were expected to learn about the history and sacrifices made by their ancestors.

John Kean also had a connections with the Roosevelt family. His Aunt Christine G. Kean (1858-1936) married William E. Roosevelt (1857-1930), a first cousin to President Theodore Roosevelt (1858-1919).

Captain Kean enjoyed many of the privileges bestowed upon anyone raised in a prominent American family. As a result, his experiences prior to coming into the military would have been vastly different from those of most of the men in this Battalion.

It would be easy to dismiss Kean as yet another Ivy League elite who was handed the reins of a Company by simply being born into a prominent family. However, the perceptions of Harvard graduates today are far different from those of the men put into leadership positions during the Great War. The Kean family had both the financial means and the social connections to protect their sons from areas of the war that would put them at the greatest risk. But these were times when many of the young men from these Ivy League schools sought to play a part in shaping events of the world. Although they were often naïve about the risks, and their perception of war was sometimes romanticized, there was an immense amount of patriotism among this group.

It may have been possible for John Kean to command a less hazardous unit, and as his letters indicate, he was certainly given a few more comforts than the average Doughboy. However, his willingness to command a machine gun battalion, and face the heightened risk of going into the battlefield, speaks directly to his character.

Kean attended St. Mark's, a private boarding school in Southborough, Massachusetts, before obtaining his undergraduate degree from Harvard. Kean was physically fit and a member of the Harvard football team. Because of his social status at Harvard, he occasionally ran into old classmates or past sporting opponents while serving in France.

The Kean family owned the Elizabethtown Gas & Light Company, a large utility. The upbringing of Captain John Kane suggests that while he was raised with privileges known only to a few, he was not handed anything. He put in the effort and time necessary to gain the knowledge and experience for his next position, whatever that might be. Kean could have walked into an office job for this company directly out of school. However, he was expected to understand many facets of the operations to be in a position to lead with knowledge. At one time, he worked as an apprentice fireman and engineer, obtaining practical knowledge of the operations. This knowledge would be useful to him when he became an executive officer in the company.

After completing his Law Degree from Harvard in 1913, he went to work for the law firm of Lindabury, Depue & Faulks of Newark, New Jersey. In this role he gained admission to the New York bar.

Captain Kean received eight years of early military training prior to the United States' involvement in the war. While attending Harvard, he served in the Massachusetts Militia and obtained the rank of Sergeant; while working in Newark, he was a member of the New Jersey Militia. Later, he was commissioned a Second Lieutenant with the New Jersey National Guard. In the summer of 1916, he spent three and a half months with the First Squadron of the New Jersey Calvary on Mexican border duty in Douglas, Arizona. In May 1917, he was called to active duty and promoted to a First Lieutenant training at Fort Myer, Virginia. During the 80th Division's forming at Camp Lee, he was promoted to Captain and assigned to lead C Company of the 313th Machine Gun Battalion.

June 2, 1918 - KEAN

Well, we finally did get away. We left camp after midnight, and marched about 7 miles. Just at dawn we got on board a boat for about a six hour trip. We then landed and sat around for about three hours. We were then marched on board this boat, where we have been ever since and where we will probably be for some little time to come as they don't run ferries on express schedules.

Everything went off very well and I managed to get aboard with my whole Company, though some of them thought it their duty to drink up the lemon extract, or something with alcohol in it, and were a little unsteady on their pins.

Cox, Thomas and I have a cabin together and it would be very comfortable except that all the port holes are closed at all times which makes it a trifle stuffy, and nearly all light go out at dusk. It has been cold and not very pleasant so far, but today is fine. In fact, for two or three days it was fairly choppy and most of the men were sick. We have daily abandon ship drills and if an old sub should get us, so that we had to quit the boat, it wouldn't take us long to do so. In fact, the only thing that I wouldn't mind about it would be losing my kit, which has taken quite a while to accumulate.

This boat is an ex-German of medium size, but it doesn't really make much of a difference to the men what size she is as they always load them to capacity so that they are pretty well crowded. However, they seem to be getting along well. Target practice was held yesterday it was quite exciting. Going out of the harbor it was interesting to see the different types of camouflage on the boats, I believe I understand the theory of it but I was hanged if I could see how it worked, except in a very few cases. We are not alone in our trip, and it gives one quite a sociable feeling to see another ship, where on an ordinary crossing one doesn't see a boat for days. It is just like having another person with you on any adventure. The food is fine and Uncle Sam must be losing lots of money from the quantity we manage to tuck away. The Y.M.C.A. have many boxes of books on board furnished by the War Service Library so that the men and the officers have plenty to read which is a great blessing. The books have a slip in the front saying that if you aren't through you can return it to any Y.M.C.A, K of C, or chaplain at any camp.

So you see they are getting things pretty well fixed and I think I shall find the same true with most things. However, if there is anything that I do want I will let you know, I believe the Y.M.C.A. canteens have tobacco etc. for sale. Probably the only things that I will want will be socks and cigars. As I have at present plenty of them, I will have a change to find exactly what I do want and then write you an order, which will be no trouble at all except for you.

June 6, 1918 - THOMAS

Am writing this while waiting on the barber. Have been on the boat two weeks now and am about ready to get off. The weather continues fine and we have really had a wonderful trip. We hope to land about Saturday, but we don't know where as yet.

We are kept pretty busy practically all of the time, either studying or looking after the men in some kind of way. They have been fine, although they have had rather uncomfortable quarters. I've been playing bridge quite a good deal, and also am up on deck in a deck chair being as comfortable as possible. The pictures and vaudeville still keep up. We will all be horribly busy as soon as we land I know, but I will try to write you as often as possible.

Just heard this A.M. that a U-boat sunk a boat just off of Norfolk. Getting pretty close, isn't it?

I hope daddy is still improving, and feel certain that he is. He would certainly enjoy this trip. But I'll admit that I would rather be on land. It is certainly curious how little feeling of nervousness there is on board. We all wear a life preserver but everything goes on as a matter of course.

The thought of a stealth attack weapon lurking beneath the ocean undoubtedly raised fear in the minds of those aboard a ship in those days. The men of the battalion travelling to France saw the need to be vigilant. Many anxious troops reported on any suspicious findings in the water, and this led to many false alarms and rumors. Thomas' letter was referring to the incident in June 1918 in which German U-boats were seen off the coast of the United States. Rear Admiral Fechteler, commandant of the Norfolk Navy Yard, reported that two U-boats were sighted off the Virginia capes; and Rear Admiral McLean, commandant of the Fifth Naval District, reported two other U-boats sighted off the coast of New Jersey, with one just off the coast of North Carolina. The Secretary of the Navy Daniels issued a report in Washington DC on June 3, 1918 that the *Jacob M. Haskell* schooner had been sunk by a U-boat. The vessel was sailing from Boston on its way to Norfolk with 11 crew and no passengers ("Navy Official Statement").

On June 6, the entire convoy converged as they got closer to the coast of France. On June 7, the *Mercury* left the larger convoy of troop ships and headed for the seaport in Brest. It sailed south with the *USS Siboney* and *USS Tenadores* through the Sea of Biscay, heading for docks located at the American Naval Base in Bassiens. To reach this inland station, the ships had to travel about sixty miles up the Gironde River. The *Mercury* anchored off the Cordouan lighthouse located near the mouth of the Gironde estuary for one day before it could be escorted up the river. The troops on the ship would have observed a great deal of activity near the coast, as French dirigibles flew overhead spotting for German submarines.

June 7, 1918 - LEINHAUSER

Had Mass this morning in the dining room. Had a rumor this morning that a sub was chased by a destroyer at 1:00 AM. I was on watch but knew nothing about it. Ocean is as calm as a piece of glass not even a ripple. Dandy weather. The convoy splits up at 6:00 PM. Part go to one port, part to another. Don't know where we go yet.

June 7, 1918 - KEAN

Still going quietly along, we expect to get within sight of land sometime tomorrow. There are several very agreeable Navy Officers on board but all in all it is a stupid dull trip. We are and have been in the submarine zone and they say that a year ago one could see wreckage all about, however, we have only seen a couple of whales.

It is a funny feeling to be using German glassware, German cutlery and German blankets etcetera, all marked for, of course, the boats. Fillings are largely the same as they were before. We get occasional wireless bulletins but not much news or many details but they say that the ports are very much Americanized and that there are newspapers printed in English.

An orchestra of the men plays music more or less, sweet at lunch and dinner and in the evening. I haven't missed a meal yet and haven't felt as though I was going through a good many others have.

June 7-8, 1918 - THOMAS

Friday. This is probably our last day on the water. It is beautiful out and I haven't anything to do but sit up on deck and look at the water. It is fine to have this opportunity. I wouldn't take anything for it. We have a pretty good idea of where we are going now and I want to be in and possibly landed by tomorrow night. I will be glad to get off of here, but the trip has been wonderful. There is not a ripple on the water.

I see by the morning bulletin that things are going pretty well in France, but it looks like a year or two more anyway. I'm selfish enough to hope we get in it anyway for a while, I suppose I'll have enough before it is over. It would be very easy to make a nice letter out of this but there is so very much you can't say. I hope you are not worrying about me. I don't think I will be able to cable, but you will get the card about Monday I suppose. I will write you again tomorrow.

Saturday. We expect to sight land now almost any time. Everybody is looking for it. It is reported now that we won't leave the ship until Monday. A submarine was reported last night by one of the destroyers and there was a great shooting of rockets etc. I doubt if it was one, but it added a little excitement. I've got a bunch of stuff to do getting ready to go ashore and out whether I have time to write again. It is all wonderful and I love it.

❧

The Battalion disembarked the *Mercury* on June 10, 1918, and marched a few miles to the town of Bordeaux. After leaving Bordeaux, they marched north to Camp Genicart, located near the Village of Lormont. There the men stayed for eight days before their orders sent them to their first training area in Northern France. At this rest area, most of the men in the Battalion would experience the culture, customs, and language of a foreign country for the first time.

June 10, 1918 - LEINHAUSER

Arrived at Bassiens at 7:00 AM and disembarked a short while after. Laid around until about 9:45 PM then marched to our rest camp which is about 3 miles out. Did not see much of the country on our way as it was dark. The scenery on the river was beautiful. Had our first night of sleep in France on a straw mattress with Giles Thornes trench coat for a cover [Gilbert George Thorne Jr. 1894-1988]. Had breakfast and then got all our luggage which we now have fixed up in our room. We have hammocks to sleep in. So do the men. Not as good as Camp Lee though. Hardly realize we are in France. Quite a few women came to camp this morning to gather laundry. Expect to go Bordeaux this afternoon with Stoddart [Robert Stone Stoddart Sr. 1895-1977].

June 10, 1918 - THOMAS

I am mailing one letter to you today but wanted to write to you as we received permission to be a little more explicit. We arrived off the French coast Saturday noon and found we were bound for Bordeaux. We came up the river and got inside submarine nets that night. Then we started up with the tide yesterday. I wanted to write to you as the trip yesterday was I think the most wonderful I have ever had. On both sides of the river as far as could be seen were miles and miles of vineyards. Every little space a tall church spire and a wonderful Château. I never saw a walled city just as it was four or five hundred years ago. The fields were all cultivated. We landed on the American docks below Bordeaux and marched 4 miles to camp. Got here about 12 o'clock. I slept on the floor but was so happy I could have slept in a swamp. Nobody knows how long we will be here or where we are going, but we don't care. The men were all wonderfully happy and singing all the way in.

I left camp with 172 and got here with 172 [enlisted men] all well and the only full Company in the Battalion. I had some pictures of the convoy sent you, I think you will enjoy. I've got my Sam Browne belt on today and feel quite set up. I have all my company mail to censor so you can imagine I'm busy. On the march last night the air was heavy with the smell of roses and lilac.

June 15, 1918 - THOMAS

We have been here now about a week and I want to drop you a few lines. We have had leave, the officers, practically as much as we wanted, and I have pretty well gone over Bordeaux. It is a wonderful old town and extremely interesting. There is of course a remarkable lack of young men and every variety of uniform you can think of. Ever so many Spaniards, also refugees from other towns. The prices are extremely high, but I am equipped at present, thank the Lord, and hope I won't spend much money.

Everybody is happy about being over but I'm tired of a rest camp. The men got pretty badly mixed up with their wine here, but it has all blown over now. Had to read the riot act to them pretty severely. We won't be here very much longer.

This part of France is beautiful. The days are very warm and the nights very cool. No cooties yet, but a few fleas. It is all wonderful to me though. The French are very nice to us, but we only see the edge of the Army. My French is improving wonderfully. I make myself understood now and I couldn't a week ago. We don't see the better class of French people, except we meet some of the officers. The censorship of letters is very funny. The men write such funny things home. One said the other day, 'as soon as we reached the shores of France, we heard the sound of guns, and an aero plane came out to meet us, twice as big as our barn.'

I don't need a thing and am well and very happy. Hope we get some action before long, and maybe we will. Love to the family. Will write again as soon as possible.

June 15, 1918 - KEAN

Near Bordeaux. We were escorted from the U.S. by a hydroplane and before we reached these shores we were met by a dirigible and several hydroplanes, thus the progress of war in the 20th Century. As I wrote you, we had an uneventful trip over, arriving a little over two weeks after we set sail. A few more days after that we embarked. We landed at about 8 o'clock and marched 4 miles to what they call a rest camp where we arrived about midnight and where we have been ever since we found the waterfront. In fact, a large part of this country is quite Americanized. It certainly was a cosmopolitan sight at the dock. The Chinese, American Turks, French Arabs and many other nationalities in many and varied costumes/uniforms.

We shortly leave here for a place nearer the front. Which I think will be within sound of the guns. For some reason we are allowed to mention the fact that we are near Bordeaux. I have been in there two or three times, it is certainly a remarkable sight to sit in the café and watch the crowd. The colors are remarkable and you see all the armies and all the people of the world represented.

᪗

On June 16, 1918, the Battalion departed Camp Genicart by train for Calais, France. This train ride, which took about 2 days, carried the men over 500 miles through the French countryside. The use of rail car to transport the troops became part of the Doughboy vernacular during and after the war. It was often used as a joke when describing the lack of comfort in transportation. The men crowded onto French box cars that were labeled "40 Hommes – 8 Chevaux," which translated as "40 men, 8 horses."

There was an obvious lack of comfort in having to spend days and nights traversing the country in these crowded box cars. Division records indicate that the train had to pass through the French town of Orleans on its way to Calais because a bridge had been previously bombed by a German raid.

June 17, 1918 - LEINHAUSER

Left Camp Genicart at 7:30 AM Sunday. Got on train at 10:30 and left for nobody knows. Am enjoying the trip immensely. Beautiful scenery all along the way. We passed through [Versailles] seen an awful lot of damaged airplanes, also an aviation field with hundreds of sheds and quite a few dirigibles. Also seen a lot of autos. Plenty of soldiers. Saw the Eiffel Tower in distance. We are traveling very slowly. Red Cross gives coffee every morning and then. We have lots to eat. Arrived in [Marseilles] at 1:10 AM. And after the usual arguments with the M.P. got started for a hotel. Stopped for the night, got up at seven and had breakfast brought to our room. Heard that our train was three hours late so we took a walk through the town for a couple hours.

Had our dinner then went to the railroad station arriving just in time as the train was about ready to leave. Very crowded so we stood almost all the way. Wonderful scenery, high mountains with châteaux on them, large crags and forest covering them. Mediterranean roads fixed, comes right into the railroad track. Road runs alongside of the mountain all the way, winding in and out, up and around. Fruit trees are in bloom, grass is green and trees have plenty of foliage on them yet. It is wonderful and getting prettier all the time. Arrived at [Calais] at 7:10 PM and took a room at the Agnletere Hotel with hot bath. Had our supper or dinner as it is now and then, went to bed to read for a while. Got up at eight with the sun streaming in our window and a regular spring day before us. Looked out the window and was surprised to see green trees and grass. Have a dandy room overlooking the Seine River. This place seems to like me. Went to Cantu to watch the tennis tournament.

᪈

The Battalion ultimately reached Calais on June 18, where they were introduced to British units and customs over the next three days. In Calais the troops received additional equipment and ordinance. It was also in Calais that the men would be introduced for the first time to the reality of wartime destruction. Multiple structures in and around Calais had been demolished by the incessant German bombing. Calais was a major port supplying the British Army and was therefore a prime target. Although this area was considered to be a rest camp, there would be few restful evenings with the almost nightly air-raid alarms warning of the approaching enemy planes.

The stop in Calais served a single purpose. It was a place to be equipped with arms and equipment necessary to train and support their attachment with the British Army. Over the next month, the Battalion would undertake intense training to complement the schooling they had received at Camp Lee. The machine guns the Battalion had trained with back in the States would not be used in the first part of their tour. They needed to be equipped with the type used by the British, and so the British Vickers machine guns were issued to the Battalion, along with the British Lee-Enfield rifle.

Because the 80th Division was going to be placed in service with British troops, it was necessary to supply the frontline with only one type of ammunition. Therefore, the American troops turned in their American-Enfield rifles, bayonets, and ammunition and were supplied with the British style rifle, helmets and gasmasks.

June 18-20, 1918 - LEINHAUSER

Arrived at Calais at 10:00 got in camp at 10:30 same camp. Old tents. Very good food though find canteen reasonable prices too. Seeing quite a few airplanes this morning. Seen a squadron coming back from a raid. Have a Chinese hospital alongside of us. The town has been bombed eight times in 12 days. Right near the Channel. Wednesday and Thursday went through Calais seen the English Channel also England. Had our gasmasks and steel hats issued. Seen British Aero factory. Also seen Belgium and French hangers. Also see big forts and another squad came home from a raid. Had ballgame beat 314th Battalion. Seen Queen Mary WAAC camp. Lots of good looking women.

June 19, 1918 - THOMAS

Since last writing we have moved around considerably. I don't know exactly what I can write and what I cannot, but anyway we are in another rest camp after having traveled for two days on a French train. The trip was very interesting but very tiresome, but the newness had not worn off for the men and they didn't mind it so much. I have stayed in camp ever since arriving except to go out with the company to draw gasmasks and steel hats.

We go to billets tomorrow or next day and are to be brigaded with the English I think. We get very little information, and it all comes at the last minute, so we have very little time to plan or to look ahead. You would enjoy France so much mama. It is all laid out so beautifully. Any anywhere you look, the landscape is just like a picture. Every single bit of space is used up for something. The French are very nice but very funny. They have an exceeding regard for property rights and also for wood. It is not an uncommon thing to see 'eggs and chips for sale here.'

They won't stand for trespass at all. Their whole customs are different from ours. They seem very glad to have us here, but are not like us at all. We see all kinds of troops, Portuguese, Belgians, Turcos, Chinese, and everything that you can imagine. I will be very glad when we get permanently located so that we can get down to work again. We see ten to fifteen aeroplanes going over at any time. It is by no means an unusual sight, and you can hear them at night too. After so much looking forward to all of this, it seems so very commonplace and just like the natural course of events. I've got a little cap now and wear my Sam Browne belt at all times. We were informed last night that all of our expensive equipment was more or less worthless. I think we could very easily replace a good part of it very easily. Well, it is not unusual and I'm not so much surprised. We will probably get a chance to show what we have got before very long. I will be very glad when it comes. We have no mail of course and don't know when we will get any. I understand some is chasing us around.

We are messing at an officer's canteen here and it is entirely satisfactory. The food is cheap and good. The food here has been alright and we have been very comfortable. I am well and happy. I have a lot to do but enjoy it.

June 19, 1918 - KEAN

Well we have moved, and are to move again soon to our bases, at present we are outfitting. We traveled for several days but luckily got mostly passenger cars. I say luckily but I am not sure the men are not better off traveling in box cars than they are in the passenger cars. We the four captains had a compartment together and managed to fix ourselves very comfortably. It was an interesting journey watching the difference in the attitude of the people and the change in the character of the country, at one time we reached the outskirts of Paris.

Where we were before the cheap wine and the plentifulness of it almost astonished the men who had been in a dry territory for so long, they thought that they could drink it all up and some of them got into a little trouble over it, of course it is always your best men who insist upon making damn fools of themselves.

However, I hope to convince them after a while that the policy of good behavior is the best, and that having wine always there is no necessity of seeing how much you can consume.

I expect to get fat at this camp as we have tea, as well as dinner. It is quite jolly don't you know. I found at our last place that censoring the men's mail was an awful job, by golly they do write a lot, and what trifle it is. I hate to write a letter as it is so much like the stuff they pull off.

On our trip we passed several places which had recently been subjected to aerial bombardment; our first sight of the actual results of the war.

CHAPTER 3
SHARING THE TRENCHES WITH NEW ZEALAND

The Battalion's move to the training area placed them with the American Second Army Corps located inside the British Zone, an area that the British Expeditionary Forces held on the Western Front that extended from Belgium to the north of Amiens. This British Zone in northern France held thousands of American troops, and it was here that the Battalion was trained and supplied by the British. The 80th Division's headquarters were located in the town of Samer. Billeting the men required the use of as many houses, barns and outbuildings available in and around the Samer training area. The French government required most residences and buildings in the land to be used for billeting troops. The owners were paid by the government for the use of their property. The American officers generally billeted with the owners of the residence, and the enlisted men found any available space in outbuildings, sheds, cellars or even barns. The 313th Machine Gun Battalion billeted in the small village of Le Turne for the next month.

During their first phase of training, the Battalion did not stay together as a unit. Some of the officers and NCOs were sent to specialized training schools organized by the British command. The typical schools lasted anywhere from four days of training to as long as two weeks. A few of the enlisted were sent to British ordnance shops for instruction on how to repair the Vickers machine gun. In the town of Haut Tingry, the Division organized training in gas defense and established firing ranges for practice using the heavy Vickers machine gun. One of the lengthiest schools developed by the British was located near Étaples and lasted for thirty days. It required nine officers and eighteen NCOs from the Battalion to travel to the British General Headquarters machine gun school at Camiers.

The billeting conditions during this time were adequate for the men, but the availability of fresh drinking water in the Samer area was a challenge and required having water hauled a considerable distance to the billeted areas. This scarcity of water, however, did not discourage the men from finding any means by which to quench their thirst when off duty. The troops were allowed to patronize the village estaminets, but were restricted to only the purchase of beer or wine. Occasionally, it was necessary for the officers to discipline troops who took the opportunity to imbibe a bit too far, especially after they received their first allotted pay.

Not all off duty experiences in the Samer area were self-serving. The good nature of many of the troops would lend their experiences from back home to helping the local inhabitants of the village with their daily chores. It was not uncommon to see a group of American soldiers helping the land owner harvest and store their crops. Perhaps it was a way to escape the monotony of billeting in a sleepy village, or maybe a simple expression of gratitude to the people who owned the billet.

June 27, 1918 -THOMAS

We are billeted in a little village about 40 miles from the front. It is comparatively quiet except for a few airplanes passing and occasionally the sound of the guns, rather muffled in the distance. You would hardly know we were at war. Everything seems just a part of the general scheme, nothing out of the ordinary. I positively haven't had a thrill up to now.

I am in a house to which the only approach is through a remarkably dirty barn yard, but my window looks out on a beautiful garden of flowers and vegetables. The roses are beautiful. The nights are almost cold and I appreciate my bed. The men are in barns, but seem comfortable and happy. I have been censoring the Company mail and haven't seen a word of complaint. The spirit is fine and it is all over our Army I hear. I think our troops are going to give a wonderful account of themselves when we get a real show. The French are wonderful people, but dirty. They have a wonderful country here. I have never seen such farms and in such wonderful shape. The women do most of the work, in fact all of it. There are a few old men. They seem to take us as a matter of course. There is a woman who owns my house with one little son. She has two young boys and one old man and a little girl about 14 who do all the work out of her farm. She has about six horses and eight cows. She does everything and is always cheerful and very nice. She gives me strawberries as big as young apples. You break them in two to eat them and they are wonderful. I don't go out of camp except with the Company. There is nothing much to do here. I'll have a horse tomorrow and can ride around a little. We don't hear any news at all, so don't know what is going on. Also don't care much. We are brought into pretty close touch with foreign officers, and they are all very nice. My striker is a wonder. He is a peach and does everything for me. I am very well and happy.

June 27, 1918 - KEAN

Since I last wrote you we have gotten our gas masks and tin hats and moved to our first billets where we are hard at work training, as all my officers, except one, and 15 of my noncoms are away at school, it makes matter slightly difficult. However, we are busy from 5:45 AM to 5:15 PM every day. And some time in the future we will move a little further forward, and train some more, and then probably to reserve and so on in. They have stripped the men to their packs and the officers down to 50 pounds, so you see we are traveling light, and much had to be sent away. They have taken what American equipment arrived with us and issued us British equipment in its place. Most of it didn't include lots of my private stuff such as Papa's cigars for Winthrop, etc. I packed it away with the Company property.

The Company billeted in a typical French village, you know, the kind about 30 farm homes in a group surrounded by rolling farming country. My Company occupies barns around an open farm yard with the usual manure pile, pigs, cows, chickens etc. Some of their letters on the subject are quite amusing, though the job of censoring them is an awful bore and takes up heaps of time. This part of France is certainly very beautiful. Extensively a farming country, with sheep, cows and other livestock for the pasture land of wheat, clover, etc.

We spent last Sunday marching to the sea to give the men a bath but after a long tiresome walk on the hard road the wind was too cold for most of them to go in. I must say, either the roads here are much harder or else my feet have become softened in my traveling for they certainly ache after much walking.

This is a very funny climate, hot when the sun is out, but cold when it's not, and cold and damp at night. In fact, it's quite unpleasant outdoors.

Cox is at present in command as the Major is away at school. We have seen countless aeroplanes flying about. Sometimes 8 or 10 together, and today there must have been a Boche about for we could hear the guns firing and see the bursts in the sky, but couldn't see the planes.

I personally am billeted in a farmhouse which is right along the road with the yard in the rear. I have a room about 10 x 7 with a red tile floor, very clean, nice certainly. A wonderfully soft bed and wash stand, two chairs, a mirror, a rosary, a crucifix and several pictures of Saints. The family consists of a man, two girls around 20, one about 15, two about 10 and a boy about 4 or 5. The latter is fine and a great friend of mine. In fact, I think I am getting along all right with them, though they are a little in awe of the foreign Captain and don't know quite what to make of us.

I eat in another farm house where Cox established a mess. There seems to be a mother and daughter there and we have a fine time talking broken French and English. They get lots of fun teasing us because we drink water, tea or coffee by choice instead of wine. When I was unpacking I found several odds and ends that I had no use in keeping, if I couldn't use them myself, so I gave them to my host. The result was that my 4 year old presented me with a bunch of roses, evidently urged on to it by his sisters.

I think our men are getting on all right in the village. We had a little trouble at first as the Australians and Portuguese had proceeded us here at various times. I guess the latter were not very popular and the former when here a trifle wild. They say the Australians are at the head of the Boche list of troops they dislike to be against.

I hope to seen the Americans there soon for the attitudes of the men all seems to be that they are here for business. They have a dirty, unpleasant job to do, but the sooner they thoroughly finish it, the sooner they can get home. They want to go home, but they want to finish the job first. I don't get much chance to write, as we can't have any light after dark and very often there is work to do after supper, which is the only time I have to myself, to say nothing of those blooming letters to censor.

June 28, 1918 - KEAN

We wear nothing but dinky caps over here, or our tin hats. I have purchased another hat which has the red and blue piping on it which seems to be the machine gun color.

We are having a good many reveries and inspections tomorrow, the Duke of Connaught looks us over.

&

With the Battalion attached to the British Army, a military review was given by Arthur William Patrick Albert (1850-1942), also known as Prince Arthur, the Duke of Connaught and Strathearn, who was the son of Queen Victoria.

July 4, 1918 - KEAN

The rest of the men from camp, with the exception of the machine guns, have gone forward. I expect that we shall in a week or so. Today, being the Fourth, we have had no formation, but this morning had an exhibition drill by an English demonstration platoon and this afternoon, athletic contests and a baseball game. As the men have not been paid for two months, I have lent them money to celebrate the Fourth. They have about 1,700 Francs of mine now and if they don't get paid some, I will be broke.

Aeroplanes are very thick, and we often see a flock or flight or squadron, or what you will, of 10 or 12. They say that a document found on a German prisoner the other day gave the location of a division.

July 8, 1918 - THOMAS

There hasn't been much to write as we are settled down to a regular routine. It is much easier though because the men as a whole are taking quite an interest in the work, and besides a few spasmodic outbreaks caused by drinking a little too much wine, life is anything that you might imagine, except exciting war times. Four of my officers are away at school and 13 of my non-coms. All but one officer and one Sergeant will be home tomorrow night.

We can hear the artillery at the front practically incessantly, but it is no more noticeable than the large number of aero planes that are over at all time. The Boche planes are easily distinguishable by a difference in the sound of their motors. We here had several air raids in the vicinity, and when they drop one of their larger bombs, the explosion sounds very close. I had very curious feelings for the first two raids, but have found a way to fool them now, that is, I go to sleep early and nothing but a direct hit would wake me so you know.

We hope to move up close to the front pretty soon, but I want about two more weeks with training back here. I'm going to school beginning Wednesday or Thursday for one week, I hope, but only have to ride about 2 miles in the morning and have my orderly bring my horse back at 4:30 PM in the afternoon. We train eight hours a day. The English don't train that much and seem surprised that we learn so fast. The English officers are all very nice.

I've got the nicest bunch of officers in the Army I think. They are a peach of a bunch of boys, and we get along fine. All of our Battalion, the men, seem to think that all that is necessary is for us to get up to the front and church will be out. They have a hard road to travel first I think, but where we get a little experience we are going to have a wonderful Army. Everybody is high in their praises of them now. I, of course, would like to see peace but I would really like to get a little action before it is over, and it would do the men good.

It is hard work making a Company in war times. I brought a full Company over, but have lost two men already. One sick in hospital and one transferred to lighter duty. But the war over here has been entirely delightful up until now.

We have been here exactly a month now, and it only seems a few days. I don't like the French much, but I guess they are war-worn and tired out. They have a great army though and a wonderful spirit. The war is on till the end and we are really beginning to make a show. With one million troops already over and more coming all of the time it really looks like an Army. I would like to see four million troops here. We could really make a show there.

I like being near the front ever so much better than back home. They don't haggle about paperwork so much, and you can really have more time for training. I hate to think about losing any of my men, but that is part of it I guess.

July 9, 1918 - KEAN

We are still in the same place and still drilling hard, shooting every day, and as I have said before. I drill all day, eat supper, censor mail, and go to bed. That is my daily routine. However, I have now gotten my Lieutenants back from school, where they have been for 16 days and I expect to have a little more time now.

Last Sunday we drove to a nearby sea side town where I managed to get a tub of hot water and had a splendid bath in a porcelain lined tub and everything. My first bath in over two weeks and my first warm bath in water that wasn't salt, or in a tub that wasn't a foot bath since leaving Camp Lee.

Transportation around here is most peculiar. You either bicycle, walk, ride a horse or bum rides on the passing autos which have instructions to give you lifts if convenient. There doesn't seem to be any other means of communication transportation and we met a British officer the other night who had been hooking his way all day on the way home on leave and still had quite some distance to go.

We put up a small purse for a series of field events, and my Company won four out of six events. We also had a ballgame between this Battalion and the 315th, but we lost it. In the morning, a platoon of Scotch drilled for us and all in all, I think the men had a fair time. It was a good thing that money was scarce as they managed to get pretty well lit up anyhow in the evening, although we had no trouble.

I met Eddy Harding walking along the road today. He said he was at a hospital 8 miles away, he is a medical Captain in the British Army. He went to Groton and was Captain of their football team my year at school, and played against me 3 years and, was in my class at college graduating from the Harvard Medical School later, and then coming over here with some Harvard Medical Unit.

We wear our gas masks daily for various periods and I have worn it for over an hour at a time. We are all getting as that we don't mind them at all, but go on about our trainees just as usual with them on. It is a funny thing to see all the men in their spare moments helping the farmers, pitching hay, milking cows, carrying milk and water etc. Of course they are accompanied by a pretty girl, more or less, depending on your taste. How they converse is more than I can make out, as none of them could speak a word of French when they arrived. I find that I can get along quite well in French and pigeon English, except that I am not very good in regard to putting my sentences and words together. My vocabulary is fair and I can usually make them understand anything I want to say even when it is merely holding a conversation, but I am afraid it is often a literal translation of the English sentence rather than the French way of saying it, as I am a little out of practice.

I hope you can read this scribble which is written on my lap interrupted by Maurice Fischer, the youngest of my family, aged 3, who is constantly showing me something or wanting me to do something. The little girls aged about 5 and 8 are getting much more friendly and I shall be quite sorry to leave here, though I don't think you would like it, as the odor of the kitchen, sort of sweat and grease is always prevalent in my room except at night when the door is closed.

I find it quite a job to get much idea as to war conditions in general over here. You meet one officer whose nerves are pretty well gone and who has had a bad time and he takes a very blue view of everything. The next one is feeling O.K. and gives you quite the opposite impression. I think there is one thing that is true, they are very, very glad to see our men over here, and so far have been extraordinarily well impressed by them, and quite agreeably surprised.

July 12, 1918 – HOLLAND

I haven't received any mail from you yet, and don't expect to for a month, yet no doubt you will get the whole bunch of letters I have written all at once. When we get mail it comes all in a bunch. This country is somewhat different than the U.S.A., it's quite nice, but not up to date like the U.S.A. of course. When one can't speak their language it makes it somewhat hard, but you can believe me, I do pretty good talking with my hands. I am well and hope everyone is the same at home. Here's hoping you receive all my mail okay. If you don't know my address you can easily find out from Barstows. I have sent it in half a dozen letters and no doubt you have it.

July 14, 1918 - THOMAS

We have all of our staff for training now and it is so very much easier to hold the men's attention. A party from this Battalion is going up for observation to the front lines. Two of my sergeants are going, but I wasn't lucky enough to get a chance this time. We will get all we want later I guess. I don't know how long we are supposed to stay in these billets but I don't think it will be very long.

Today is the French Independence Day, corresponds to our Fourth of July I believe, but it is raining and we are out in the country so won't see much celebration.

The Company hasn't been paid in about 2 1/2 months and I have loaned all the money I had to them so haven't left camp since arriving here. I don't care much though as I had rather stay around here anyway.

I'm in command of the Battalion for a few days, but it is just about as easy as a Company. I suppose there is a big draft on always now. I think it will keep on now, by the number of men that are being sent over. I don't see much war here. There was another air raid last night over a neighboring town but it didn't bother me, as I was asleep. My striker told me about it this morning.

All my non-coms, and all my officers have returned from school except two. They have gone for a little longer course and will not return for about two weeks.

The French are funny people. They go ahead with their work at all times, here really, pretty close to the front, and they certainly are taking advantage of the fact that we are here. Everything is desperately high, and it is next to impossible to buy anything. I understand it is the same way everywhere, also in England.

You hear a good deal more of the war than we do. We never hear anything as a matter of fact, except that we get a London paper every day or so. You see the front is so wide it is next to impossible to keep up with more than a very small sector of it, and that very indirectly. We will give a good account of ourselves if we ever get up there.

Tom Thornhill is my transport lieutenant [Thomas Murrell Thornhill 1894-1972]. He is doing fine. His wife said she was coming to visit you this summer.

July 14, 1918 - KEAN

I am leaving for a few days inspection of the front tomorrow. Spent last night in one of the nearby British base cities and had a fine time. Went and dined with Eddy Harding at his hospital on Friday. Saw Alan Gregg who was in my class and Mike Grinnell of New Bedford who was a couple of years ahead of me. Also met Bobbie Morgan of N.Y., brother of Harry, and Charles who is at a M.G. school near there. They showed me where the Harvard Unit was located that was bombed last year and caused such a fuss. I remember reading about it in the bulletin.

July 21, 1918 - HOLLAND

I have received mail from the U.S. in 20 days, that's pretty quick. I am well and never have the blues, and hope you are the same. I haven't any news. If I had a postal card I would send one of them once a week. Answer soon all the news. Love to all.

July 21, 1918 - THOMAS

Some of our officers and NCOs have already been up in the front lines. They had a peach of a time. I was due to go Thursday morning, but we were expecting to move at any time so didn't go. We had all our final inspection yesterday and I think we'll move.

I guess you see a lot more news of the recent fight than we do. We know that the French and Americans have spoiled the German plans entirely and are about to put over one of the victories of the war. I wish we could get in and think we will by Fall. I've got a pretty good idea that the Germans will have a lot of peace talk in the next month or two. We are certainly making a name for ourselves now. Our troops have been wonderful so everybody says.

I've cut my equipment down about 15% up till now. Thank the Lord I don't have anything else to buy. It keeps on getting on my mind that we won't get in, but I guess there will be enough for all, and we ought to serve our time by Fall. I'm very anxious to see how I'm going to behave under fire. Not to be bragging at all – air raids rather love me to death. One of our officers was in a hotel not far from here when an air raid took place. They dropped a bomb right on the top of the building and it failed to explode. That was pretty lucky, wasn't it?

We are about trained to a standstill now, and are about over it I guess. From now on we should be getting a little actual experience. All the schools are over except one, and that will be getting over pretty soon I hope. These schools are the bane of existence over here. Always there are some men to go to them. One of my lieutenants and one of my sergeants are away now.

I believe that everybody is to take a fifty mile hike in the next few days. It will be the first of long hike we have ever taken and should be fine for the men. They take training over here a lot better. Diving to the fact that the Battalion has not been paid for nearly three months we, the officers, are totally busted. All the money we have had has been loaned out to the men. They should be paid pretty soon however and that will help considerably.

One day last week I bet five-hundred airplanes went over. It is wonderful but so common that it ceases to be a novelty.

The most remarkable thing about this Army is their adaptability. They are wonderfully at home. They feed hogs and cut hay or anything else. The lady whose house I am billeted says she wishes we would stay here always, as while we are here, no one has stolen her chickens and pigs and have a guard over her property and many in the house, and when the airplanes come over bombing and if she gets very frightened she could run jump in the bed with me. I accused the Adjutant who lives next door, but he pleads not guilty.

Everything is going very smoothly now. I hope we will have things in good shape for a real fighting company, but for many days.

July 21, 1918 - KEAN

Strange as it may seem, I have just received a box from you from de Neuflize which looks uncommon like cigars, much obliged. I don't know how they go by, but here they are.

Well, I have been to the front and don't think I shall be a hero, for though I quite agree with Winthrop [Robert Winthrop Kean 1893-1980], that when they merely pass overhead and burst a couple of hundred yards away, the shells are quite entertaining. I don't like to do as we had to do twice one night. We sit in a little shelter and watch the shells burst in a field, then when the flurry had stopped, we start and walk across the field. I couldn't help wondering whether he wasn't going to open up again, of course, even if he did your chances of being hit are small, but just yet I haven't got to the stage that Winthrop has reached, and I was always glad to get another sheltered spot.

We had done about all the training we can do here and the next thing is to get the men accustomed to shell fire, having them sail overhead etcetera, and not pay any attention to them.

July 21, 1918 - KEAN

I was sorry to hear of Mr. d'Hauteville and also to read about Quentin Roosevelt [1897-1918]. I think he was the best of the family and most like his father.

I got an envelope from Winthrop containing an account of the attack near Château Thierry made by our men the first of the month. I suppose he must be with them, as all that was on it was a date and his initials.

Monday I left for a trip to the front. Two officers from the Battalion and 8 Sergeants, together with the same proportion of officers and N.C.O's from the other battalions and M.G. Company. We were divided into two parties and mounted on the regular London [not legible]. We gaily set forth and were transported to a place in the line just over the boundary of Belgium. I was attached to a Company and spent most my time in a command post, but we couldn't move during the day as we were under observation, but at night we made a tour of all the guns and emplacements.

One night I took a trip to the very front line and looked at the Lewis gun emplacements, they showed me a house about 50 yards off near which they said the Boche had a bombing post, but I didn't see anything of him, though I heard a good deal, and he frequently dropped various kinds of explosives my way. I was up there four days and came back again Friday afternoon. The silence around here seems quite strange. It was just like going to the country from the city, for there was a continuous stream of our shells going over head, even when he was quiet. It was a most interesting and instructive trip and I think my Company is about ready to go up and become acclimated to shell fire etc. so that when they get accustomed to it, and know how to take care of themselves, they will render a good account of themselves.

One of our bulletins the other day contained an extract from a gunman intelligence report on one of our Divisions. It was not complimentary and very true, saying that the men had a naïve confidence, and had not yet lost their nerve, and had the big brother attitude.

I think in a little while when Uncle Sam gets a few more Divisions broken-in, the Hun will really regret it for until the men get sick of the war, and still have their eagerness, nothing in the world at present can lick or stop them to my way of thinking.

❧

Following the preliminary training in the Samer area, known as Phase A, the Machine Gun Battalion was introduced to frontline combat by participating in a new training stage. These stages were referred to by the Division as Training Phases A, B, and C. Phase A concluded on July 22, and was a period of training in which no platoon or large unit was permitted to go to the front line with the British until the Battalion's initial stage of training was completed.

The Phase B training for the Division took place from July 23 to August 18 and consisted of supporting the British 3rd Army, who at the time, held a front along the L'Ancre River of about twenty five miles, just opposite the 17th German Army.

The British Army developed a defensive line that spanned about twelve miles in depth. The Battalion's Phase B training included sending individuals to the frontline attached to the British for a 48 hour tour. After individual men were transferred in and out of the line, the officers arranged for an entire platoon to spend four days in the frontlines under the command of their own platoon leaders, but still be attached to the larger British Army units. Finally, after the rotation of the platoons, a complete battalion from the regiment was required to relieve a British battalion at the front. Initially, there were plans for a Phase C to relieve an entire regiment, but this phase never took place. Nevertheless, this was the American Battalion's first experience of life in the British trenches.

The Battalion's Phase B training period took place at the beginning of the Allied offensive in what is now known as the Hundred Days Offensive or the Third Battle of Picardy. The Allied offensive started August 8, 1918, and pushed forward until the end of the war. The 313th Machine Gun Battalion did not remain in this sector during that entire period, but instead, they used this battlefront as part of their first tour of combat training before moving on to a different front.

The battlefront for the British in Picardy started with the Battle of Amiens. It forced the Germans to retreat out of France and fall back behind their Hindenburg Line. The 80th Division supported the British 4th Corps which was made up of the following British Divisions: 5th Division, 37th Division, 42nd Division - East Lancashire, and the New Zealand Division.

The New Zealand Division, which held a front from Puisieux towards the Albert-Arras railway, about 9 miles of front line, made use of the American troops by absorbing the 313th Machine Gun Battalion and the 317th Infantry in with their troops.

Phase B required the 80th Division to move its headquarters into Beauval, a commune in the Somme region. This move by the Division started on July 4 while members of the 313th Machine Gun Battalion were still training in the rear area at a British machine gun school. The specialized machine gun training did not commence until July 20 which kept many of the troops in the Battalion separated from the larger unit. After the initial training was completed, the Battalion was finally able to leave the Samer area on July 25 and travel by rail with orders to billet at Doullens. Both Captains Kean and Thomas remained at a British machine gun school receiving specialized instruction while the rest of the Battalion moved to the frontlines for the first time.

The late arrival of the Machine Gun Battalion to this sector meant that their Phase B did not begin until July 30 when individual officers, NCOs, and a man from each gun team could arrive in the trenches for a two-day tour of the front lines. Their rotation was followed by the advance of an entire platoon entering the front on August 1, 1918 for a four-day tour with the New Zealand Divisions in the area around Hébuterne and Gommecourt.

The strategies coming from the Division during this period called for the first significant changes in leadership throughout the Division. Major Foley, then commanding the Battalion, was promoted to Lieutenant Colonel and was made Division Machine Gun Officer (DMGO) for the entire 80th Division. Foley's promotion to DMGO called for a new commander to lead the Battalion, and on August 1, 1918, the position was assigned to Prescott Foster Huidekoper (1887-1939), the former commander of the 317th Machine Gun Company.

Huidekoper, a New York native and Harvard graduate was first commissioned in the United States Calvary in April 1917. Captain Huidekoper came from a family steep in military and American history. His second great grandfather was Colonel Joseph Shippen who served in the expedition that captured Fort Duquesne during the French and Indian War. His Uncle Henry Shippen Huidekoper, served in the Battle of Gettysburg with the 150th Pennsylvania Infantry and was awarded the Medal of Honor for his actions. In 1918, his first cousin, Major Frederic L. Huidekoper, author of the 1915 book, 'The Military Unpreparedness of the United States,' served in France as the 33rd Division's Adjutant. After a few short

HUIDEKOPER

commands with various infantry units, Captain Prescott Huidekoper eventually joined the 80th Division when they were still training in the United States. He sailed to France as an officer assigned to the 317th Infantry Brigade. His promotion to Major came just two weeks after taking command of the 313th Machine Gun Battalion. This assignment meant the Battalion gained yet another Ivy League officer to join their ranks.

With the Battalion's move closer to the battlefront, it put the Division within sound range of the German artillery for the first time. It also put the troops in closer proximity to more frequent air raids by German enemy planes. The town of Doullens was large enough to accommodate several battalions and housed a large hospital used by the Allies. The town also provided the troops with a number of shops and cafes to occupy their occasional free time.

Captain Kean and Thomas were still away at their specialized machine gun school when Huidekoper was placed in command of the Battalion.

July 24, 1918 - KEAN

As strange as it may seem, I am going to machine gun school for a month. School is on the shore, quite a proper place to spend August, and it is near Harding's Hospital. Cox and Thomas are also going, and I am looking forward to it as rather a vacation. The Company has left here and we leave tomorrow. I feel it is quite strange, without anything to do in this little village.

I am glad you received 'The Bayonet.' I wonder where it is published, and what it contains. I subscribed for you and Uncle Jule, and I think myself. I am enclosing Nénette et Rintintin, which they are selling in the cities as sort of lucky dolls. Also a picture taken of mass on Sunday being celebrated in my Company kitchen and mess hall, and the Battalion guard house, right next to my Company billets.

The villagers here have all been fine and I sort of hate leaving this place, but I am glad to go to school and glad to have the Company get more advanced training. My hostess keeps a little cup filled with flowers for me and I think Maurice is going to miss me a little, though I haven't played with him much lately.

July 25-28, 1918 - LEINHAUSER

We finally got our orders to leave Le Turne, one half of the Company leaving in the morning and the other half, I have charge of, scheduled to leave in the afternoon. The move, after a few false starts, was successfully carried out at 3:45 PM.

Jerry aviators gave us a sort of farewell exhibition. Wednesday night, from 12 midnight until 2:00 AM, at intervals of about 10 minutes, there were bombing planes flying over bombing Boulogne, Camiers, and Étaples, also trying to hit the railroad which runs down the coast from Boulogne. The British have innumerable anti-aircraft guns along here and the shells bursting in air, plus search lights flashing all along the coast, mingled with the roar of the German bombs was quite a celebration.

Étaples is a large British base where men come back from the lines for rest and re-equipment. It was here that the bombs did the most damage. Several striking the railroad and one striking near a barracks in which a company of Scotch soldiers were sleeping, quite a few killed and wounded. The town of the Étaples itself has been very badly bombed and consequently is in bad condition.

We left LeTurne at 3:45 PM, joined the 315th Battalion at Frencq and arrived at Étaples at about 7:30 PM where there was much bristle and confusion loading horses and transport, but we finally got away at about 8:30 PM for an all-night ride on the train. At 4:00 AM we pulled into Doullens. Here the men were billeted for the first time. Some of the billets being good and others very poor and dirty, which was soon overcome as we spent all day Friday and Saturday cleaning up. Doullens is a city of about 15,000 population, very old and of very little interest except that there is a very hard proposition keeping the men sober. Cafés abound and so do drunks.

In 1914, the Germans got within 8 miles of this place so most of the people are still away as the large percentage of them left at that time. The British have large bases here and in adjacent towns. This is in the British sector called the Artois sector which is part of the Somme sector between Albert and Arras.

⋄⋄

Leinhauser's reference to 'drunks' may explain an incident that occurred while the Battalion was in Doullens and is recorded on a Military Charge Sheet dated August 8, 1918. One of the enlisted men of the Battalion was charged with 'Intent to murder, and feloniously strike', Roy E. Blakeley (1893-1951) of the Battalion in the left side of the chest with a pocket knife.' The accused soldier pleaded 'Not Guilty.' The officers ruled the soldier guilty with the exception of the words 'with the intent to murder.' He was required to forfeit two-thirds pay of his pay for three months. There was no mention of the extent of injuries suffered by Blakeley (Headquarters Correspondence).

July 29, 1918 - LEINHAUSER

Hamilton is in command of our Company and he went up in the line today on a reconnaissance with other officers of this Battalion and some New Zealand officers. Our drill field is about 3 miles outside of town in a very pretty place, on top of a very high knoll, overlooking some perfectly wonderful country. Here we see quite a few planes. About the first actual battle planes we have seen as there are quite a few airdromes near here.

July 29, 1918 – HOLLAND

I received your two letters, I have received four or five from Marie. I was sorry to hear that the kids have been sick, I haven't felt a bit sick in any way since I was on the boat, and the majority of us felt kind of unnecessary after we had been out a week. Lawrence and Walter are still on the job, I don't believe I could go home and go to work again, this is soft over here.

July 30, 1918 - THOMAS

We are still in billets and working pretty hard. The training is ever so much easier over here so the men give it more attention. They are fine too. Nobody complains, although it is pretty hard for them sometimes I guess.

We, the officers, are pretty well fixed. I've got a room with a bed and sheets. My striker always sleeps in the room with me and does everything for me. I get plenty to eat and am really very comfortable. The drinking water over here is poor. The French seem to live entirely on wine. You can get excellent champagne or good white or red wine for ten francs, $1.75 a bottle. We usually have a little with our meals. I haven't been out of camp much except with the Company. We are close to a pretty good town and I guess I'll go in sometime before long.

Our priest, Father Roche, [Thomas Bernard Roche 1885-1947] is mess officer and one of the best little men I ever saw. He speaks French well and is very handy to have around. My mess Sergeant also speaks French. I bought the Company a calf for today's dinner. Yesterday, it strained my French to the breaking point to put over the deal. Much 'oui, oui', and 'monsieur le general.'

We passed in review before the Duke of Connaught yesterday. Being more or less unused to Dukes, I can't say what kind of Duke he is, but he was a very nice looking old gentleman.

We have got part of our horses, but are to get more later on. It would be wonderful here with a car. The roads are beautifully kept everywhere you go. We have air-raiders over quite frequently, but they are more for observation than anything else. I think all things considered, this is a very pleasant war. As yet, it all seems the most natural sequence of events. I haven't had a thrill and no excitement whatsoever. We get a London paper occasionally, but really don't know so much about what is happening as we did back home.

We wear overseas caps now. All of my company were issued size 6 7/8, and as you can imagine, the looks are not all uniform. Four of my officers are now at school so I am pretty busy. Also about 16 of my non-coms are at school. The rest are showing up fine. Wonderful spirit and can't get too much work. It would break my heart to lose my Company now. I've had a few pretty tough times with them but have pulled them through pretty well and want to keep them for a while.

I'm glad I'm here though because after being here six months I'll have enough foundation to talk for the next 40 or 50 years.

July 31, 1918 - LEINHAUSER

Bobby Stoddart left for the trenches today with his platoon. Thorne and I went to a tank show today given by the British and Canadian tank corps. It was real interesting. There were about 50 tanks of different sizes and shapes here ranging from the little Whippet which weighs about 15 tons and can go about 15 mph, to the big Mark V weighing about 30 tons traveling only 4 mph.

The small tanks have only two men for a crew. One a driver and one who operates the machine gun with which they are equipped. The large Mark V has a crew from 6 to 8 men. One being the driver the rest operating the guns of which there are in the female tank having five machine guns and two six pounders or cannons which have a diameter or bore of 2 inches. The male tanks tank is only equipped with machine gun of which there are seven.

With nearly all combat units of the Division under command in the With nearly all combat units of the Division under command in the British 3rd Army zone, the British battalions were getting front line relief by synchronizing the American battalions to relieve them in the trenches. Those units not going to the front rehearsed manning the rear defensive lines. The nature of the machine gun units required that they be rotated to the front, but maintain at least one third of the men in constant defense of the rear lines. The 313th Machine Gun Battalion left Doullens for the frontlines and marched to Bois de Warnimont. There they waited for orders to be given as to which British unit they would relieve. Because this operation was still part of the Division's training program, instructions were given from General Pershing that the American Divisions were not to engage in offensive operations. Although an occasional advance did occur from a unit within the 80th Division, it was known by the higher command that the German Army was holding their line but also slowly evacuating from this sector.

August 3, 1918 - LEINHAUSER

Got ready this morning for our first trip to the trenches this morning. We left Doullens at 2:30 PM for about a 10 mile hike and arrived at the Bois de Warnimont at 2:00 PM where we camped for the night within hearing of the artillery which worked all night.

A large 12 inch naval gun mounted on a flat car was fired at regular intervals all night long from a position just in front of the wood in which we were camped. Every time it went off it sounded like an earthquake. But we were soon to get more experience and more used to that.

August 4, 1918 - THOMAS

School is getting along very well. We are getting quite a good bunch of staff here and I really think it will be of considerable help to me, but I wish I was back with my Company.

You very probably see more about the actual war than we do. We get the London papers a day late and also Paris editions of the New York Herald and Chicago Tribune. The troops have been doing wonderfully; I know that and we are really getting an Army over here now. A year or two more will certainly see this thing well ended I believe. I hope we will get a chance before long. I know our Division will do wonderfully if we ever get up.

There are a big bunch of American Nurses and Doctors very near here. We see quite a few of them. As a matter of fact, it is all we have to do. Most of them are either from New England or Chicago, a pretty good crowd. It is nice to be with Americans again. Your own country looks pretty good from here. If we ever get over going to school and settle down it will be fine.

I suppose the casualty lists are coming in pretty well now. Over here it is very noticeable.

Two other Captains (Kean and Cox) of my Battalion are with me and it makes it all together very nice. I want to get back to the Battalion, however, and am glad I only have three weeks more. If Germany knew what preparations were being made for them they would get out as quickly as possible.

August 4, 1918 - KEAN

Last Saturday as school didn't open until Monday, I went into town and ordered a new uniform for myself. While I was there I ran into Malcolm Peabody [Malcomb E. Peabody 1888-1974] who is a Red Cross Chaplain with the Base Hospital No. 13, Harvard Unit. He took us over to the hospital introducing us to Lieutenant Colonel Roger Lee, Commanding Officer [Roger Irving Lee 1881-1965]. We then went to tea at the nurse's quarters.

Last night, Cox, Thomas, and I dined with Eddy Harding and attended an informal dance at the nurse's quarters. This you see is not such a bad war after all, spending August at the sea shore and going out to dinner and dances. I haven't received any word from the Battalion, but believe our Major has been made Division Machine Gun Officer, so that there is a vacancy there, and we don't know what sort of a thing they are going to spring on us, or what is going on in our Companies. Therefore, we are sort of torn between enjoying our vacation and anxious to get back.

I am going to write the names of my last lodging and boarding house keepers, as I suppose our billets nearly should be called, Madame Ficheux and daughter Blondine fed me, Mademoiselle Alice, Julie, Martha, Laire, and Mr. Maurice Ficheux lodged me. This is in case I ever want to know them later when I have forgotten them.

∽

On August 4, 1918, the 313th Machine Gun Battalion was attached to the New Zealand Machine Gun Battalion. Major John Hector Luxford (1890-1971) of the 3rd New Zealand Rifle Brigade provided his observations of joining with the American Army. "By this time the American Army was almost ready to take its place alongside the Armies of France and Britain; but before it did so, its officers and men were given a final period of training with various British and French units in the line.

Towards the end of July, five officers and 114 other ranks from the 313th and 317th U.S. Machine Gun Battalions joined the New Zealand Machine Gun Battalion for instruction, and on 4th August the whole of the 313th Battalion became attached to our Battalion. Otago Company, less one section, was withdrawn from the right subsector, so that each of the American Companies could have a three days' tour of duty in the forward defenses. The American Company was smaller than the British, only comprising twelve guns and 160 officers and men. The American gunners adapted themselves to their new and trying duties in the most remarkable way, and soon established a warm friendship with our men.

The American Battalion Commander and his staff received their baptism of fire while making an inspection of the Divisional sector with Lieutenant Colonel Duncan Barrie Blair. Every portion was visited and many explanations were given. After returning to the Battalion Headquarters the party summed up their impressions with the words 'most illuminating.'

After the 8th August, conditions in the sector began to change and a feeling manifested itself, that the enemy was about to make a graceful retirement if it could. The gunners increased their activity at night against the channels of communication, hoping that if the retirement was being arranged there would be a few less Huns to take part in it.

It was not, however, until about 7:30 AM on the 14th of August that it was definitely known that the withdrawal had commenced, nor was it certain to what extent the withdrawal would be made" (Luxford).

❧

Charles E. Ray, a single, 24-year-old machinist from Erie, Pennsylvania was drafted into the Army in September 1917. His leadership abilities allowed for two promotions while training with his men at Camp Lee, and before sailing for France, he reached the rank of Sergeant to become one of C Company's respected NCOs. Sergeant Ray's experiences during the war were shared by him in a memoir written for his family. His vivid details of the events of those days in France provide yet another perspective offered by a soldier in this Battalion. A portion of his writings recount the initial days spent at the frontline with the British, confirming what we know about the Battalion's fondness for their New Zealand gunners. It also gives a good sense of the life these men experienced while living in the British trenches.

Charles Earnest Ray (1891-1990):

"My experiences in the First World War started when I arrived in Europe with the rank of Sergeant and was immediately shipped to Calais, France. There we were, equipped with English equipment including their machine guns, horses and limbers. We were given English underwear, their hobnail shoes, trousers, shirts, gas masks, etc. The only thing we had to make us look like Americans was our blouse and hat, and the American buttons and emblems.

We came under English officers and were attached to a New Zealand machine gun battalion and sent into the Somme near Doullens, where the trenches were 12 to 14 feet deep with a parapet to fire from. In the bottom were duck boards to walk on, some floating on mud and water. The dugouts went out of the side of the trenches and down about 30 feet below the earth. That was where we slept when we went off watch. This was one of those fronts where the English or New Zealanders would hold the trenches one day and the Germans the next.

The beds at the bottom of the dugout were made of scrap wood with chicken wire for springs and one bed over the other, with old blankets or coats as mattresses. By the Germans sleeping there one night and

RAY

maybe the English or New Zealanders or Aussies the next, we found ourselves with quite a combination of cooties and rats. I never saw such big fat rats which sometimes took you for dead when you were sleeping. There seems to be only a few people who know that American soldiers were sent into the English front with English equipment and given their rations. The hardtack was so hard it could only be eaten by taking two rocks to break it into pieces, then let it dissolve in your mouth. There were times when it tasted good too! I remember their jam was excellent.

We did find the New Zealanders and Australians a group of fine men to soldier with. They were seasoned soldiers and we just rookies. They had probably spent two or three years in the trenches if they were lucky, as a machine gunners life was short" (Ray 85).

∽

August 4, 1918 - LEINHAUSER

We left the woods at about 1:00 PM and hiked about 3 miles to Couin which was the base for the New Zealanders to which we were attached. The New Zealand officers greeted us right warmly and after having our lunch we started for the trenches arriving there at about 5:00 PM and relieving Stoddart's platoon which went out. Here we had our first experience with shellfire. None came very close so we didn't mind that much. Plenty of shells going both ways, but it seems we sent over about 5 to 1. I spent my first night in the trenches in an old German dugout which was about 50 feet deep and quite safe, unless one came in the doorway.

August 5, 1918 - LEINHAUSER

This sector was held by the Germans in 1914. The trenches are in good repair but it is terribly muddy. The ground is one mass of shell holes of all sizes and particularly over lapping one another. Barbwire is plentiful also. The German lines are about 1,000 yards away. No shells fell very near us as the German artillery seems bent in shelling the remains of a village which is in back of us. The New Zealanders played a good joke on Jerry today. A couple went out in front of our position about 600 yards to a patch of woods which is about 500 yards square, started a fire and then cleared out. The Germans, thinking the wood was occupied, started up a terrific shelling which lasted about an hour. Trees and dirt were flying all over the landscape, but as far as I know, no one was hurt, although about 100 shells fell in the woods.

August 6, 1918 - LEINHAUSER

I took a walk around the trenches today. I kept on walking, met very few men and was surprised at how few men were actually required to hold a trench. I was up within plain sight of the Jerry's frontline before I knew it, so I got back.

This afternoon we watched quite a few Germans coming down a hill about 9,000 yards off. We were using a telescope and could see them very plainly. We have two machine guns set for night firing. The first guns I set.

The method of laying the gun is this. It shall be done by use of a map and instruments. First, the position of the gun is located on the map, then the target, usually a road, bit of trench or strip of woods, but in this case one target was a well and one was a section of road, is chosen from information given by airplanes or other sources. The distance between the two is measured by the scale of the map. That gives the range. The direction is then measured with a protractor which gives the number of degrees the target is from North. Then a compass is taken to that gun position and the corresponding numbers of degrees cited through the compass. A stake is driven into the ground which gives the direction. After dark the gun is mounted, an elevation proportionate to the range is put on it by use of an instrument, a bit of phosphorus is put in the stake making it visible for use as an aiming mark, and the gun is ready for firing. Then all through the night at different intervals the gun is fired for a few seconds, thus showering machine gun bullets all over and around that particular target.

This time we were rather lucky as the [Germans] we had seen in the afternoon were part of a trench relief going in, and unfortunately for them, they had to use the road which we had chosen for a target. The result was that the relief was pretty shot up before it got to the trenches. This information was gotten from some prisoners which the New Zealanders captured the following afternoon who said that their relief was subjected to pretty bad machine gun fire from the previous night as they were coming in.

August 7-9, 1918 - LEINHAUSER

While we were doing this the German artillery was also busy. They usually did any time the machine guns started, and they got five New Zealanders who were bringing up water on a narrow gauge railroad track. Wednesday evening we came out of the trenches again. We left about 7:30 PM and were taken out on a light railway to a place called St. Leger, arriving there about 11:00 PM. From there we hiked to the Bois de Warnimont again, where we spent the rest of the night again.

Left the woods at 9:20 AM [August 8] and started back to Doullens, arriving there about 12 PM after a quick march. Spent the afternoon getting cleaned up and getting some sleep. On Friday [August 9] we left Doullens again, this time for the rifle range at Orville. Got there about 10:30 AM, made our camp which consisted of pup tents and did some work on the range.

August 10-11, 1918 - LEINHAUSER

Spent all day shooting with good results. About 11:00 PM we heard a plane flying over, so we came out of our tents and soon after heard a bomb go off. We found out it hit our Brigade headquarters at Doullens, completely wrecking a beautiful château. We set up a gun and soon the 'Archie's,' the name for anti-aircraft guns, began to roar and the whole sky was lit up with searchlights. All at once one large beam of light picked up the plane which was beating it for home, but the searchlight followed it right along. Other lights also playing on it. When the plane got directly over us Hamilton and I let loose a belt of ammunition at it without result. The plane kept right on going until suddenly from the dark we seen a thin stream of blue fire dart out, which we knew for tracer bullets fired from another plane, then two more streams from different directions, and the battle was on. Suddenly there was a burst of flame from the big bomber and she started down. The other planes following it down shooting all the time. We see it hit the ground with a huge burst of flame and another plane was finished. After a while another came over but he did his dirty work and got away O.K. as the lights were unable to pick him up.

Sunday [August 11] range work this morning. Some of the men went out to see the plane which was brought down last night. It was one of the new type, carried an eight man firing crew, all of which were horribly burned and mangled. The plane was 140 feet wide and had five engines of which was used for electric lighting the plane. Later we seen the account of it in the paper which gave the same figures.

❧

The plane that was shot down that evening was a German Gotha G. V; the aircraft was one of the largest planes built by the Germans at the time and first introduced in August 1917. The plane carried a crew of fifteen and was put into service primarily as a night bomber. This aircraft partially destroyed the 159th Brigade's Headquarters building on August 10, 1918 with surprisingly few injuries to the men in and near the building. The plane was ultimately brought down by an English single-seat airplane and crashed near Rubempré killing two British soldiers who died as a result of ground impact and the plane's exploding ordinance.

The following day, the wreckage became an opportunity for the troops to scour the location for possible souvenirs and to gaze at the spectacle of the enormous machine that had been torn from the sky the previous night.

August 10, 1918 - KEAN

I am still at school and enjoying the vacation. Friday we had an examination, but it wasn't half as difficult as I thought it would be. There is little that I haven't had already, of course there is much that I don't know. Still no news from my Company or the Division.

Some of the officers of the Division have been sent back to the U.S. as instructors. I rather think it was because they didn't care much for them here. People here who have received mail from the Division say that Major Foley is now a Lieutenant Colonel and Division Machine Gun Officer.

Major Garry [Leland Beekman Garretson 1880-1941] is in command of the 315th Machine Guns and Captain Prescott Huidekoper in command of our Battalion. Huidekoper used to have the 317th Machine Gun Company, and unless they make him a Major when Cox returns to the Battalion, Cox will have command as he out ranks Huidekoper.

I would be just as glad to have Huidekoper the Major as he was about two years ahead of me in college and I know him pretty well. One of the Lieutenants from our Battalion, [William M. Whittle 1896-1960] went as Company Commanded of the 314th Machine Gun Battalion and is the senior officer there and so is in command of the Battalion.

Therefore, you see why we miss not hearing from the Battalion and knowing what is going on. I think we chose rather a bad time to go to school or rather be sent to school. Another thing is that our Division was somewhere in the rear of where the latest push has just been made and that we hear various rumors that they are close behind the attacking troops and then that they aren't. Of course we all want to take our Companies in the first time they go, even if only for a little while. They are our Companies and we brought them up from childhood and we want to be with them at first.

Latest news is that they are not in and so we are feeling a little better than we were on Friday when we thought they were. We were sitting here quietly at school and feeling pretty low.

They say the [German] morale is pretty low just now and from the way things seem to have been going lately, I think there is a slight possibility of his lying down by winter. If he doesn't, he certainly will get all that is coming to him next spring. I hear that the slogan of the troops down in the American sector is 'Hell, Heaven or Hoboken by Christmas.'

A blooming Boche aeroplane has been flying about this morning and the Archies have been having a splendid time. I guess he was photographing and we shall probably have several nights of bombing. He does it about every two weeks, and was here last night, and as he is a methodical fellow, coming regularly, he will probably be her again tonight.

August 11, 1918 - THOMAS

You see from the papers, I suppose, of the fine things the Allies are doing. It looks like they are over the top of the hill finally. It is awfully hard to have to get it all second hand though. There is a big hospital near here, and the wounded are coming in by trainloads every day. They are all in wonderful spirits, and didn't have much trouble going over from all accounts. We will be in pretty soon, I think. We only have two more weeks of school, but although I want to be back with the Company, I am getting a lot out of this course now.

Every now and then it leaks through that someone or other that you know quite well has been killed, but it seems so a matter of fact that it is startling, but you don't really realize how commonplace it is to be over here.

I rather had the idea before coming that it would be so different, but it is not at all. You do exactly the same thing you do at home. I believe it will be just the same throughout. We'll very probably get a bunch of action before Christmas. I hope so, because after I've been in a few times I won't care after that.

There are a bunch of changes going on here. Major Foley has been made a Lieutenant Colonel and one of my Lieutenants a Captain. One of the other Captains in my Battalion is going to be a Major, I think. That makes two since September out of the 313. That will make me 2nd ranking Captain instead of 8th now. But promotion in our branch is slow and I don't care if I never get it anyway.

They are going to raise a real army aren't they? Will take over a big part of the war I hope. The preparations we are making over here are marvelous. In one place I saw about 4 miles of wharves, an ammunition plant, a railroad, refrigerating plant and warehouses beyond all description that our people have built.

August 11, 1918 - HOLLAND

I sure was glad to hear that you received the allotment at last, but you don't say how much it was. The weather has been good with the exception of a few rains. I think the climate agrees with me better over here than it did in the States. I have been in the lines and I liked it much better than I thought I would. I had the pillow you gave me until a couple of weeks ago and I gave it to a French lady. One can't bother carrying so much - one blanket, toothbrush and a razor is enough for me to care for. I have 120 Francs or $24 U.S. money. One can't buy much of anything, only wine and cigarettes, and of course I don't use much of either, just enough to be sociable with the boys. Oh yes, we have lady bartenders and there's a kiss that goes with each bottle of wine.

They call a soldier over here a 'digger,' everyone says, 'Hello digger,' and a German is called 'Jerry.' I am going to town to spend the afternoon and evening, this is Sunday. I haven't seen any boys from home over here, only Hazen [Carle Barton Hazen 1896-1972] and he is a bugler in this Company. Write all the news.

CHAPTER 4
THE FIRST CASUALTIES

Before being drafted into the Army, Joseph Paul Devir (1892-1973) was living in Philadelphia, Pennsylvania, and writing sports articles for the *Evening Public Ledger.* This past occupation of reporting facts led him to write a history about the men of Company A called, '*War History of 313th Machine Gun Battalion, Company A, 80th Division.*' In this publication, Devir reflects on the company's experiences during Phase B training, and in particular, the Company's fondness with serving alongside the New Zealanders. His platoon went into the front lines during the first week of August 1918.

Devir writes, "Here is where A Company gets its first taste of trench life. The area in question, Gommecourt, was formally held by the Germans. Knowing the lay of the ground in this section, the Germans keep its artillery everlastingly hammering the area. Allied artillery is plentiful also in this sector and the banging away of the canons is a common noise. Many New Zealand machine guns are located around and among the Company. This is where our fellows got hip to some trench warfare stuff. To A Company men, the soldiers from England's colony, New Zealand, measured up to the finest of manhood and it can be said that these men acted like brothers to us Yankees. When A Company was to return from the trenches they regretted to leave the New Zealand soldiers" (Devir 22).

The next Company to be rotated into the front lines was the B Company. When they entered the lines as part of the British training program, the B Company too was assigned to relieve part of the Otago Company, a New Zealand Machine Gun Company. On August 10th, the Otago Company kept one officer and twenty three privates attached with the Americans and supported the advancing New Zealand Infantry. The Germans were withdrawing from a sector just southeast of the Serre Ridge near Hébuterne. The New Zealand Infantry was pushing forward to position themselves near a German trench known as Kaiser Lane. The B Company experienced a casualty free training tour of the trenches.

A few days later, on August 15, C Company came into the area under the cover of darkness to relieve B Company. The senior officer of C Company, First Lieutenant Minard Hamilton, was the highest ranking officer in charge of the Battalion while Captain Kean was away at school.

HAMILTON

Minard Hamilton was born in Tenafly, New Jersey, to parents George Hamilton (1844-1929) and Bertha Torrance Hamilton (1861-1963). From all accounts, Hamilton enjoyed a privileged life as a young man. Hamilton's grandfather, William Hamilton (1806-unknown), purchased an eighteenth century mansion that was built by the Campbells of Knockbuie and located on the shores of Loch Fyne in Argyll, Scotland. This castellated mansion, 'Minard Castle,' was the birthplace of George Hamilton and the origin of Lieutenant Hamilton's first name.

George Hamilton immigrated to the United States in his early thirties, married Bertha in his early forties, and was involved in the business of importing tea from the Far East. While George Hamilton had the means to educate his son, Minard Hamilton was not formally educated in a postsecondary institution like many of the officers in this Battalion. However, the lack of a strict education did not appear to hamper his future successes.

Minard was known to be very personable, well liked, an avid reader and a very athletic person. He was an ardent squash player and competed as a member of the Englewood Field Club, a private club located in Englewood, New Jersey. It was at this club that he played polo and spawned his love for the sport of riding. His passion for horses led him to join the United States Calvary. At age 25, he enlisted in the New York National Guard, and in October 1915, he was attached to the Squadron A Armory, known as the Madison Avenue Armory, located between Madison Avenue and Park Avenue in New York City.

Hamilton received his first genuine military experience when he mustered into the services in June 1916, as a Private in D Troop, as part of the Squadron A Calvary. He served in the Mexican Punitive Expedition on the southern border of the United States. His squadron was sent to the border when the United States Government was on the hunt to capture the Mexican Revolutionary leader Pancho Villa.

After one month of service, Hamilton was promoted to Corporal in July 1916. His troop remained on the border for about six months as a border patrol in the event there were attacks made on the United States by the Mexican contingent of troops. However, diplomacy prevailed and Squadron A returned to New York City and Hamilton mustered out of service in December 1916.

Before Hamilton left for border patrol, he was working for James W. McCulloch (1857-1938) of the Preferred City Real Estate Company in New York City. It is not known if he resumed his real estate job after returning from border patrol, but within a few short months, Hamilton was back in the military again and preparing to go to war.

In April 1917, shortly after the United States declared war with Germany, Hamilton attended the Reserve Officers Training Course in Fort Myer, Virginia. From May to August, he joined hundreds of other young men in Virginia for a course that prepared them to lead a platoon into the frontlines.

Hamilton was commissioned as a Second Lieutenant in the Calvary Officers Reserve Corps and his first assignment was with the 313th Machine Gun Battalion. By the end of December 1917, he was promoted as a First Lieutenant with the Battalion.

The writings of Lieutenant Hamilton are introduced here for the first time and provide significant insights about the experiences of this Battalion throughout the war. While Hamilton did write letters home to his family prior to August 14, it was at this juncture in the war that he decided to begin writing his story for possible publication.

August 14, 1918 – HAMILTON

I have written no diary since reaching France two months ago, largely because I could buy nothing to write in. I have therefore chronicled my doings in letters to Gordon [Amy Gordon Hamilton 1892-1967] and have gotten most things I think. I have just received this little book from Aunt Louise [Louise Meisel Torrance 1871-1952] and as today marks a new era of my military career shall continue the diary from this date.

We left Doullens bound for the trenches today. The time we came in before was just a Cooks Tour, today is real business. We are going in to relieve another Company and will be quite on our own. The Captain is still away and I am in command of the Company. We marched in the afternoon to a place called Bois de Warnimont where we camped for the night in the woods. Nothing of any consequence happened, we had a jolly night of it. I fell in with some Scotch officers who were very cordial. They asked me to dinner and lent me their water cart for the men. I spend a large part of the night scouting around the woods for patrol tins to carry water in. A large family of tanks have been living in the woods, and where they are you generally can find plenty of cans. I found plenty of tank tracks, but no tins and after getting awfully tangled in the barbed-wire in the dark managed to get back to my tent and went to bed.

August 15, 1918 – HAMILTON

An orderly arrived during the night saying that we will not relieve today. So instead of an early start we stayed in bed and felt the way you do when you hear unexpectedly that it's a holiday and you don't have to catch the seven fifty-two.

I spent the morning riding around on a horse trying to locate my men's rations. After great trouble and delay, and worry, I found that they had been lumped with the rations of another Company and they almost got double and we almost went shy. Their Sergeant tried to tell us that their quantities were just right for one company, his company, but he jolly well lied. I got back to camp late in the morning and there received orders to make the relief as before. I assembled the Company and told them a few truths about the New Zealanders, gave them my blessing and left them to follow me in.

I went on alone on my horse. Reached the line safely, I rode my horse right up to my dugout, saw the Captain I was to relieve, who said 'Cheere-O' in the usual way and sat down and arranged the necessary details. The Company came trailing along some time later, went up into the line and we went back to our dugout to await those sweet words

'Relief complete.' We waited and waited, and smoked and talked, and one after another the runners came trailing in from the different platoons. At last they were all in so Captain [censored] said 'Good bye' and I had taken over.

August 15, 1918 - LEINHAUSER

Left Doullens again for Bois de Warnimont where we again spent the night, leaving the woods at Noon on Thursday the 15th and arriving in the line again at 7:30 PM.

This time is much more war than the first time. The line had advanced 3,500 yards and the Germans were fighting pretty hard. We spent a very unpleasant night. When we came in we received of a shower of gas shells which was very uncomfortable, but did no damage to us. No dugouts this time, but only a little hole in the side of a trench. Preston [William B. Preston 1888-1959] was with me and had I been willing, he would have kept digging all night to get on the hole deeper. He always wanted to go in just one more foot until I said 'not another inch, I'm going to sleep,' which I did.

The shells were breaking all around us and some hit within 15 yards of our hole. The wall of the trench was full of shell fragments the next morning, but no one was hurt. Old Jerry was sure putting the stuff over.

August 16, 1918 - LEINHAUSER

This was a very bad day for us. The shells were falling continually and all around us. Our guns were the forward most guns and under observation, so during the day the guns were taken off their tripods, which were carefully camouflaged. One shell hit fair on the tripod making a complete wreck of it. Another hit the guns which were in the bottom of the trench along with a lot of other equipment, which was lifted sky-high and scattered all over the country. One gun was completely destroyed. Quite a few of the men's coats were torn to shreds along with their mess kits, which were never found. A couple of their bivvies' were caved in, and two were buried, but suffered no hurt.

My four guns were about 900 yards apart. About midway I established a cookhouse in an old communications trench. At 2:15 PM two men went to bring the rest of the section dinner, and on their way back with the food a shell struck right between the two killing them instantly. They were thrown 20 yards and horribly mangled. Two of my best men too. They were the first men I lost. Luckily for us the Germans let up during the night so we got some much needed sleep. Our artillery opened up during the night and did some good work. The Germans are retiring.

August 16, 1918 - HAMILTON

Got about one hour's sleep between runners, and messages, and telephone calls. The forward guns had been very badly shelled and some of the runners had to lie in shell holes for hours before they could get through. I set out as soon as it was light to visit my guns. I saw the Second Platoon and they were getting on fine, digging in and not getting much shelling. I then got up to the Third Platoon and they were getting it hot. There was an advance of about 4000 yards over this ground yesterday and they were in an old German trench. This trench was shallow and knocked about by shell fire and had no dugouts except a few that the Germans had blown up as they left. There was practically no real cover there at all and they had been lying flat in the trench all night under very heavy fire. The trench was exploded by machine fire and was certainly a 'pas bon' place to stay.

As I came along the trench some of the boys said 'Look out! He shoots a machine gun there.' As I ducked, an old Fritz fired and the bullets went just too high. He was a long way off anyway and didn't have a decent shot. While we were there the shelling got noticeably worse. Up to a certain closeness you don't mind the big ones a bit. Well, these began to get within that certain closeness. I went along the trench looking at my guns and talking to the boys. It was their first real shelling and they were scared all right and I don't wonder. The shells, mostly 5.9 and 4.2's I think, were coming in one after another and it wasn't local a bit, he was fairly plastering the whole sector. A big shell comes like an express train. If it is going past, you just hear her whistle, if she is going short, you just hear her explode but if she is coming toward you, first she whistles, then she shrieks, then she roars, then the whole earth rocks and you wonder if you are still alive. You can tell because the sound is getting louder every instant and it is then that you flatten yourself against the shallow wall of the trench and cover under your tin and pray to God it will miss. They are bad by Jove, they are certainly bad, and it was bad there this morning. I had no idea I could get into a shell hole as quick as I did one time when I was standing outside the trench looking for a machine gun position and I heard that unmistakable increasing scream of a shell coming close. Well sir, I was in the shell hole, out of sight, with a rapidity that would make a prairie dog sit up nights practicing it. No, it was not bon at all, and I knew it, and when I went away, I prayed that no one would be hurt, but felt sure that somebody would be.

It was an awful walk around the guns and I got in for lunch. I went back to the Third Platoon to see if I could not get them into a better place. The shelling was still bad, but considerably less. I met a lot of the boys out on the track waiting for the water cart and I knew from their faces that something was up.

'Lieutenant. We have bad news. Privates [Siefert] and [Marshall] were both killed by a shell as they were carrying the rations up to the trench.'

Two of my best men! Good true Americans full of fight and good spirits. I had been talking to both of them an hour before, gosh it made me feel bad! Siefert was six feet six and weighed about 140 pounds. He was older than the rest of us, over thirty I think, had been all over the world, a big simple homely sort of chap that wrote simple, homely, kindly letters to his mother and carried his bible in his heavy pack to the front line. The boys called him 'Slim.' He had a sad face with a perpetual grin. Marshall was one of my best gunners. The first casualties in our Battalion.

I had to move two guns in the evening up a little closer, and luckily they got in without any casualties for they really got caught in some heavy shelling and I certainly was grateful when I got a message saying that they were in position with nobody hurt.

In the last few days I have walked and ridden at least 70 miles, and altogether have had only about 8 hours sleep.

❧

Leinhauser and Hamilton wrote about the first two casualties of the Battalion. The men killed were George W. Marshall Jr. (1895–1918) and Louis E. Siefert (1888–1918), both were unmarried men from Pennsylvania, and both were members of Leinhauser's platoon.

Marshall was a 23-year-old former steelworker from Greene County, Pennsylvania, and previously served one year as a Corporal in the Army's 10th Pennsylvania Infantry Regiment. His draft card indicated his request to be exempted from service due to a physical disability. The exam board did not approve his medical exemption and drafted him into service. Marshall's younger brother, Frederick Marshall, (1897-1918) was killed in action just a month earlier in France while serving with the 110th Infantry Regiment, 28th Division.

SIEFERT

Louis E. Siefert was a 30-year-old former drilling operator from Warren, Pennsylvania. After the family received word of his death, they permitted the following letter from Seifert, written to his sister Lillian Mary Siefert (1891-1959), to be published in the *Warren Evening Times*. On July 23, 1918 Siefert wrote, "Received your letter yesterday dated June 28. Have not got one from mother for a week. I have moved again, and am in a town now about one half as large as Warren. Have been having it rather easy for a few days. We moved Friday and have not drilled until today; am on kitchen police tomorrow; will have it easy and lots to eat, so rather like it. I got the children's pictures O.K. and they look fine.

It is three months today since I left and it seems like a year. The time goes fast here, but when you look back it seems as though I have worn O. D. for a long time. Bill Lessler [William Lessler 1887-1958], Frank Raisor [Franklyn Ford Raisor 1889-1918], and Fred Witz [Fred Peter Witz 1896-1963] are all here. I found Bill Saturday evening, and yes, he and I hunted the other boys up. We have not been paid yet. Have been expecting it every day. You asked about the weather here. In southern France, the weather is warm; they raise pigs and lots of other fruit. It was only a few miles from Spain; then up North it was colder than at home, and here it is about like it is at home. I believe [censored] is the nearest city from here.

Mom wanted a picture of me, and I don't know when I can get one taken. This town was re-taken not very long ago and the people have not got organized right. There are hardly any men left here. Wish I could tell you all about what I have seen. I saw an old fort that Napoleon built that is over a mile around. Everything is old here. I don't care much about looking at old stuff anymore; the novelty has worn off. I surely have seen more in the last three months than I ever saw before. I am writing with the pencil that Maurice [Maurice Phillip Simmons 1874-1935] gave me the day I left Warren. I will not write to mother this time, as you know I am alright, and will write to her later. I think Maurice had better stay where he is and he will think so too, if he does as you said he was talking of doing.

We are still in the British sector. There isn't room to tell you how we like it. Was watching a Frenchman butcher a pig tonight in the courtyard, they burn the bristles off with straw. Well, I will close; hope you are all well. Tell dad and mom I will write to them in a few days. Write often and tell me all the news. Tell the children I said 'hello.' Does Gerald [Jerold Norman Simmons 1914-1962] still think I am on the train? Well, Goodbye" ("Another Warren Boy").

∽

August 17, 1918 - HAMILTON

I visited my forward guns with apprehension early this morning. Everything was very quiet and there were no shells coming down at all to speak of. No other casualties although they had some very close shaves. I went over the entire line and tramped steadily for six hours before I got back. It was a big walk, particularly as I had had no breakfast whatsoever. The only thing that kept me going was a cup of hot tea that one of the boys gave me up front. I got back, had something to eat, and went right to sleep. I certainly needed it today. It is very quiet after yesterday's bedlam. I believe old Fritz has gone back to the Rhine and we will be moving on again.

This dugout is O.K. It is well under ground, comparatively dry and roomy. I have a table, three chairs and a sort of bunk. There are shelves up and hooks and I could live here happily forever. The table has an oilcloth on it, two guttering candles, and a mass of papers, maps, letters, tobacco and food. I need a maid to keep it straight, although my wild eyed orderly does fairly well considering. Over in the corner is the switchboard and the operator. Everything is in code, and when he gets going fast, his utterances are unspeakable. We burn a million candles a day and altogether consider that it's the Hell of a war.

Today is August 17th and it is a big anniversary for me. I got a telegram from Gordon all the way from Colorado Springs saying 'Lieutenant Minard Hamilton 313th Machine Gun Bat. A.E.F. Love Gordon.' It was about the best thing I ever got in my life.

August 18, 1919 - HAMILTON

Moved Company Headquarters about a mile up. We were getting too far back. It took all morning to get set and I didn't get around the guns, although I hear they are O.K. I now have an old Battalion Headquarters with all kinds of room. It is very stuffy, but jolly fine. These artillery chaps are awful fools. When there is a move they push their guns up awfully far and fast. I saw a Battery yesterday of field guns and pushed way forward on a ridge and what do they do but get out on the sky line at 12 noon and do physical exercises, with two German observation balloons in plain view. The consequence was that about an hour later I saw the Germans put 130 heavy shells on that place in less than an hour. I watched the shelling, which was just far enough off to make us duck a little when they exploded. You could hear the big shells coming and see them burst with a deafening roar and a great cloud of black smoke. Every time a shell burst you would see a lot of men appear out of the ground and scurry for cover, just the way you see birds come out of a tree when you throw a stone. The shells were bursting right among them and somehow it was jolly funny to see them come scurrying out of their holes. I don't think anybody was hurt such, although they hit one gun square and blew their cook house into minute fragments of bully beef, jam dixies and hot coffee. Old Fritz always has been very expert at blowing up kitchens. It isn't nice of him at all.

Oh, one more word about those big shells. I can't say I'm very religious, and I never pray, but by gum I was nearer prayer yesterday than I've been in some time. When your tin hat feels like a peanut shell and you are trying to make yourself as flat as a shingle, and you know darn well that the old shell has your name and present address on it, you will either pray or curse. I did both, and they seemed about equally effectual. The men mostly cower and curse, and I don't blame them for these shells certainly move you very deeply.

We were due to stay several more days in the line, but this afternoon we got word that we would be relieved tonight. The relief came in eventually, and after making the relieving Captain sign for innumerable trench stores, I left him with my blessings to all the delights of 'Kaiser Lane' where the 5.9's come in regularly every thirty seconds.

I rode down to the transport lines on a little jigging white mare who objected to shelling and who made an otherwise delightful moonlight ride into a series of buck jumps and shys. Anyhow, I got down safely and after a long wait was joined by the Company and we hiked on to Bois de Warnimont into camp. It was a long and trying one but we got in finally and I was in bed by 3:00 A.M.

August 18, 1919 - KEAN

I received a letter from Hamilton, my 1st Lieutenant in charge of the Company, saying they had all been up to the line by Platoons, but hadn't yet been in as a Company. He enclosed my pay check, also his account of some of the money loaned the Company.

I hope John Pershing organizes his field army soon, as I have said before. The boys with the main American Army live like kings, and can get anything they want from the Y.M.C.A, Red Cross, or Commissary. It would make everything easier if they could get it, I think.

Food is all right, but the British ration is not as plentiful as ours and doesn't fill the tummy, though it has as much nourishment and the men seem to keep well on it. Bread is pure white, but not plentiful and sugar is pretty scarce. I believe the ration calls for about a shaving stick full per day, per man.

August 19, 1918 - LEINHAUSER

A very quiet day. Very few shells have fallen today, although they put over some 9 in the last night, but they were a few hundred yards back of us. Puisieux, the town just on our left, is the scene of quite a few little scrimmages. The New Zealanders and Germans occupy a part of the village and at one time they both occupied a part of a ruined church.

Every night we were subjected to machine gun fire from that

direction, but without any damage. We watched the artillery work on a road across the valley from us. An observer watched the road, and as soon as anything with life in it comes in sight, the signal to fire is telegraphed back. If one is lucky he gets out, but more often he doesn't, as the guns are accurately laid on by trial shots on that particular place.

This evening I was lying on the parapet of the trench watching the artillery work when I heard a shell coming which seemed to spell my name. So I simply rolled back and tumbled into my bivvy. The shell burst just in front of where I was laying and fragments flew all around and over me.

We were relieved about 8:00 PM this evening and went back to Couin, arriving there at 12:15 AM. From there we hiked out to Bois de Warnimont again and left the following morning arriving back in Doullens at 1:30 PM. We spent the afternoon getting ready to move again. We don't know where, but rumor has it that we will hike 15 miles to get there.

August 19, 1919 - HAMILTON

Everybody was dead tired as we made a leisurely start and did not get going until after ten. The Company walked but I trotted on into Doullens ahead of them to see about a hot bath for the men when they got in. Two miles out an orderly came along on a bicycle and said that the Company would entrain for [censored] at 2 o'clock. Bad news. I hurried my tired horse in, reported to the Major and told him that the thing was impossible as the men wouldn't get in until after 1:00 and would have to get something to eat and pack up before they could move. He said he agreed and would see the General about it.

Later, orders came out that we could not leave until the following morning. I had a bath in my room in the afternoon and flooded out my landlady. The water was an inch deep on the floor until my lunatic batman came in with a mop and cleaned the place up. Very tired and early to bed.

August 19, 1918 - THOMAS

I'm on my last week of school I'm glad to say, but have got quite a good deal out of it I think. We have quite a bunch of practical work here, but will be awfully glad to get back to the Company. I expect by the time this reaches you I will have had my baptism of fire. I hope so anyway, because I don't want the 80th Division to go in without me. My Company has already been in, I think, and are all old stayers by now, I guess.

My lieutenants seem to have all been too busy to write me, but one of my sergeants here got a letter saying, two of my best sergeants have gone to ROTC and two of my lieutenants have transferred, both being promoted. I think that is fine, but it means more work when I get back.

All kinds of changes are going on in our Army. I don't know what is going to happen to the Battalion, but hope I can stay there. So many promotions have been going through that you don't know your Company from one day to another, but it makes you rather keep at it all the time and is more beneficial, I suppose, than anything else.

August 20, 1918 - HAMILTON

We marched out of this place at 7:30 AM. The men carried their full field equipment and were loaded down pretty heavily. We had a fine cool day and came along in fine style. We marched until 3:00 PM with a two hour halt for dinner. The men were foot sore and weary but stuck to it gamely and we had none fall out. Although some of the other Companies did. We hiked about 12 miles altogether and came to another small French village [Franqueville] and went into billets again. Billets are never too good and this is about the usual thing; old barns with straw in them set about a filthy court yard full of miscellaneous assortments of animals, broken down farm implements and the inevitable manure piles.

No they are not too good. I'd jolly side rather be in a pup tent. Certainly the men would. Incidentally, my room is not so bad with its clean stone floor and new wall paper. The bed however has no sheets. I shall have to speak to the landlady about it. These French peasants are pretty discouraging people. They seem so old and worn out and stolid and you never see any young people or hear anybody laugh. They have born too much, too much, oh, much too much.

August 20, 1918 – HAMILTON

I have been in and out of the trenches and it is all jolly interesting. Slept in a dugout for three nights under shell fire, fired a machine gun at

115

the Hun, saw a night attack and a dead German in a shell hole. I told you I was going in on the 20th, didn't I? Five weeks from the transport to the trenches is better than I hoped. I took in a little party from my Company on a purely sightseeing tour. We went by lorry from here to a little village a few miles behind the line where the Division to which we are to be attached had its headquarters. All along the way we saw the back yards of the big show – guns and guns and guns; Tommies, Tommies, Tommies; ammunition dumps, big shells, little shells, shells, tanks, aeroplanes, wire and back area trenches. Unceasing activity of every kind. They are fixing it so as not to be caught again as they were in March, and are digging trenches back for miles. If they had done it before, a lot of mess this spring would never have happened.

At [censored] we got down from the lorry – 'disembussed' they call it, and were fed hot tea by our hosts before going on. A lot of sectors can't be entered by daylight, but this is a poor one or a good one as you can ride your horse up to the front line by daylight, well almost. As we went along we began to pass the big guns. They went 'beaucoup de boom, boom, pas bon' just when we didn't expect it, and it made us jump. I heard such a lot about the artillery, and at last found them sitting more or less placidly along the road, rather bored, served by their rather bored gunners who bawl shells much as the chef in Childs' 'Plate of wheats, five.' They have so many shells to shoot each day; they have never seen a German yet and have been doing the same job for years.

The F.O.P. is somewhere in front, up to his waist in mud, and has had quite a lively time. He sees, actually sees Germans once in a while so he calls his battery and speaks thus, 'K25 Beer 3796, working party 6 men,' and his mate at the end says, 'Righto, cheero,' and hanging up the receiver bawls through the megaphone 'BatERRRRRRRRRRRRRY? Elevation --- Deflection --- Five rounds rapid fire,' and then goes back to bed.

Out in 'No Man's Land,' five miles away, six Huns hear these shells come screaming down the wind and flatten themselves into a shell hole. 'Whang, biff, bow, zang, bluie!' So the war goes on, but incidentally there is nothing nice about big shells. They don't disappoint as to size, noise, danger, or number. Their one merit is that one can hear the big fellows coming and you go where they ain't. It is only 'pas bon' when one has to go where the shells are. In ordinary circumstances it is awfully bad luck to be hit by a shell. In trench warfare, with all out doors to get hit, I wonder why there are any casualties at all. There should be none. I think I'll have to try a tank for some excitement.

The front line nowadays isn't a line at all, but a handful of isolated posts thrown out towards the enemy. You never know exactly where he is, or he you. No Man's Land has no well-defined limits; it is all No Man's Land. The consequence is that instead of a few well defined trenches running, there is a large area defended in depth, torn by shells, crisscrossed by wire, riddled by trenches, running every which way. The most unexpected thing is the vegetation.

Everywhere are weeds and grass and in some cases wheat and other crops. Most of the trees are bare and full of bullet holes, but some have escaped and one even sees trees trying to grow pears and apples in that howling wilderness of war. I had fancied a sea of mud and up turned earth and in many sectors it is so, but here it is green and verdant. You can't stop the summer; you may be able to hold her back a little, but in the end she arrives even here, and spreads her mantle over this tortured ground which has suffered some of the bitterest fighting of the whole war.

The Village of [censored] exists on the map only. I did find one bit of a wall standing; the rest is gone so completely that you might imagine it had been destroyed by the original Huns and not their descendants.

We were living in the old German front line before the BIG RETREAT after the Somme, and one could look across their trench, their huge, wide, deep, solid, Hunnish trench, across waves of barbed wire to the pitiful shallow exposed trenches of the Allies. It is just as it appears in pictures, two trenches facing each other across two hundred yards of No Man's Land and the surprising thing that the pictures don't show is that the German trenches are so good and the English trenches so bad. I slept three nights in a German dugout and I know, 30 feet deep, beautifully timbered and shored with Belgium's best timber, I believe, roomy and best of all perfectly dry. I think it must have accommodated 30 men at a pinch.

In this sector everyone is awfully optimistic, crazy about the Yanks and frank about their praises. They certainly have the supremacy of the air and more artillery.

Yesterday I went out on an awfully funny party. Two of us had to meet up to reconnoiter a back area line of defense – trenches and wire already put in and we were to site in nine machine gun positions. P[censored] and I started off early in the morning without horses and orderlies to ride to [censored] were we were to pick up the New Zealanders who were going with us. We rode slowly because the way was jammed with traffic of all kinds, limbers had been marching all night now, passed with their drivers slouching in their saddles, their great coat collars turned up, all pretty tired and worn out. Canadians mostly, and they looked pretty low, being up all night, no fun anyway you do it, even dancing, and as for riding, we arrived at our destination after ten miles to find our New Zealand officers in a bit of wood, a jolly fine lot. Excellent lunch with a white table cloth and butter, 'Cold beef or Cottage Pie, Sir?'

After lunch we went out with Colonel [censored] to make the reconnaissance. [Colonel Duncan Barrie Blair, commanding officer New Zealand Machine Gun Battalion. Wounded at Gallipoli 1915-16.] The Colonel has one [-] cracked leg, so bad he has to drag it and he jolly well ought to be back in New Zealand instead of commanding combat troops. He does famously however, sort of skipping on one leg and dragging the other and I had to [-] to keep up. We did not go on foot, of course, and the Colonel on account of his leg has made a practice of riding a horse where and ordinary man would walk cautiously; and you must have a good horse and a dashed good seat to stay with him. I had a cart horse not made for riding at all; he was games to the last and galloped until his eyes bulged out of his head.

So we started, the Colonel, several majors, I was out-ranked horridly by everyone, and myself. The Colonel riding first would half turn in his saddle, hold up one finger, then dig in his spurs and over the hills and far away before you could say Jack Robinson. It had been pouring and had been rough going. 'This is madness,' said one of the New Zealanders, through his teeth; 'the Colonel ought not to be allowed out; we can't keep this up.' But we did. I felt as if I were riding to hounds and the lust of the chase came upon me.

Mind you this was a reconnaissance and we were supposed to get a good view of the country. I didn't see much all afternoon but the ears of my horse and the stream of mud sent up by the horse ahead. Through the barbed wire, over ditches, uphill, down dale and always, whenever we tried to slow up, the old bird of a Colonel would turn in his saddle and hold up that one finger before disappearing in a cloud of mud. He would jump right down into a trench a ride his horse along the firing step where it is all a man can do to walk. 'No dugouts here,' he would call and we thanked God for I have no doubt that if there had been one he would have held up his one finger and gone clattering down into it. We were riding thru a wheat field full tilt when P[censored], tearing along behind us, was suddenly swallowed up by the wheat. Two of us galloped back and found that he had charged head on into barbed wire; the horse had turned a complete summersault throwing both quite clear but had then sat firmly upon P[censored] until asked to desist. They were an awful mess, the horse badly cut about the forelegs and P[censored] not a little shaken up.

As the Colonel had by this time entirely disappeared into the mist of the horizon, the only thing for us to do was to plod our weary way homeward. We did finally arrive at the New Zealand Camp and after a cup of tea, felt better. The Colonel came hobbling in after a good while and insisted on our staying to dinner as our horses could not be ridden another step. The old sport sent us flying back in a staff car like two bally generals.

Today I can scarcely walk and P[censored] is in bed. We had a 'tres bein reconnaissance' if you please and if we ever have to defend that line we have not only seen the ground, but we have had it in our ears, nose and mouth. Yes Sire, we know the GROUND.

The fog of war hands over everything and nobody knows the future, but the Yanks are doing fine work below Soissons and I'm proud of 'em. I'm afraid their having rotten casualties, but is better so as it shows they are really in it. The Germans are better trained and are much nearer their base, but give us a chance and we'll have them by the ears and BY GEORGE THEY KNOW IT. A little while and it will be over. I don't see how they can stand the pressure of another year.

The First Casualties

CHAPTER 5
PREPARING FOR THE BIG SHOW

The 80th Division was arranging to move out of the British Sector and had begun its next chapter of the war by joining up with the American First Army. As the Germans were in retreat from the sector the Battalion occupied, so ended the Division's first-hand experience in trench combat and their participation in the Somme Offensive in Picardy. Although the men of the Division did not have the opportunity to relish the successes of the advancing New Zealand troops, they would later take pride in knowing that their new friends brought notable successes to the Allied cause.

As the Division was leaving the area, the British Third Army launched what is now known as the Battle of Bapaume, on August 21, 1918. This push advanced their infantry north of the L'Ancre and gained the line of the Albert-Arras railroad by the end of August. General Byng's Third Army drove the Germans out of the Somme plateau. News eventually reached the American Battalion that Bapaume was taken over by the New Zealanders.

The Division began their preparations in the American Zone by moving their headquarters from Beauval to Bernaville, one of the four rallying locations designated for troops to turn in their British style equipment and have new equipment issued. The locations were also designated areas for loading troops onto trains for their passage across France to join up with the American First Army. During these few days the men began turning in their British style arms and ordinance and began to accept their American equivalents. Not all equipment, however, was turned in. The men retained their British helmets and gasmasks for the remainder of the war. The 313th Machine Gun Battalion was ordered to march to Prouville, just west of Bernaville, and prepare to entrain on August 22, 1918. The trip took two days travel across parts of France that had been untouched by the war. The Division was heading to the American Zone that established itself in the Province of Côte-d'Or.

August 21, 1919 - HAMILTON

Dull day, the usual checking of equipment, and cleaning, and polishing. Some of the men are drunk again and everybody is tired and out of sorts. I applied for transfer to the Aviation today and was turned down flat by the Major. Leinhauser and I both applied. He said we knew too much about machine guns, well we do, we know that machine guns are too darn far back. I want to see some more action and go over the top with a tank or an airplane.

Tomorrow we go on again. God knows where. Sufficient it is that we will again hit the trail for 'Heaven, Hell or Hoboken before Christmas.' I have an idea that we will see some real action soon, but my ideas are seldom if ever right.

Captain Kean will be back directly and I will relinquish my command. This has been a pretty good experience, I have, I think, gotten away with this job to date and it has increased my confidence in myself a great deal. The last month has been the most interesting and also the most trying one that we have been through and I feel jolly lucky to have gotten through it without mishap. The only thing was losing these two men, and I don't see how that could have been helped. It was an accident, and accidents are bound to happen in the front line. I only feel glad that it wasn't twenty instead of two.

August 22, 1919 - HAMILTON

Today is a day of rest and meditation of which we have had very few lately. Last Sunday we were in the trenches, and the Sunday before that we were at the rifle range at [Orrville]. The Sunday before that we were in the trenches, and I rather think the one before that we were on the train. Today we are writing letters and getting our hair cut and just settin'- it is all right. The weather is lovely, but it certainly is surprisingly hot at noon and surprisingly cold at dawn.

We marched from [Foncquevillers] at eight o'clock this evening. Everything was ready and we got off with as little bustle as if we were going to evening parade. Generally, when we move our baggage there is lots of trouble and rushing around and swearing, but this evening was a cinch. It was very hot but there was a full moon and we marched along singing and everyone in fine spirits. In really hot weather all marching should be done after sundown. We marched five miles and entrained. The entraining was the best we've done, very quick and no confusion. Somebody deserves a lot of credit. I always think that troops on the move, particularly at night, is great fun. The limbers, pushed by a squad of shouting, sweating Yanks go up the planks and onto the flat cars in no time. The horses take longer and all along the train cursing drivers are trying to pull, push, persuade, force, carry, yank, cajole and induce unwilling steeds up the steep ramp into the dark box cars. '8 chevaux 40 hommes' is a reality at last.

The men aren't so badly off after all. There is clean straw in the cars and although they have no private baths, they can at least lie out flat and three can sit in the doorway and let their feet hang out just the way you see them in pictures. Everything is loaded at last and the train slides out of the siding. We are off once more.

August 22, 1918 – HOLLAND

I received a letter from you a week or more ago, and one the other day, but I haven't had time to answer. Perhaps I could have taken time, but a soldier gets tired and lazy as well as other people. I receive mail from you and Marie every time the mail comes. We get our mail just the same at the front, they bring it up. I sure was glad to hear you received your allotment.

Yes, I saw one boy from Union, Wayne Smith [1890-1963], he and I used to go around quite a bit together and Lobaugh [Howard Norman Lobaugh 1892-1918], I haven't seen him.

When you mentioned about Blanche Baldwin having a soldier over here, I was wondering if that long guy had come, and I have forgotten his name, but he belong to the same order as I did KP, so I knew him.

I got a letter from Julia and she said I guess I am forgotten. Ha, we have more to think about than girls over here, of course if I don't get mail every time it comes, I am disappointed. No mother, I don't expect to be home for Christmas this year, but maybe next year. I am quite sure next year it will be a happy day for the ones that come home and an unhappy day for them who have boys that doesn't. I am First-Class Private now and that means three dollars more on the month.

August 23, 1919 - HAMILTON

Spent a poor night as these compartments are not too good for four, six foot men to sleep in. I was awakened very early by the continuous rub-a-dub-dub of heavy artillery over towards the east. A long way off, but somebody is catching it hot. We seem to be going south but it is hard to tell. It is frightfully hot and these troop trains just crawl along.

I have not seen a paper but I hear that the British have captured [Bapaume] and the French have gone ahead for 10 miles. That is rather a joke about [Bapaume] because that is just where we were and missed getting into a real big party by two days. If we hadn't pulled out I might easily be in [Bapaume] today.

A long dull hot day interrupted by the men riding on the tops of the cars and getting lost in the station and all the manifold ways they can manage to keep the young American officer on edge.

August 24, 1919 - HAMILTON

They got us up at 2:00 AM to say that we would detrain in one hour and for everybody to pack up. We got our kits together in the dark and lay down and went to sleep again. It was six o'clock before they woke us and told us to get off. We got off at an American made station, under American officers and unloaded by American stevedores. After two months of wandering among the French, British and New Zealanders we have come to our own people; next to going back to America nothing could have made us feel better.

The British, or English rather, are all right but our boys don't like them too much. They don't like the broad 'A', they don't like the English tobacco and most of all they don't like the English ration. It isn't enough for these big Yanks and nothing else could so militate against brigading us together. We don't like their grub. Anyhow it is all over, our training period is over, we are now quite fit to go into the line with our unbeatable army. I can't say where we are except that we came through Paris yesterday and we are further from the line now than we have been in some time.

We detrained, had breakfast by the road side, shaved and hit the trail. We marched until 3:00 in the afternoon. About 12 miles I think, pitched tents and camped for the night.

❧

The nearly 300 mile train ride carried the Battalion for two days through the French towns of Amiens, Beauvais, Paris, Melun, Montereau and Sens. The designated area to detrain on August 23 was Poincon. The men arrived at Châtillon-sur-Seine on August 24, but the stay in this area was short. It was only a temporary rest area for the troops to allow for the replacement of equipment.

The men were assigned to billet in the town of Beneuvre, an agreeable little village for the troops. This region of France was one of the most picturesque places on their tour. They enjoyed good weather during these few days and soaked in the beauty of the lush rolling hills, vast pastures, and cold running streams. The bonus was the availability of the Burgundy wines that could be purchased at reasonable prices.

August 25, 1919 - HAMILTON

Up at 4:30 AM, very cold, damp and dark. We got off after an easy start at 7:00 AM. We hiked all morning and then came to a place where there was a nice pasture with a big brook at one side [Recey-sur-Ource]. We stopped there for dinner and everybody had a swim. My morale went up from 5% to 90%. We resumed our march at 2:00 PM and came on to her in all about eighteen miles for the day. Here we have camped in a big field on the side of a hill. It is 'tres bon' and everybody is happy. We drew our first Yank ration today and it looked like a million dollars. This country is pretty. It is rolling and not thickly populated. The people are very friendly and quite enthusiastic when we go through, very different from the way they are in the north.

August 26, 1919 - HAMILTON

My word these August mornings are cold. Before the sun gets up the damp penetrates to the bond. We got off at 8 o'clock and marched about six miles to another little French village [Beneuvre]. This is the nicest one we've been in yet, very small, very clean, very untouched by the war. The roofs are red tile and the kids wear clean smocks and everybody has a flower garden.

There was a mix up about the men's billets so we put them in pup tents in a field. I'd like to keep them there, I think they are so better off. Spent the day trying to get some Company matters straightened out, talked a lot but did not accomplish much.

My billet is delightful, a big room with a stone floor. The bed as usual is OK only this bed is OK-er than usual. Madame is a wonder. She is the ordinary age, about 120, but far more agreeable than any other to date. She came in this evening, arranged flowers, made the bed, and brought some water, all the time talking a blue streak of French the purport of which was utterly impossible to follow. God knows where all the middle aged French people are. The men are all at war of course, but you don't see women even. You don't see anybody between twelve and eighty and that's a fact. Grandparents and grandchildren, the middle generation, seem wiped out entirely.

August 27, 1919 - HAMILTON

I don't think I'm much of a Company Commander but I have a pretty good time at it I must say. I busted my mess sergeant yesterday and think the kitchen is going to run better, it has been very unsatisfactory. I busted him and expected him to be sore and instead he has been around all day helping on little jobs and as pleasant as you please. I have busted about six non-coms during the Captain's absence and made about the same number of new ones. I don't believe the Captain will be too darn pleased but I don't think I've been wrong yet. I've got to get a Company of my own. Messing around another fellows outfit is poor dope; either that or for me a nice quiet tank.

August 28, 1919 - HAMILTON

One year ago yesterday, I reported at Camp Lee and was assigned to the colored infantry. So I have been in the Army proper for just one year. Captain Kean returned from school today and I have turned over the Company to him. I busted a tooth yesterday, a tooth and a mess sergeant; I busted them both on the same question, hard tack.

The food shortage among the French people is really quite serious, much more than I first thought. This old lady here I don't believe ever has a thing to eat but cabbage. I gave her a piece of good white American bread today and she took it in both hands like a hungry child and hugged it close. She is 82 years old, I found out today. The old man is 79. That is the way of every billet I've been in - two incredibly old people and one dog. This dog is a big collie and he goes out every evening and brings the cows in all by himself as it is a long way. It is pretty remarkable that he does it. These are master cows too, as big as elephants almost. The collie dog is darn nice, but he's on rations too and is beginning to get pretty fed up with the meatless days. He says it is a hateful, pig of a war, when the bugle blows revile, I darn well agree with him.

August 29, 1919 - HAMILTON

Very dull day. This is the only notebook in France and I won't be able to get much more in it. After all the bustle and excitement of last month a dull day seems much duller, and besides, Captain Kean is back and he has to do the worrying.

August 29, 1918 - THOMAS

We had received word just before leaving that the Division had moved, so we came all the way across France after them. A matter of course, three or four days. We were greeted with the alarming news that we had to go through Paris, and we got there at 2:00 AM at night and stayed until 12 Noon, so we looked around a little. It was wonderful and I have to go back again sometime. An hour and a half of my precious time was taken up by sending my watch home. Be on the lookout for it.

I'm in a new part of the country altogether now. We don't know much what is going to happen, but hope to get some action soon. My Company has been in the line already, but got no casualties. From what the lieutenants tell me the Germans are all dead now, if the letters sent home are correct. It was just like coming home to get back. One of my Italians had knifed a gentleman of the company, one was shot by unknown parties, and one kicked by a mule. Aside from that all is serene. They are in wonderful shape and anxious to get back to the line. The

Battalion is being changed all around. A lot of promotions going through all around. I haven't heard any rumors of mine, but it bothers me less than anything I can think of.

Up until now I have played a very small part in this war, but hope to get my chance. It is getting pretty cold here now but the weather is beautiful. We had a wonderful moon just before we left the coast, but it was bad luck as the Boche came over every night and slung bombs all around. It is a very helpless feeling.

I guess you see from the papers about all of the news over here. We never get very much news here, but when I last saw the papers everything was wonderful. I don't think there is going to be any let up from now on. I really don't believe there will be. I would like to get some action, because my Company are all old veterans.

We have talked to a bunch of men who have been in and all my Company too, and they are enthusiastic about it.

August 29, 1918 - KEAN

Well, we finished our courses and then received orders to join the Division. This caused us to travel for about three days. We arrived in Paris at 2:00 AM and as we had a bunch of men in tow we couldn't leave them or stay over.

Prescott Huidekoper is in charge of the Battalion and Rob Cox has been transferred to the 314th and given charge of that Battalion. Captain Garretson having been given command of the 315th Machine Gun Battalion. This makes me senior Machine Gun Captain in the Division, I think.

It certainly is nice to get where you have an occasional American Y.M.C.A., Red Cross or Quartermaster to buy things. I had some chocolates made in N.Y. and some American cigarettes and tobacco for the first time in quite a while the other day. But I wouldn't have missed my month vacation for anything as it was the best time I have had since I have been in the Army. This place is another stupid little town quite different from the first one we were at and I guess it takes after the country which reminds me a lot of the foot hills of the Berkshires.

Unfortunately, when my Company was in the line, I had two men killed outright by a shell. It happened they were both good men, and they were the only causalities in the Battalion. I was sorry to lose them.

We now have turned in nearly all our British equipment and are partially equipped with American stuff, getting loads of it every day. Now that we are away from the British, I don't mind using such expressions as 'cheereeks,' 'Good lyer,' 'Wind up,' 'Best of Luck,' 'Wash out,' 'cushy,' 'bon' for good, pronounced as written. Also 'no bon.' None of which we would deign to use when at our former locality. The food here is also much better and hence the men are more cheerful, though I have got to whip them about a bit and get them into shape again, for I don't think they are up to what I would like them to be.

✄

On August 30, 1918, the entire Division began to move out of the rest areas and began to stage in preparation for the Saint-Mihiel Operations. The Battalion was ordered to march to the Essarois and establish a bivouac until further preparations were made for movement of the entire Regiment. The next move was to the Stainville area, about 45 miles south of the Saint-Mihiel salient.

August 30, 1919 - HAMILTON

This seems we are all set for a very enjoyable stay here. We had started a canteen and a YMCA and the Battalion was to give a show and everything as fine as you please. However, it was too good to last and at 2:00 AM this morning we got orders to move again. We pushed out at 8:00 AM and marched fifteen miles. The men are getting pretty good at route marching but it is poor fun at best.

August 30-31, 1919 - LEINHAUSER

We left Beneuvre at 8:00 AM on another hike. Eleven miles of marching and we had a good swim in the head waters of the Seine River. We made camp and had a fine night. Good swimming holes here. Hamilton and I went fishing, but no luck. Everybody is feeling good and the weather is ideal. We left Essarois the next morning for Châtillon-sur-Seine. The 319th Infantry is ahead of us and it is awfully slow marching.

129

August 31, 1919 - HAMILTON

I have got another note book so don't have to write small. I have a letter from Louise at Paris [Louisa Low Haydock 1890-1978, Red Cross Relief Worker]. She said George was killed in action on May 28 leading his platoon [George Guest Haydock 1894-1918]. He was shot dead through the head in the Cantigny attack. Louise perfectly splendid about it, but it has been a hard blow. She also says she is engaged to a man named Hackett [William Henry Young Hackett 1886-1963]. Another girl gone to the bow wows. I never supposed Lou would fall in love, but if she has it is a fine thing and somebody is very fortunate. Louise is a priceless person. It does sort of knock my props out though, men I care for getting killed and girls I care for getting married. It just seems as though life had gone back to essentials, marriage and war and death. It leaves a fellow without a thing to lean on but luck.

Another long hike. We were on the road for 10 hours. We are going on maneuvers and the roads were full of troops. We camped in an enormous big stony field. There are pup tents as far as the eye can reach. After making camp I went down and watched the transport come in. They are fine fun and always make me feel like a small kid again, the way I used to when prairie schooners went rumbling by in Buffalo Bills Wild West show. They came in this afternoon, white with dust, lumbered wagons, ration and baggage wagons, officers mess carts, motor trucks, rolling kitchens, bicycles, ambulances, water carts, staff cars, pack mules, and God knows what else. They came rumbling out of a cloud of fine white dust that sticks to the driver's faces, hat and clothes. Behind the rolling kitchens walk the cooks et al. Cooks aren't too military anyhow, and on the march they look like so many tramps. They come trooping in carrying sticks, some of them have pets and you see cats and dogs and other animals. I saw one cook yesterday loading an enormous yellow hound dog who was straining on the leash and pulling the cook after him, they were a ridiculous pair. All the rabble of an army finally sifts into the transport and they are funny, my word they are funny. Bobbie Stoddart and I sat on a wall yesterday for an hour and never stopped laughing once.

In the evening Bobbie and Lin [Stoddart and Leinhauser] and I went into town in the motor sidecar to get something to eat. Everything had been eaten up, but it was great fun tearing along the dark roads without a light. The motorcars over here never have any lights, and the towns never have any, except for an occasional candle flickering in a pup tent. There never are any lights at all.

September 1, 1918 - LEINHAUSER

We got up at 8:30 AM and marched a detail of our men to mass at Saint Nicholas church in Châtillon-sur-Seine. We got back about 11:30 AM. Hamilton and I went out on a motorcycle. Had a nice 3 or 4 hour ride to Recey-sur-Ource. We stopped at Prusly-sur-Ource for our supper which was fine. It was served in the cleanest hotel I have seen in France by a nice old Madame. I met a young girl who could speak English. We got back home about 7:00 PM.

September 1, 1918 - HAMILTON

After yesterday's big march we rested most of the day. In the afternoon Lin and I went off in the side car in search of chocolate. We went 15 miles at a terrific speed to a Y.M.C.A. We got white dust all over us but it's a lot better than walking on your flat feet. The Y.M.C.A. as usual had no chocolate but we bought some biscuits and I bought a pipe and a can of Prince Albert. I'm going to try to smoke it.

We were out of gas and went to steal some, and the way of the transgressor was hard because the gas we stole was 90% water. Luckily we found out before trying to start it as water in the carburetor does not produce the speed that Lin and I like. The tank wouldn't drain, so we spent a jolly hour mopping it out with a piece of waste on a wire. That left us out of gas entirely so we stole some from a nearby 'dead' truck. My morals in regards to stealing no longer exist. I take whatever I need and as everybody else does the same, things change hands rapidly. Gosh knows what we are going to do when we have to be honest again. After all, it all belongs to Uncle Sam so it is in the family anyhow.

September 1, 1918 - THOMAS

We have been hiking for three days, but rest a little while this afternoon. I have just been down to take a swim in icy cold water, so feel clean and very much better. This part of the country has been simply wonderful. The night before last I had my shelter tent in the back of the most wonderful château you ever saw. Part of it was 600 years old. Tell sister that the dungeon-keep and everything was there. There was the most wonderful terraced garden, with wonderful roses, innumerable summer-houses and fountains, and enjoining a park of about four hundred acres. I had a wonderful time looking at it, and the countess came out and took a picture of me shaving. She took us all through the [not legible] and complained about how badly things were kept, because all the men were away. But it was simply wonderful.

We hiked about 30 km yesterday, but the weather was wonderful, the country beautiful and the men in the best shape imaginable so we didn't mind it a bit, and came in complementary fashion. This is by far the prettiest part of France we have been and it is really wonderful. We see ever so many American troops and the people are fine to us. The whole business is fine, as the saying is here 'well it's a hell of a war, but is the best war we've got,' and everybody is happy.

We're going in soon, right away I hope and my Company is fine. It's in better shape than it has been, and with the exception that they are in the habitual state of wanting to borrow money, are perfectly happy. It's a wonderful life.

Last night, just after Jimmy had brought me my supper, a little girl came and stood around. I gave her a slice of bread with molasses on it, and she took it and burst out crying. She told me she had seven sisters and brothers. I got rather fed up on the French where I was before, they were so darned mercenary, but these are wonderful. I'm still bothered with schools. I have only two lieutenants now, but can get along just so, they have left me a few of my sergeants. They are fine. I sent two of my sergeants to officers training camp the other day. One of them was a man named Duff [Joseph Miller Duff Jr. 1889-1918]. He coached the University football team several years ago. Bob Lassiter would remember him [Robert Lassiter 1877-1953 was the War Fund Chairman, American Red Cross, Charlotte NC]. This National Army is wonderful.

Sergeant Joseph M. Duff Jr., an enlisted member of the Battalion, apparently impressed Captain Thomas enough to mention him in a letter home to the family. Duff was a 1912 graduate of Princeton University. He was a standout player on the varsity football team, a 1911 'All-American' and proclaimed to be the 'Best guard in football history' ("Joe Duff Chosen to Coach").

DUFF

After graduation he was asked to stay on at Princeton to serve as an assistant football coach. The following year he received an offer to become head football coach at the University of Pittsburgh. Duff delivered two winning seasons for Pittsburgh in 1913 and 1914. Following the 1914 season, Pitt found an opportunity to hire legendary coach Glenn Scobey "Pop" Warner. Coach Warner helped Pitt win the College Football National Championship in 1915. That same year, Duff obtained his Law Degree from the University of Pittsburgh and went on to work in his brother James' law firm, Duff, Scott and Smith. His brother James H. Duff (1883-1969) became the 34th Governor of Pennsylvania in 1947.

It is not clear why Joe Duff was not initially commissioned as an officer in the United States Army. At the time of the national draft registration, Duff was already a college graduate. He enlisted in the Military Training Association, and was already situated at the Reserve Officers Training Camp at Fort Niagara in June 1917. At the end of his training at Fort Niagara, NY, he was not assigned to a specialized unit as many of the other candidates listed on the roster. It is possible that he was not commissioned because he was recruited to work as an attorney for the United States Justice Department. In 1917, he was responsible for prosecuting men who attempted to evade the draft.

However, this role as a government prosecutor did not protect him from being called up under the terms of the Selective Service draft. In March 1918, Duff was inducted into the Army as an enlisted man and sent to Camp Lee to join the Battalion. He set sail for France with the rank of Private. It was his time in France with D Company that he was quickly promoted to the rank of Sergeant. His commission as a Second Lieutenant came on September 30, 1918. He was transferred out of the Battalion and reassigned to lead a machine gun company in the 32nd Division, 125th Infantry. After only ten days with his new unit, Duff was killed while fighting at Gesnes-en-Argonne, part of the Meuse-Argonne offensive. His body was buried in a temporary gravesite in Dur-sur-Meuse, France.

Lieutenant Duff's brother, Captain George M. Duff (1886-1953), a Chaplain serving in France with the 305th Infantry, sent a telegram back home to his brother, James to notify the family of Joseph's death.

The remains of Lieutenant Duff were returned to the family about three years after his death and a funeral service was held on September 9, 1921 at the First Presbyterian Church in Carnegie, Pennsylvania. Duff's brother George, then pastor of the First Presbyterian Church of Elwood City, presided over the funeral and his remains were interred in the Chartiers Cemetery in Carnegie, Pennsylvania.

CHAPTER 6
FINDING HUMOR IN THE MISERY

The 80th Division was staged in reserve of the American First Army's planned attack upon the Saint-Mihiel salient. The Battalion travelled for twelve hours north on a train through the towns of Châteauvillain, Chaumont, Saint-Dizier and finally reached the station at Révigny. They took a second train and traveled southeast in order to reach the village of Ligny-en-Barrois, the location of the A.E.F's General Headquarters. Upon arrival, the Battalion bivouacked near Ligny-en-Barrois for one night. The following evening they moved to Nant-le-Grand. Due to the overall secrecy of the A.E.F operations, the troops could not be seen marching in the open as large formations, nor were they to take part in training maneuvers during the day. The wooded areas provided the best cover for the Battalion during the day and the officers wrote in their letters about having to perform training exercises in the evenings.

At this juncture in the war, the men of the Battalion were never given the overall scope of the planned operations, nor were they told the details of the impending attack. This information remained secret, and the lack of understanding what their part in the campaign would be, was often expressed in the letters home to the family. At times they believed that the newspapers probably knew more about the Army's plans than the Battalion itself. What we now know is that General Pershing was assembling several Divisions in the American Sector for the eventual attack in the Saint-Mihiel operations.

September 2, 1918 - HAMILTON

Labor Day. Not very much like the ones we have at home. On the move again. We took the train at 2 o'clock. Entraining is becoming second nature to us and we do it now easily and quickly. We rode twelve hours and if anybody thinks it is not cold in France in September, let him just try a box car without straw at 2:00 AM in the morning, which is the time we detrained. The men were absolutely frozen stiff. We unloaded our horses and ourselves and marched out. We marched until dawn and camped in the woods. The men were so tired and cold and sleepy that they couldn't walk straight and when the order came to 'fall out' they flopped in their tracks pulled their blankets around them and were asleep all inside two minutes.

September 2, 1918 - KEAN

When I got back to my Company from school I found things in fair shape, but not as I like them. I don't know whether it was the fault of my Company, or of my Lieutenant. I think the former.

The Company has hiked about 200 hikes in the past two weeks. Luckily I have only been with them for about 75 of them, as having no horse, I have to push along on my flat feet, which is not at all to my liking. Cox is now in charge of 314th Machine Gun Battalion.

September 3, 1918 - HAMILTON

We didn't do a thing all day. The sun came up and shone down on us through the trees and we turned lazily in our blankets and looked up at the blue sky and said it was a 'good war.' One man told me that it was the first warm sleep he had in France and it was certainly darn fine. I didn't get up all day and only woke up for dinner.

We marched again at 8:00 PM after a good hot supper. Quite different from last night. Everybody was well rested and feeling good. It was fine marching along under the bright stars. Over to the north we could see the occasional flashes of big guns and the German flares going up. We were back the front once more. We made camp at about 2:00 AM in another woods and bivouacked on the ground.

September 4, 1918 - HAMILTON

Another peaceful day. I can't remember doing anything at all except putting up a master tent with the Captain and camouflaging it over with green leaves and branches. There is no water here. We have to go miles for it and I don't suppose I'll ever have more than half a cup of water to bathe in again. Half a cup of water to bathe, shave and clean my teeth. I don't exactly consider that it's enough. It is surprising how you can get along though. A good water supply is certainly a great blessing and a great luxury and something you never get in the Army.

There are a lot of things you never get in the Army, noticeably cream, fruit, and chocolate éclairs. I'll be glad to go back to civilian life again and get some.

September 5, 1918 - HAMILTON

I am breaking all my teeth on the Army hard tack. I broke one a week ago, another clean off at the base two days ago and another today. It is rotten, especially as there is no immediate chance of having them fixed, and if I go on this way, I'm going to be a toothless old wretch by the time I go home again. The dentist [Joseph Harold Parsons 1894-1918] we have isn't bad, but he lost all his tools on the way over and now uses a chisel and a pair of wire cutters on all comers. He has me intimidated.

It rained today and we didn't get much work done. Gil Thorne is away at school and I have to take his platoon.

September 5, 1918 – THOMAS

I started this letter some time ago, but a discussion arose as to what day of the week it was. Everybody had forgotten and conjectures made it all the way from Monday until Saturday. We have been on the go steadily since I wrote you last. We are in pup tents and I think everybody is enjoying it. I am for one. We march usually by night. My Company is in wonderful shape. With the exception of the usual morning incidents, such as the barber going on strike, someone missing reveille, one or two sick, the path of life is exceedingly smooth. As long as you keep their stomachs full and work them till they can't stand, everything is sweet. Around payday they all get drunk of course, but this is to be expected.

And they are a wonderful pleasure. To see them in comparison to one year ago, all of them tan and strong. Their uniforms all fitting them close, and they are all on the eve of the great adventure, and they want it.

News is too encouraging now I'm afraid, but we are promising ourselves Thanksgiving dinner in Germany. This wondering life is fine. It keeps you busy. Packing up in an hour and hiking 20 miles is nothing. Living in tents is fine. Applegate, [Edward Maskell Applegate 1885-1924] one of my lieutenants, complained this morning that his melon was not good. This with breakfast consisting of bacon and eggs, cantaloupe, toast, and coffee, served by our orderlies in bed. We had to laugh about the discomforts of the poor soldier, as all of us are happier than we have ever been. The extra food we pay for of course. The weather has been just right for camping out. Cool nights and warm days. There is no water here. That is the great trouble. We have to go about 6 km, about 4 miles, to water our horses. I haven't bathed for a week, but the men all managed to get shaved for inspection. I just heard that we pull out tonight, but that suits us fine as we have been here two days. To keep moving is fine, and it helps the men. They get seasoned.

We have been over here three months tomorrow. It doesn't seem like three weeks. I'm glad we got here when we did. Another year will probably see us begin to go home, but it doesn't seem like almost a year and a half practically since I went to Fort Myers, does it?

Jimmy, my striker, can talk a lot better than I can. I'm making quite a little progress, however, and hope to do better. These men write the funniest letters you ever saw. They describe the most horrible engagements you ever saw. Very often in the same letters there will be several with the same general description. It means some Tommy or Poilu has told them the night before. However, one of my braves always appears as the hero. They will do it if the chance comes however, I know.

September 5, 1918 – HOLLAND

I haven't written to you for a week or so, and I haven't received any mail for three weeks. I suppose I will get a bunch someday. I saw Tom Delaney [Thomas Owen Delaney 1890-1951] one night. I was talking a bath in a brook and he was also, so I spoke and he knew me at once. He is fat and looks good. I also saw Jay Bennett, he worked with me three years in the Union City chair factory.

The weather is good, only the nights are a little cold. I suppose you will celebrate the 18th of this month, all I'll be home to celebrate it with you next year. I have several letters to write but I don't believe I will answer half of them. If people hear from me once a month they should feel satisfied.

I get six dollars more over here. We get $0.10 a day for Foreign Service, and then I am a First-Class Private now, and that pays $0.10 more. I saw a clipping out of the Erie paper, the heading was 'the hardships of a home guard.' They had to ride all night in a day coach and sleep on a cot with only three Army blankets. They only got ice cream once and had to hike 2 miles. When we read that, maybe there wasn't a laugh and I would hate to see them over here with some real soldiers. We don't think anything of hiking 16 or 18 miles with a heavy pack and take a flop on the ground anywhere for the night. Lots and lots of times we don't bother unrolling our pack to get our blanket. All the boys have a red face and look good, of course we are tanned from the sun. We don't wear the campaign hat over here, just a little skullcap. We call it a ducky.

September 6, 1918 - HAMILTON

My pipe doesn't go very well. I think I'll cut out smoking entirely for the duration of the war. After all the excitement of the past month, this is pretty tame lying in the woods here trying to do a little drill and trying to pull ourselves together before we get into a big party.

A year ago today 'A Company' of the 313th M.G.B. began its existence and began drilling recruits and giving lectures to eager going things about morals, feet, discipline and sanitation. 'A Company' is having a reunion tonight in celebration of their first year, and had ice cream, or its French equivalent, bread again, ad lib. I was not invited, although I thought I might have been as Captain Cox, John Curlee [John McFerrin Curlee 1894-1967] and I formed the Company.

Captain Cox has now gone to the 314th as their new Major. Curlee is in the 317th Infantry, and I am in 'C Company.' The only two of their original officers are Mackey [Sidney Augustus Mackey 1888-after1959] and Lunden [Walter Carl Lunden 1894-1969]. Of the original officers of the Battalion about half survived the first year. The Major and two Captains and one Lieutenant were promoted and sent to other outfits. Several transferred to the Infantry and several more to the flying corps and about ten were bounced for various reasons.

The men we have are pretty good, although I don't care particularly for any of them, at least, I don't care for most of them. Bobbie Stoddart of this Company is a fine fellow and I'm very fond of him. He is a good officer and a gentleman. Leinhauser also of 'C Company' is one of the world's chosen few. He is six foot six, broad shouldered, clear eyed, the kind of man you only see three times in a life time. About 26 year's old, marvelous athlete, master mechanic, and first class soldier. Not a vestige of conceit, although I've hardly ever seen a man with more to be conceited about and almost absolutely unselfish. His men worship him and would follow him to Hell and back. He's the very finest type of American, although both parents are pure German.

Captain George Thomas of 'D Company' is one of the other good fellows in the Battalion. His Company looks up to him and loves him like a father. Personally, he's an awful old rounder and has been all his life, and is a living proof that fast living does not necessarily beget hardness or coarseness. He is one of the gentlest, kindest, most lovable fellows I've ever known, without a trace or egotism. He is good all through in spite of his outrageous morals and is worth about sixty of the kind that talks about morals and doesn't play the game square.

September 7, 1918 - HAMILTON

Today I went on a liaison problem with a lot of generals. It was a tactical maneuver in liaison, which after all is the most difficult thing in modern warfare, especially when on the move. Nobody ever knows what to do with the machine guns, so they say, 'The machine guns will be in reserve'.

We were in reserve the entire morning and I lay down behind a hedge and went to sleep. It was a pretty good war. Later we got orders to move up a bit so we moved up to another hedge and went to sleep again. Then we went to the critique and heard all the generals talk, and so home at last. It was a dull day and if I hadn't run over a man in the Ford car I wouldn't' have had any fun at all. It happened this way.

Four of us went out to the problem in a Ford car. The confounded thing had no brakes and no horn and I must say was pretty dangerous to all concerned. We didn't learn that the brakes were no good until we came to a steep hill. Captain M[censored] was driving and I was on the front seat with him. The first thing I knew I saw we were rapidly catching up with the Major who was in a side car in front. We were gaining speed with every second, to miss the Major we turned out, skidded, turned over on our side and continued down the hill. About this time I thought I'd get off as my services didn't seem required. I had no sooner gotten off than she righted herself and owing to sliding on her side was going at a reasonable speed, so I got on again and by holding her in low we got down the hill with no harm done, but the worst was yet to come.

We reached the rendezvous and there Captain M. left and they asked me to drive it. I said that I could drive a Ford better than Henry Ford himself, so we started. It was a narrow road and there were a lot of troops on the left along the road. In front of me a couple of squads of this Battalion were marching. They were just ahead when they suddenly halted. I found myself driving down on them at a speed of about 5 miles per hour and unable to stop. I applied all brakes and jammed her in low and tried to slide between the men on the left and the last man on the right of the column in front. It was no use and the next second I hit him square with my right mud guard. Ordinarily he would have been pushed clear but it shoved him against the next man and he bounced off and over him we went bump, bump, bump, bump. It was a horrid sensation too, going bumping over him and not being able to stop the damned car. I couldn't get it stopped either for 50 yards. I went back feeling pretty blue, I certainly hate running over people. A great crowd had gathered, Major Wise [Jennings Cropper Wise 1881-1968] who was there got very excited and shouted, 'That's the first ambulance we've seen in six months and it's killed a man.' That made me mad because in the first place, whether he was killed or not there was nothing to get excited about. Men are killed over here every minute and accidents are bound to happen. In the second place it wasn't an ambulance, it was a small Ford truck, and in the third place he wasn't killed because he sat up immediately and said

'Thank God that wasn't a tank,' and then lay back and said 'Carry on with Mechanism.'

However, he was hurt all right and they sent him away to the hospital, but fortunately nothing serious and he will probably be about again in a week or less. I felt pretty blue about it. If I had only put her in reverse I think I could have stopped in time but it all came so damn quick.

We move again at 9:00 PM tonight. We have been here three days and I was just getting everything all set and comfortable when Bang! off we go again. Another midnight march either 12 miles or 12 kilos I'm not sure which and don't care much. The best thing about night marches is that you generally rest all the next day, and as tomorrow is Sunday I think it would be particularly nice to lie in the hay, don't you! .

Since restoring my diary, have written no letters of any kind. It was wonderful getting so many letters and made me almost homesick although it's funny to be homesick for Dobbs Ferry.

September 7, 1918 - KEAN

Since leaving my billets, a week ago Thursday, we have been camping out. I have erected my cot, however, for the past three nights and have been quite comfortable. It is almost like militia maneuvers here as we seldom here any guns fired. I expect that soon, however, we will get a plenty.

Several men of the Division have been awarded decorations by General Julian Byng [Julian Hedworth George Byng 1862-1935], who was in command of the Army to which we were attached. If we had stayed where we were, we would have had it pretty hot and busy. They say that two of my Platoons got shelled almost as heavily as the New Zealanders, with whom had over seen it.

We haven't had any hot weather to speak of all summer. In fact, most of the time it has been cold with a hot day here and there scattered throughout. Washing is very scarce as you know and it is now nearly a week since I have had more than a canteen of water at any one time. However, we get along all right.

I hear from my Lieutenants, who have just received mail, that the thermometer was up around the hundreds when their letters were written.

It is never tiresome or stupid to get letters no matter how old they are. I think you have been worrying a lot unnecessarily, as except for air raids. I have only had four days under fire so far, and was more comfortable than many times since and before.

Since July 23rd I have only spent two nights in doors. Our food is pretty good. We get plenty of sugar, white bread, some butter, jam, and the rest of the things depends greatly on how the transport is running, as we never seem to be near a rail center. Potatoes, rice, breakfast food, oatmeal, hominy, etc. are scarce.

Last Sunday, I went with Garry to an Officers Club run by the Y.M.C.A in the town near us. He met a friend from Morristown, she sold us some regular American sucky candy which was quite a treat. I don't see all the currants that I expected to find in this vicinity, but last night, the First Sergeant [Frank Ferdinand Fee 1884-1934] presented me with a large cup of stewed elder berries. They were very good, but I couldn't eat them all and put them under my cot. The result was that this evening I found about ten drained yellow jackets in them. They seem to flourish in September all over France as they were thick at Camiers too.

P.S. September 9, 1918 Marched several miles the other night getting well rained on and ended up in a town where I am billeted and have a bed again. Cox is also in the town which makes it very nice. The Company are located in the château grounds and though they must be pretty uncomfortable, they seem to be happy and cheerful.

∗

A Division Field Order required the movement of the 80th Division to Ligny-en-Barrois, Tronville-en-Barrois, and the Nançois-le-Grand areas on the evening of September 7-8. The Battalion was ordered to march to Guerport, about 2 km from Tronville-en-Barrois.

September 8, 1918 - HAMILTON

The march last night was a mess. We groped our way out of the dark woods at nine and took the road. A thunderstorm was coming up and it was dark as pitch, you could only see the man in front when the lightning flashed. Word was passed back to cut out the whistling and cigarettes so we had to stumble along in the dark in silence. The road was awful, all loose stones and it was poor sport. In front of me two bicyclists from headquarters were trying to ride and couldn't keep their balance in the dark and went crazily from one side of the road to the other until they went crashing into the ditch. They did it the entire way and it rather got my goat. Later it came on to rain, and as usual, everybody was drenched before the order was passed back to 'put on slickers.' Then these damnable overseas caps are worse than useless in a rain and when they get wet through the water runs down the back of your neck and into your eyes and it is rotten. They are just like a wet sponge on your head. So we all got wet. Then we got lost too and had to sit in the wet ditch while another battalion marched through us. Hillbillies from West Virginia, and they looked a mile tall, silhouetted against the sky as they went by with their rifles slung over their backs and their steel helmets. Very wet and very cheerful, marching in step and well closed up. These fellows are Yanks, all through, and make fine soldiers. We got in eventually; the men went into tents and the officers into billets.

Today we have rested. I did not get up until 2 o'clock and didn't do a thing after I was up but lie around on the bed and talk to Bobbie and Lin, it was a good war, I think we are winning. Incidentally, we are winning. The British advanced seven miles beyond Péronne today and the Hindenburg Line has been pierced in several places. Unless we get into it pretty soon, there won't be any Huns left.

September 9, 1918 - HAMILTON

More rain and not much to do. At home at Camp Lee it never seemed as if anything funny ever happened. Over here it is entirely different. Funny things happen all the time, and if a man had any gift for writing them down, an account of the A.E.F. would be a scream. Life runs pretty swiftly and I would give a lot to be able to snap shot the little amusing things as they occur, because generally in the excitement of moving on they get forgotten, and also so much depends on the setting, which is hard to reproduce on paper.

Now the other night we were halted in a small village filling canteens. It had been a long wait and the men were cold and shivering in the dark. Word was passed up from the rear that another battalion was coming through us. Soon along came Captain Leland B. Garretson on his horse. Captain Garretson of Morristown, New York and the Essex Troop. Captain Garretson with his Mexican Border ribbon on his breast and a limber full of his other decorations. Along he came, just made a Major, riding at the head of his battalion with his staff on a tall horse. He came to 'C Company' sitting in the ditch very cold, very hungry, very tired, very fed up, and asked them sternly 'What outfit is that?'

No reply, and then, a voice from the ditch 'We're Storm Troops. Bup! Bup! Bup! Bup!'

He almost fell off his horse. 'What's that! What's that! Who said that?' No reply. 'What C Company?!'

'Bup! Bup! Bup!!!'

'I shall report the whole Company to Captain Kean,' and he rode off in the darkness fairly sputtering, leaving C Company in hysterics. He did report us to the Captain later, but nothing came of it and nothing will come of it. C Company has been well taught not to give it's designation to strangers and although they all knew Captain Garretson, well, it was a dark night and you can't be too careful.

September 9, 1918 - THOMAS

To begin with, we don't have the gun you spoke of but will probably get it before long. We have a darn good gun however. I see a Paris edition of the New York Herald, a day late, practically every day, also the London Daily Mail. That keeps us pretty well posted, including the Worlds Series.

As to our Army, it is good. Of course we have profited by the French and English experiences and that, passed on, has been invaluable, but also there is quite a good deal of pros and cons which only time can help. The personnel cannot be equal anywhere. Where there are errors, it is the officers. You find the same here that we find in civil life, some hyped on promotion, some that strange variety of a damn fool whose success is due to pure and simple gall, and then the vast majority that are doing the best they can and laughing at hardships. The errors are in judgment of course and my only hope is that the war will last long enough to show up some of the blatant asses that are forced on you. The men of my Company are the best I've seen of course. It is gratifying to look at them now and realize what they were a year ago. They are trained to the notch and as fit as they can be until they get the old experience.

Last night we hiked until 2:00 AM, went through one of the worst rainstorms I've ever saw and they all slept on the wet ground, and came up smiling today. I got thoroughly wet myself, but was lucky enough to have a billet, so after I got them fixed up I got Jimmy Ferraro, my striker, and got comfortable. I got away with a case of Scotch a week ago, so we had a little party at 4:00 AM consisting on canned lobster, Roquefort cheese, hard-tack, and Scotch, which is what I call a large party for these turbulent times.

This Battalion will always be with this Division. The Division itself has been in II Corps already and at present I think it is in the First Army, III Corps. As a matter of fact, I don't really know. We have covered practically all of France. My Company has been in the line and acquitted themselves exceptionally well, but I was at school. I haven't been in any kind of a show, and only scared once or twice by a little bombing. As Cothran [Perrin Chiles Cothran 1885-1959] wrote me the other day, he was scared as hell, but not yellow. I figure that is about my fix.

The chief joy of my life is my striker Jimmy. He is tireless and can do anything. Talk about living. Here's one menu tonight. Hamburger steak with onions, baked beans, French fried potatoes, French toast, orange marmalade, preserved plums, Roquefort cheese, coffee, champagne and a liquor, and you can see that when the noble sacrifices are talked of, it is a little embarrassing.

Of course we don't get that much often, but we can always get eggs. Our mess is reasonable. Jimmy produces most of it. God knows from where. I asked him tonight where he got the potatoes. He said, 'I ask to sell um, they say no. Nobody knows me, I steal um.'

We are really spoiled by having a good Division. We follow some Divisions into place that leave rotten reputations and rotten billets. They leave billets of all kinds, something unheard of with us. We have got a real Division and am confident one that will make a reputation. But the Army is not for me. If I can get out and get a good job afterwards, that's what I'll do, so look out for me. There will be too many opportunities afterwards and too many hangers-on in the Army. Army life in peacetime is not much fun anyway.

I've got a poor little undersized Jew named Kaszlewicz [William Kaszlewicz 1894-1980] in my Company, whom I had never thought worth a damn. He was on sentry duty at a gun position up in the lines, and a 5.9 hit in the trench right next to him. He didn't even quiver. It was a dud, and Applegate, making his rounds a little later, asked him about it. He said, 'Oh, that came in a few minutes ago.'

All my bunch were happy in the line. They want to go back. I guess you know that the M.G. are trying to get a Corps. We are in tough luck now as our command is indefinite. It will work out in time but it has horrible disadvantages now. It's a wonderful weapon and if properly handled has absolutely unbounded possibilities. In the recent German attack in front of Château Thierry, one machine gun held about a 500 yard front for a day and a half. The Germans are good with them, as a matter of fact, we are learning a lot from them.

September 10, 1918 - HAMILTON

Another wet day and it still is a good war. We stay at home and loaf, the loaf of that greatest of all loafers, the soldier. Lin and Bobbie are talking about their wives and showing me pictures of their children and trying to tell me that the hand that rocks the cradle does NOT run the ranch. It makes me almost wish I had some of each myself.

Our horseshoer, an enormous man with no teeth writes faithfully to a little wife in Erie and signs himself invariably, 'Your loving horseshoer, Cline.' [Wilmer Harold Cline 1892-1946] Wives are tres bon and as I've said before, I would like to have somebody back home who was worrying not about shot or shell, or typhoid or gas, but simply whether I had on any wooly underwear. Mother thinks about that of course, but nice as that is, she has been doing it for the last 25 years and there's no novelty in it.

The past few days I've had more to eat and less to do than any other time since I've been in the Army. We've just laid around here, rough housed, talked, smoked and played poker. We had a fine vacation generally. The flies are awful though. The French don't keep things clean and they are in swarms.

The French aren't too nice I must say, and although I'm glad to pay my nickel to the account of the Lafayette-Rochambeau debt, and all that, I'm not quite as stuck on the French people as I was at first, or as I thought I should be. It's pretty, but not half as pretty as America. It's well kept, but not as clean as they keep things at home. The climate is not nice and you can't get any water to drink. The people themselves are all right, but they don't wash, or clean their teeth, or keep their kitchens clean, or read the papers, or - but after all they have been up against it for four years and naturally they aren't the same as they were before.

September 10, 1918 - KEAN

Some of the country reminded me quite a bit of the Berkshires. We have passed several châteaux in our wanderings, and when there were officers I knew in the billets, we stopped long enough and I inspected them. Once we were near the scene of 'Graustark' [Fictional location used in the novels of George Barr McCutcheon].

The Company is now encamped in a château grounds, but I am in a billet. As it has been raining for the past four days, they are a trifle damp, but seem cheerful. The American rations make all the difference in the world for their good spirits. Yesterday, we spent part of the day having a boiling ant party for those with cooties, alias gray backs, or seam squirrels, etc. They accumulated them when they were in the trenches, and also from some of the trains they have travelled in for the Poilu and Tommy are covered with them and so are the dug outs and the places where they lived.

We have also had quite a time cleaning up this town, the last Division that was in here left it in pretty bad shape. It was quite amusing to see the French get annoyed when we invaded their yards. They keep their houses clean, but that is all. The other night, while we were marching here, we ran into quite a thunder storm. It was pitch black and the lightening, occasionally making everything as bright as day, blinded us every now and then. So that with getting soaking wet, we didn't have such a delightful journey as we might have. Cox has a billet almost across the street and it makes it nice to see him as I missed him.

September 12, 1918 – HOLLAND

I haven't done hardly one thing for a week, only sleep, and then there's times we have it a little tough. It has been kind of cold and rainy for a few days. I was sorry to hear you've sprained your knee. We would call it a 'blighty.' That's what they say when one gets hurt or wounded and goes to the hospital, he got a 'blighty.'

I have learned a little French, but not much. We don't pay so much attention to them. They are not very classy through the country, but around the cities, there is sure some class. I have seen a great many of the large cities, and I have seen the ruins of a few villages, and believe me, they are ruins, just a pile of bricks and cement. There are some sites to be seen over here that one could get all kinds of souvenirs, but he hasn't any way to carry them. Here's hoping you are well and happy as I. I don't worry, it's not as bad as one's imagination.

September 12, 1918 - HAMILTON

The war seems to be called off on account of wet grounds, and we are back at work drilling and drilling and drilling. We actually worked all morning before the rain commenced. God knows what's going to happen, but we are still here and maybe we will stay and maybe we will go to the war.

I received orders today to report to the doctor for physical examination. I reported not having the smallest idea what for and was put through the usual thing. I passed O.K. and find now that it was the examination for promotion and that my recommendation for a Captaincy has gone in. It was out of a clear sky and I had not the smallest hint of it, nor do I particularly want it. Dad will be glad and the family too, I reckon, but it's a Hellish responsibility and I haven't felt ready for it.

I don't know yet whether I will stay in this Battalion or not, nor do I know whether or not the thing will go through, although they practically always do. All I know is that I passed the physical and will have to leave C Company because C Company has one Captain already. In one way, I won't be sorry, I haven't gotten along so well with Captain Kean, or rather I have gotten along pretty well, but don't like him for a damn.

On the other hand, I love Bobbie and Lin and feel as though I knew the men of the Company like children. I know their first names and their girl's names and all about them, hardly a single man in 170 that I haven't felt as though I knew well. It has taken six months hard work to do it and now I've got to start all over again, and learn 170 different ones. No, I think I'd really rather not change. I don't know why they promoted me anyhow. I am quite junior in the Battalion, at least there are seven or eight ahead of me, and that isn't going to make it any more pleasant. I swear promotion is all luck. If things had been different by a hair I would be a second lieutenant until the end of the war, but they weren't, so I'm not, and it's the Hell of a note.

∽

The Saint-Mihiel operations commenced at 1:00 AM on September 12, 1918. When the American First Army attacked, the Battalion was held in reserves along with the entire 80th Division. The Germans were being pushed from the Saint-Mihiel salient and operations were succeeding as planned, but General Pershing wanted to ensure that pressure continued on the German retreat. He authorized a portion of the 80th Division to be attached to the French 2nd Calvary Division to attack the withdrawing enemy. Orders were given to the 320th Infantry and the 315th Machine Gun Battalion to proceed to Woimbey, just north of Saint-Mihiel. From there, the troops crossed the Meuse River into previously held German territory. Their stay in this area was short as the enemy showed no signs of a possible counter attack. The Division's units were instructed to return back to Woimbey to await further orders. The balance of the Division remained in the Tronville area during the Saint-Mihiel operations and continued to drill and hold instruction.

September 13, 1918 - HAMILTON

In the past month we have done darn little fighting in proportion to the amount that we have travelled. We've been completely around France three times and have just been in the line a few times that I've written you about.

There seems enough war left over here to give everybody a chance and although it's been slow coming, we will get our full share of gore and glory one of these days. Try not to worry too much because I am going to come through and worrying is the last thing that we do here.

It's been a pretty good war ever since reaching here. It has been very wet and we've not been able to do much work, and so have just played around in our billets and had the most remarkably fine food. I have gained about ten pounds in a week, and really feel most extraordinarily well.

At present the only thing that I need is chocolate, which cannot be had here, and socks. If you could occasionally send some it would be great. I would like to get on the average one pair of heavy wool socks per month.

I have been recommended for Captaincy and took the physical exam yesterday. It has to go to Washington, and it will probably be at least two months before it goes through. Don't put Captain on my letters until I tell you because it might never be approved.

September 13, 1918 –THOMAS

I suppose the papers have told you of our little push. I think we will have plenty of excitement before winter comes for good. Here is the kind of General we have. I quote from yesterday's bulletin: 'To the members of the 80th Division. I know how disappointed you are not to be actively involved in the present operations. When I told the Commander-in-Chief yesterday what fine shape you were in and how keen you were for action, he authorized me to tell you, in his name, that you must not be over anxious, and that you would get your fair share of important work' [Major General Adelbert Cronkhite, September 12, 1918]. That's pretty nice, isn't it? The men thought that it was fine.

Nothing is surprising anymore. We may go anytime or stay here a month, but we don't care. The men, sleeping out in this wet weather are happy and cheerful. It does you good to see how tough they are. We had another little order today about cutting down our bedding rolls still further. I have my trunk and a big box all the way across France now, and have more stuff here. If I ever get a vacation it will be spent picking up my belongings. But nobody kicks and you can't be a down beater as long as the men have such wonderful spirits. But it is a good war still and I'm highly in favor of it.

I wouldn't change places with anybody I can think of in the machine guns, but this job isn't going to take so long to finish. But I have personally played such a little part in it. I really do feel ashamed not to have done something. My only first lieutenant took my Company up into the line, and I of course was off at school. My company is, by the C.O.s confession and my own, the best in the Battalion. I wish you could see them. They are wonderful. But my Non-coms run it now.

151

I sent my top-kicker off to school for a month. He complained that he couldn't acquire his full amount and quota of French wine with the Mrs. around, so I gave him a holiday. If we get in before he gets back, and he knows it, I'm afraid the school will have a deserter.

I put one of my new Sergeants in and life keeps up its own sweet trend. If I could only explain to you how commonplace it all is, you wouldn't bother. You sit around and drill and train and kick about everything. You get orders to pull out in an hour and a half and you pack up. Maybe you move, maybe you don't. You might go to the front, you might not. Everybody knows their job and orders are delivered, that's all. Jimmy packs up my things and I curse everybody in sight, just to keep my hand in and sustain my reputation. Everybody has found out long ago that I'm harmless, but a few well-chosen adjectives adds considerable help.

I'm not going to write any farewell letters, because I don't feel that way. But by any chance, if I should get mine, I want you personally to go through that trunk of mine at home. There may be a few things in it that I wouldn't want anybody else to see. As the English say though, the war is top hole and everybody is having a fine time. But at the present writing, my dear daddy, your precious son is anything but a hero. I think if you applied that term to any of my braves they would resent it horribly. Just as the New Zealanders are about British decorations. You ask one where he got a Military Cross or Distinguished Service Order, and he says, 'Oh, that came up with the rations one day.'

September 13, 1918 –THOMAS

It stays pretty cold over here. I don't think we have had more than three or four days this summer that you would call warm at home. We have had a fire in our billet the last two nights. Not because we needed one especially, but because it was cheerful and we could sit around it, and imagine all kinds of things. Also we are in a part of France where you can buy a little wood to burn. You never saw anything like the way they guard their wood.

I'm staying in a billet now with an old woman and her husband and a young girl about 15. The old woman washes for me and the young girl cleans. The bed has real linen sheets and always big mirrors in the room, but chickens and hogs live in the same house. This family doesn't require much though and seems thoroughly happy. They want money for everything though. They are very, very mercenary these French people.

I am enjoying myself to the fullest just at present. If we could get a nice town with billets for the men we could be pretty comfortable I think. They get so they can stand anything though and don't complain no matter what happens. They are old soldiers and write home that they are known as 'shock troops.' Where they get that I don't know.

September 13, 1918 - HAMILTON

The First American Army has attacked around Saint Mihiel and have gotten all their objectives. They have wiped out the salient and have captured over 20,000 prisoners. The best news of the war and I feel pretty badly that I wasn't in it because I certainly expected to be in the next big push. I reckon I'll be in the next one sure. The old Boche is on the run at last and we are going to win the war sure.

The men over here that are doing the work only think of three things, food, letters, and sleep. They aren't one quarter the heroes that the people at home are who have to live on two pounds of sugar per man, per month and have to pay for the bally war. The soldiers really have a darn good time and get the deuce of a lot of undeserved credit.

September 14, 1918 - HAMILTON

The Saint Mihiel push is progressing satisfactorily and as per schedule. We expected to move today but after several contradictory orders we didn't, although our baggage did. We therefore found ourselves confronted with the proposition of three or us sleeping in one bed, which was never built for more than one. Bobbie and I are about the same size, but Lin is the whale of a man, six foot six and broad in proportion. I knew darn well the thing wasn't possible, but they said we ought to do it because it would be 'unique.' I consented because I was curious to know if it could be done. Well we did it, and slept very well, at least Bobbie and I did as we were on the inside, but Lin complained bitterly and said he couldn't stay in the bed unless he dug in his fingers and toes, and if he did this he couldn't sleep. So he got up in disgust at a very early hour and went to mass.

CHAPTER 7
'WAR IS A FUNNY PROPOSITION'

The Division moved from the Tronville area to a location around Souilly. The Battalion bivouacked in the woods about 1 kilometer southwest of the village of Vadelaincourt. They were resting in a patch of woods just north of Oches and east of Ippecourt.

General Cronkhite established his Division Headquarters at Ippecourt, while the town of Vadelaincourt supported an active airfield for the Allies. A sketch of the Battalion's location was drawn by a member of the unit and the words 'Hide M.G.' sketched on a map referring to the name of Major Huideikoper's Machine Gun Battalion (Headquarters Correspondence).

September 15, 1918 - HAMILTON

Another Sunday of peace and rest, it seems too good to be true. They generally fix it so that our worst days come on Sundays. I wonder what it will be like to go home and have the easy leisurely Sundays we used to have at home. Sunday mornings at Dobbs Ferry, my word. I don't think much about going home I must say, in the first place it is as remote as the end of the world, and in the second, I don't mind this most of the while and have a darn good time.

I expect there will be some bad days coming, but if a thing is really bad it generally is interesting enough to carry it through. So far I've struck nothing so bad in France as getting up early after a late dance at home and really doubt if Hell has any worse torments. Nothing is very bad unless it concerns just yourself. In the Army you generally have your men to think of and they make you forget your own troubles, but Oh! Oh! Oh! that awful feeling when you try to get out of bed on a cold morning after being up until 5:00 AM.

Where we are living now our own boys do all the cooking. In most billets, so far, we have had Madame do it, but here Madame didn't want to do our own housekeeping. Incidentally, Madame's husband, like all other Madame's husbands, was killed in the war in 1914. Anyhow, we have these two boys to look after us. Bergiotis [Nicholas Bergiotis 1891-1956] a Greek, whose father is a priest and whose brother is a lieutenant in the Greek Army. He kept a candy store in Erie before the war and he is a fine cook. The other one is named DeMarte [Ralph DeMarte 1893-1964] an Italian. They are the most willing pair in the world and certainly do a lot to make life worth living. Always smiling, they walk miles to find fresh eggs for us and we live like kings on the food they cook. He is a fine looking chap with his dark eyes and white teeth.

It's always the same about moving, first you hear you're going to move, then you hear it's all off and then you are very doubtful either way and then when you least expect it, Bang! you get your orders. It was this way this afternoon. We had given up hope of getting orders and were down in the creek having a bath, we finished that and walked leisurely up to billets and there found that the Battalion was moving in six minutes, and we weren't packed. We got packed in a terrible rush and just joined the Company in time to move out with it. This time we embussed.

Embussing handled very effectively by French officials and into French busses. It didn't take over fifteen minutes to get 700 men loaded. The French busses are O.K. Driven by the most picturesque bunch of bewhiskered brigands that ever eased a car into high speed. Darn good drivers too with beards like the Bolsheviks. All the busses were Renaults and hadn't been washed since the Germans took Brussels, but their engines sang a sweet song of good care and careful adjustment, and after all, that's what counts. If they had been Tommy busses they would probably have had every axel cap shining and every spoke spic and span, and the engine running on one cylinder. If they had been Yanks they would probably have had the bad points of both. Anyhow, that's got nothing to do with it, these were French and they were all right, although I'd just about as leave walk 30 miles as ride in the military lorries. They certainly are poor sport and after four hours of it cramped on the hard seats, we were glad enough to disembus and take to our legs. We walked a mile or so and bivouacked in a thick wood. We just flopped where we stood.

September 16, 1918 - HAMILTON

Slept cold on the damp ground. I had nothing but my trench coat and believe me it's not enough. These night operations are all right and although not too pleasant during the doing of them, generally make for a day of rest and meditation the following day. Today was one of the latter, and we lay in our tents and speculated as to the duration of the war, our next probable move, the scarcity of chocolate, The Saint Mihiel operation, etc.

We counted up during the day the different places where we have spent the night since arriving in France. I figured up over 25 separate and distinct stops, which I rather think is going some for a three months stay, and I must say that if we can fight like we can move, the Kaiser had better spend his next vacation in the Siberian Steppe's because Germany won't be safe much longer.

Seriously, it all has been darn well done, and we have moved practically all over France and always have connected with our rations and our baggage and our animals with extraordinary success, somebody by gum! Somebody on the lines of communication is O.K.!

September 18, 1918 - HAMILTON

The beautiful weather turned to rain during the night and as the tent leaked, it wasn't too good. A wet pup tent being one of the poorest of habitations.

War is a funny proposition. If the fellars that decided on going to war had to go first themselves, there would be a darn sight less of it. These boys in our Company come from Erie, what do they know or care about the laws of 'visit or search.' What do they know or care about the rights of Serbia or Albania or Poland? What do they know or what do they care about making the world safe for the democrats? The answers to all these questions is 'not one continental damn.'

They are fighting because, in the first place, they were jolly well drafted and couldn't help themselves, and now they are pretty good sports about it and are more than ready to see it through. Personal feelings about Germany, they have practically none. They fight like good Yanks because that's the sort of a cuss they are and they will do any darn thing they might be asked to do. They are going to fight the Germans, but they would go after the French just about as willingly, and the Tommies a good deal more willingly. As for that, they would just as leave fight against Arkansas or North Carolina or St. Louis or any other darn country, and I don't know that I wouldn't just as leave myself.

I saw an airplane brought down this evening. He came over about 5:00 PM this afternoon, a big observation plane sent out, I guess, to see if there are any Yanks here about. He was all alone, and seemed all alone, when the Archies cut loose on him. He came almost right up above us when zip, from out of the clouds, a little fighting plane came flying. He was going two feet for every one that old Jerry went. Jerry saw him and turned and beat it for home, and mother, the little Newport after him like a flash. Three other French planes took up the chase and things began to get exciting. Pup! Pup! Pup! went the machine guns and the Boche turned and dove into a big bank of clouds with the chase swerving after him like a sparrow hawk after a crow. They didn't appear for some time when they came out of the bottom of the bank much lower than before, the four French planes had their nose on his tail, all five diving towards the ground, like falling stones and firing all the time. Suddenly, we saw the Boche straighten out and crash nose first out of sight behind the trees. When he went down the four other planes swung off and circled the spot and in the distance looked exactly like buzzards wheeling over their prey. We all shouted and threw our caps in the air and although its good warfare to put four to one, and that's the way to win battles after all, it wasn't a fair fight, and it made me feel a bit sick at heart. Four battle planes against an old strawberry of an observation buss, hell, that's no game at all.

September 19, 1918 - HAMILTON

Rain all day and everybody pretty uncomfortable. At five o'clock we got orders to move again and at 6:45 PM we pulled out. The rain kindly held off while we were packing up. We went North towards the war. It was a rotten march because aside from the fact that it rained off and on, the roads were jammed with traffic and we had to halt, and move, and then halt again every few minutes which tires men more than anything in the world.

A machine gun battalion with their transport strings out along the road for miles and with all the backing and filling we were doing, it was no wonder when the Adjutant rode up and said, 'You might as well halt here Captain Kean because the leading two companies have lost us.' So we halted and sat down by the side of the road and waited two long cold hours before contact was reestablished.

We then went on again and after another hour came to a steep hill with a wood at the top. We scrambled up as best we could, the men staggering under their heavy packs and finally reached the top, and plunged into the most dismal swamp of a wood that I ever saw. It wasn't so bad after we got in for the brush had been cleared away and we threw ourselves down on the leaves and went to sleep. The hill up to the woods was so steep that the limbers couldn't get up and they only did manage it by doubling up the horses, putting as many as 10 horses on some of them. They were at it the rest of the night. Machine gun transport isn't always as good fun as it might be. It was almost 4:00 AM before I finally hit the hay.

⁊

The Division was in an area known as Camp Gallieni, a stop in the vicinity of Bois la Ville, about 6 kilometers southwest of Verdun. They stayed in this area about four days making pre-battle preparations in the issuance of food and ammunition as some of the officers ran reconnaissance missions to the forward area.

September 20, 1918 - HAMILTON

Nobody got up this morning until late. My orderly brought me some coffee and bacon about eleven, and after that I managed to find the courage to get up. This wood is the best we've been in. Big beach trees and comparatively no underbrush. Leinhauser and I walked up to the top of the hill and inspected a French fort [Fort du Regret, Verdun], a wonderful piece of work and absolutely impregnable against infantry assisted by ordinary artillery. What they didn't figure was 42 cm stuff, and a fort like that is about as safe from really heavy artillery as if it was made of cardboard. Still they are very cunningly devised and thought out and as I'd never seen a regular fort before I was glad to see this one. We went down the hill to where a tunnel had been built, and there, by lifting a door off its hinges, gained access to a flight of stairs going down. We felt our way down 30 steps as dark as a 'Stygian cave forlorn' [Taken from *L'Allegro* by John Milton]. We then came to a big room and a passage sloping slightly up. We felt our way along this for maybe 200 yards, not having the least idea where we were going, or if it was safe, and then we decided that we had better go home as it was no use loosing ourselves in any French catacomb. So we cautiously groped our way back and out. We are going back there with a candle tomorrow and explore the place further.

In the evening I went up on the hill again to see the fireworks. It was a wonderful night with a full moon and we sat on a bank high up by the fort and admired the view. Below us in the valley, hidden by the mist, we could just dimly make out [Verdun], the far place is across the valley in the row of hills surrounding it now, all held by the French. You can just make out, in the distance, the German line 7 or 8 miles away.

Not a shot along the whole line, as far as the eye can reach, the valley lies before us bathed in moonlight as peaceful as the Berkshires. Occasionally, a flare or a signal rocket reminds you that there is a war, but that is all, not a sound except a motor horn or two on the road below. If people knew I was here looking at this they might be thrilled, I must say I was thrilled myself, within my sight [censored].

September 20, 1918 – THOMAS

We haven't had much of anything happen to us. We are still camping out, at present on the top of a high hill from which we can see the German front. We hiked here through the rain last night. Got lost and didn't get in until about 3:00 AM. The men were complaining bitterly that they were getting tired of chasing the war. They said they had followed it for almost 4 months. But after about the worst night I have almost ever spent, there was not a single man in my Company on sick report this morning.

I would like to give you an account of where I have been. I will one of these days. This morning I visited a French fort. We went all through it and then had coffee with about six French officers who came back to camp with us. They seemed to be as interested in us as we were in them. You can't imagine what a wonderful frame of mind it is to be in such as we have now. If we were ordered to go to Italy tomorrow, I don't think it would be even considered out of the way. You just live from day to day and nobody ever remembers what day of the week it is even.

September 21, 1918 - HAMILTON

After dark Lin and I walked down to [Verdun] and saw the most picturesque ruins in France. Imagine a well-built town with large, well built houses as close together as they are in New York and every house wrecked beyond belief. Hardly an intact house in the town. We saw it under a full moon and it certainly had an evil aspect. Not all the houses are completely destroyed but there is not a living soul in the town, with the exception of an occasional soldier, there is no one. A city of death and destruction piled up in a mass of white ruins in the moonlight. The cathedral seemed damaged very little, it afforded too good an aiming mark for the Hun artillery, I guess. The streets of the city had all been cleaned up, not a brick or loose stone on them, in striking contrast to the houses on each side.

Old Fritz burst a couple of shells high up above the town while we were there just to show there were no hard feeling, but otherwise, the place was as silent as a cemetery in a snow storm. Another night and not a shot along the whole front, with the exception of some big long range guns in the woods below who fired in a desultory way during the night.

September 21, 1918 - KEAN

The front is not very far away, but it is very quiet, and you wouldn't know we were anywhere near it. If we keep on walking we are bound to run into some fighting soon, unless we turn around.

The other day I saw my first airplane brought down, it was about five o'clock and three Allied planes drove a Boche down about ten miles away from us. We could see it quite plainly and everybody cheered.

We have the most peculiar weather, it seems to rain every day from 3:00 AM to 10:00 AM, and then in the afternoon the sun comes out. With the exception of the last two days when the sun came out, it was quite warm, but most days have been cold and rainy.

This afternoon I have been demonstrating a German machine gun to the Company so that if we capture one we can turn it around and use it. It is much like our guns.

September 22, 1918 - HAMILTON

In the last eight weeks I reckon I've spent six of them in a pup tent, and although fond of outdoor sports, and all that kind of thing, a pup tent in wet weather has no good points whatsoever. They are 7 feet long, by 6 feet wide, and 3 feet high in the center, but as the roof slopes very steeply, you can just barely sit up in them. When it rains the tent will leak wherever you touch the wall on the inside, and as you always touch the wall a little, the tent always leaks at least a little, at any rate, mine always leaks some, and generally leaks a lot, and I can't see any sport in that. The front end of the tent is open to the weather, and that doesn't help matters much, as the rain generally comes from which ever direction you face your tent. No, there's no doubt at all, puppie tents were devised for overnight stops in fair weather. After living in one for a month in the rain they are a great bore. Incidentally, you only get mediocre results from trying to heat a pup tent with a candle, I know because I've tried. Candles are lovely things and make a fine light, but they don't heat a tent for a darn.

The men are wonderful, never a word, hardly, of complaint, and I don't guess their feet have been dry in 6 weeks.

CHAPTER 8
CROSSING DEAD MAN'S HILL

General Pershing and his First Army were preparing to enter into an offensive, that is now known to be the deadliest battle in American history, the Battle of the Meuse Argonne. It involved more than one million American soldiers and by the end of the operations it took the lives of 26,277 Americans. The key objective of this operation was to destroy the German supply lines that fed enemy positions to the west and northwest of Sedan. This was no easy task as the Germans spent years building fortifications to protect their positions. The Allies needed to push through these stout defensive lines, one being the significant Hindenburg Line, known to the Germans as *Kriemhilde Stellung*. Aside from the deep fortifications, barbed-wire, machine gun bunkers and concrete trenches built in defense, the Germans took abundant advantage of the natural terrain to give themselves a strategic advantage over an opposing enemy attack.

The First American Army launched their attack on September 26, 1918, between the Meuse River and the Argonne Forest. The 80th Division was part of the III Corps who positioned the 4th, 80th and 33rd Divisions from left to right on the enemy line, then spanned from the Meuse to Malancourt. The III Corps objective was the control of Dannevoux, Nantillois, and Montblainville. The 3rd Division was held in reserve. The German 7th Reserve Division was their opposing foe.

The 313th Machine Gun Battalion found themselves supporting the 320th Infantry who had an objective of reaching Brieulles-sur-Meuse, a strong point of the Hindenburg Line.

The Division's long range artillery, the 155mm caliber Howitzers, started pounding the intended path of the advancing infantry from 2:30 AM until H-Hour. It is unlikely that the infantry, or anyone else advancing that morning, would have been capable of sleeping during the early hours of constant artillery pounding. The 75mm caliber artillery then joined in at H Hour with a rolling barrage in front of the Brigades where the infantry advanced to their first positions.

Lieutenant Colonel Oscar Foley, the former 313th Machine Gun Battalion commander, was the acting Division Machine Gun Officer on the eve of the attack. He ordered the machine gun battalions to put down a barrage just over the heads of the advancing infantry.

The Division faced their first attack just beyond Béthincourt. The H Hour jump off point was the Ruisseau de Forges [Forges Brook], a small stream located near the battered ruins of Béthincourt. The path of the Division's advance was on a northerly course through Béthincourt to Dannevoux, a distance of about 5 miles. The planned path of advance took the 80th Division through these key points on the map: Fromeréville, Germonville, Bois Bourrus, Chattancourt, Hill 295 - Le Mort Homme, Ruisseau de Forges, Béthincourt, Hill 281, Bois de Sachet, and Bois de Dannevoux. Through this passage the Battalion became familiar with the reputation of Le Mort Homme, also known as *Dead Man's Hill*, one of two hills that overlooked Béthincourt located in the Verdun sector. The hill was north of the village of Chattancourt and earned its notoriety from the bitter fighting that occurred at this site during the 1916 Battle of Verdun.

The 80th Division staged their frontline to cover about 2,000 meters, with Béthincourt as their center point. The infantry organized in columns with the 320th Infantry on the left [2nd and 3rd Battalions] and the 319th Infantry on the right [1st and 2nd Battalions]. Plans were given to advance toward the enemy at a rate of about 100 meters per four minutes. The speed was dictated based on a curtain of shelling placed down by the artillery in front of the advancing infantry.

Just a day before going in, some of the officers and NCOs of the Battalion proceeded forward to reconnoiter the area through which the infantry would advance and spot locations to place their guns. This opportunity for planning and preparation would be in stark contrast to what the officers were given for later battle engagements.

September 24, 1918 - HAMILTON

Today was a nonentity; the only items of interest were my night operations which were several. Bobbie, Lin and I, with three sergeants, left Battalion Headquarters at 12 midnight in a Ford. It was the same little Ford truck in which I had run over that fellow in A Company and we certainly would have run over a few more had it not been for Lin's remarkable facility for putting her into low and reverse at the same time thereby bringing the detachment to a halt. We made fair progress seeing that the roads were jammed with troops and their transport. I never saw so many before. At one place, where we had to go across a narrow bridge, we were halted for a long time. A regular 42nd and Fifth Avenue jam of traffic. I didn't like it much and when he began to crack a few big shells over our heads I thought still less of it. Then just as we were getting clear, the car stalled on a hill and it wouldn't crank. About that time I was quite upset as he was just getting the range so I spun her like mad and she went.

In the next town they told us not to go in because it was being shelled, but we went on and they stopped shelling long enough to let us go through. We then got out and hoofed it over the most damnably shell torn ground I ever saw for a couple of miles up to the frontline. There as usual, we got lost and prowled around over the top at imminent risk of being spotted by one of our own posts as a hostile patrol. They would say in a tense whisper, 'Halt - who's there!' and I'd tell them, and they would say 'Have you the pass word?' and I'd say, 'Hell No.' and it seemed quite satisfactory in every case.

We finally located ourselves and laid out the positions for our guns. We couldn't lay them out before daybreak, but as soon as day broke, old Jerry sent up a tall balloon which made us step lively to get it done without being seen. We went back to our Ford and so back to the Battalion who had in the meantime moved forward.

September 25, 1918 - HUIDEKOPER

Midnight. The Battalion took a position on the northern slope of Le Mort Homme in front of Blanchard trench. The Battalion P.C. at the junction of Hamburg trench at Boyou Biche. Battalion strength 23

165

officers, 698 men, 48 Vickers machine guns. The guns played for barrage on targets to the North of Bethincourt. The transport is at Bois des Sartelles (Headquarters Correspondence).

September 25, 1918 - HAMILTON

I had been up all night and as it was 12 o'clock noon before I had something to eat. I curled up in my tent dead weary. At 4:00 PM the Captain woke me to say that we attack at dawn and we will move up to the line at once.

We pulled out at 6:00 PM and came through very well. Although the roads were again jammed with traffic, we didn't get a shell all the way in which was great good luck. I expected every moment to have bedlam break loose, but not a sound. We marched some 10 kilos to the line there, unloaded our kit and pushed on two more kilos to the front line.

Carrying a machine gun outfit with ammunition is no joke either. We got into place about 2:00 AM and spent the rest of the night digging ourselves in.

Ralph Clarkson was a 26-year-old machinist working in the coal mines of rural Sewickley Township, Pennsylvania, when he registered for the draft in June 1917. Clarkson was a Corporal in the Battalion and was attached to Company B. He maintained a diary while in France and wrote this passage on September 25, 1918, "We marched 15 kilometers to Hill 262, LeMort Homme, near Béthincourt, a ruined city at the foot of the famous Dead Man's Hill in Death Valley; Hill 304 was just a few kilometers to our left. At midnight, we mounted our guns just over the crest of Dead Man's Hill" (Clarkson).

The first opposing German positions were about a mile north of the jump off point, and the American Infantry received little resistance in the first 3,000 meters. A significant resistance came at Hill 281. The Division later discovered that some of the enemy hid underground during

CLARKSON

the initial artillery barrage and as the first wave of American infantry passed, the Germans rose from their dugouts and fired on the rear of the advancing infantry (Crowell 31).

September 1918- LEINHAUSER

We went out on a reconnaissance party locating machine gun positions. We left camp at 12 Midnight in a Lorrie without brakes and had some trouble. We were stopped in [Fromeréville] and Jerry and some shelling got 5 men. We got back to camp about 11:00 AM, tired to death, crawled into my tent and fell asleep until 3:00 PM when we got orders to move at 6:00 PM. We left for the frontlines with our fighting equipment. We arrived in [Chattancourt] at about 11:30 PM after hiking about 9 miles. Fortunately it was clear. We unpacked our limbers and each man loaded himself down with ammunition and off we started for Dead Man's Hill. It was about 2 miles of the hardest going ever. Finally, we reached our positions and then sent most men back for more ammo. We are taking part in a push extending 65 miles and involving over 600,000 men. At 12:00 Midnight the artillery opened up and such a night you never saw. We are opposite south of Béthincourt. The horizon, as far as you could see, was just one blaze or continuous line of flashes of every caliber, and the war was terrific. This continued until 5:27 AM when the barrage started and the infantry left the trench. Just multiply all that racket by about 10 and then add more and you will have just the noise the artillery made. Our machine guns, of which there were 120, all opened up at 5:30 AM and then Hell was let loose. You couldn't hear yourself think. This continued until 7:00 AM when we ceased firing and are now on [-] orders. It is now 1:00 PM and the infantry at last reports they had advanced 5 miles and have only about 4 more to go to reach their objective, the river Meuse.

Airplanes arrived in the attack and at times there were almost 100 in the air at once. Jerry lost 2 planes and one balloon. Also there were about 3,000 to 4,000 prisoners that came through in this morning. The Company fired about 5,800 rounds. At present, there is only little shelling and quiet lines of communication have been established. Bombers and motor trucks are also only up where the fighting was. The engineers built a bridge in 3 ½ hours across a fair size stream. Our balloons are working up closer. Jerry planes are more numerous now that we are almost all down. Just saw Jerry planes get [-] of our balloons. Started to move to Béthincourt at 6:00 PM but only got about half a mile. There is only a single one-way road and it has to supply the 3rd Division. Talk about traffic jams. MPs control it like regulars. We laid around for about an hour and then went each to trenches for the night. No blankets for us or the men. We found a large Hun dugout with bunks and [-] in. I got up at 4:30 AM and lit a fire in the stove that we found there. We had hot coffee, hot beans and crackers. It is raining again.

September 26, 1918 - HAMILTON

The attack was to start at 5:30 AM. The artillery, which had been gradually gaining momentum during the night, grew to a roar at 5:27 AM and at 5:30 AM our boys clambered out of the trenches, and went for the old Hun. One year of training for this and by George they looked good too. Great big sunburned Yanks as cool and cheerful as if going squirrel hunting. I was thrilled, but not excited. Those of us who were not to go over with the first wave sat behind our guns and poured a steady stream of machine gun bullets on the place where Jerry was supposed to be. The counter barrage was much less worse than I had expected and we had little shelling and no casualties. The infantry got through wonderfully, and at present 1:00 PM, we are still going strong.

We expect to move up after waiting for the 'tout de suite' long strings of German prisoners who are filing by, and a few wounded who are straggling back. Everything is going fine and we are winning. Of this push, we are a very small part, there being I believe some 300,000 French and a like number of Yanks mixed up in it. If they have made as good progress elsewhere, as we have here, it is tres bon.

I have been up all night, two nights running. We waited all day expecting any moment to get orders to go forward. All day long we hear rumors of how we have fared. I hear that the [4th] Division on our left is badly held up by a big woods, and all day long we could hear the rattle of machine guns, and the roar of artillery, trying to pin him down so that our infantry could step around and take him in the flank. I hear also that our Division has gone right through, like a bat out or Hades with very few casualties and have taken all their objectives. By Noon the Engineers had gotten a road through and our light artillery are going forward. Later I hear that one of our Regiments is held up and the other has gotten way beyond, and they are in a very precarious position. I hope they don't get cut off. The new road is blocked with troops going forward as far as the eye can reach, going forward, going forward, by gum the whole gang is going forward!!!

Late in the afternoon we got orders to move and we went down the hill carrying all our kit. Our transport is left way behind. Down below we saw how the Infantry had crossed the swamp on sort of rough pontoons put down by the Engineers. In the hollow below we were held up by the road being blocked by ten million infantry and God knows how many red cross, ammunition, ration and baggage wagons, to say nothing of side cars, cavalry, motor trucks, guns, etc. We waited 9 hours and didn't get on, so we went back a little way and bivouacked. Just before we went back, two German planes came sweeping over the long lines of transport firing down at us with their machine guns. They flew directly over our heads, only a few hundred feet up, their bullets spitting into the ground all around. We handed it back to them with our rifles and made a fine racket, but hit nothing. But as they hit nothing either, the affair was a draw at least. I thought it was damned cheeky of them to do a thing like that. We had no blankets and it certainly was cold. The men lay in the bottom of the trench and froze, and the officers of 'C Company' found a good German dugout and likewise froze.

September 26-27, 1918 – DEVIR

This is the beginning of the Allies most powerful offensive to defeat Germany. German prisoners are seen coming in. We move forward. Our outfit is in reserve. Allies begin the moving up of supplies, etc. Traffic is held up at Béthincourt. The Engineers are busily engaged in making a double driveway of a former small roadway which is banked on both sides by old Hun dugouts. During the blockade of traffic, five German planes come over and cut loose their machine gun fire on the congested road. Their shooting was poor for only a single horse was hit.

On September 27, while men are laying along an old road early in the morning a few soldiers trip over to see some former Hun trenches. All were hungry and several boys build fires in the little bivvy to heat up

Corn Willy. Corporal Milton Neuroh [Milton Elias Neuroh 1887-1965] and his squad were heating up some bully in a bivvy and an explosion occurred. A hand grenade buried in this place went off and it sent mess kits a flying. Corporal Neuroh's face was scorched by the powder (Devir 25).

September 26-28, 1918 – HUIDEKOPER

At 5:30 AM all of the Battalion guns opened on the first target and fired slow fire until H Hour plus 45. The average range was 2,200 meters. From H Hour 45 to H Hour plus 73 all of the guns lifted to the second target. The average range was 3,000 meters. After the barrage, we remained in the same position until 3:00 PM. We then marched to the foot of the slope south-west of Béthincourt and bivouacked for the night.

At 6:00 PM Company D was ordered to report to the 320th Infantry and marched to Hill 281 where they remained in reserve.

On September 27, the Battalion moved to the slope on the northern edge of Béthincourt and bivouacked. Company D remained on Hill 281.

At 3:00PM on September 28, Company C was ordered attached to the 2nd Battalion, 317th Infantry. Company D rejoined the Battalion at 6:00 PM (Headquarters Correspondence).

September 27, 1918 - HAMILTON

4:00 AM my teeth were chattering, at five we got up and lit the little trench stove that was left there some time before by a kindly German. Its warm glow certainly improved the aspect of the war and we managed to make some excellent coffee, and heated some beans, which with the good new hardtack, made a fine breakfast.

One more word about the barrage. Our Divisional artillery were engaged for the first time, and they were good. Although the noise was less than I expected, it was more noise than I ever heard before at one time, and the whistling of the shells over my head sounded just the way Bairnsfather's pictures of bombardments look.

They seemed to be going over in flocks, dozens at a time. Incidentally, I saw flocks of ducks very much bewildered by the hub hub, flying every which way, and one bird in particular, a thrush, flew right down into the shell hole where I was laying and almost hit on my finger.

It flew zigzag between the shells, and I reckon though that judgment day had arrived.

We had one shell hit in our trench, within three feet of my men. Four men were near it and nobody was hurt, which was the nearest to a casualty we had, although we had plenty of splinters flying around and early in the morning we were gassed.

Anyhow, we got out at 6 o'clock this morning, September 27th I think, and went forward into the German lines. We didn't get very far; the infantry has gone so fast that we'll never catch them again. Our transport managed to get through okay. We expected all day to go into action but we didn't. They are having all kinds of trouble with communications. Our Division got a road through very quickly, but the one on our right and the one on our left failed utterly, and they had to use ours.

It is too narrow to allow traffic to pass and has been a steady stream of wagons going forward for two days. They are lined up one solid row for 10 miles at least. I can't imagine why Jerry hasn't shelled it, or bombed it, because he certainly could have done a lot of damage. I guess he has been too busy elsewhere. It's impossible to find out the real dope on the situation. I think our infantry are now on all their objectives and whether they are going ahead another jump, nobody knows. The operation on the whole seems wonderfully successful, but it's pretty hard to tell yet. The rumble and roar of artillery is absolutely continuous and the fog of war covers everything.

We sat on our guns all day expecting orders, and when night came, we got our blankets off the limbers and lay down to the first good sleep I've had in four days. My Yeager blanket is the real thing.

September 27, 1918 - LEINHAUSER

Left for Béthincourt at 7:00 AM and arrived about 9:00 AM, only 2 miles. The road is still jammed at 7:00 PM with a steady stream of traffic coming in and none going back. We are staying in Béthincourt tonight. We visited the trench that we fired on and saw traces of our barrage, but there were few Jerry signs. He held the line very lightly and was terribly scared of us and all in. We also saw the new country we are going to fight over. It is a beautiful country with fine villages and nice

171

woods. The Germans left a lot of fine equipment, maps, and instruments. They left soft drinks, one keg of beer, cigarettes, and some food. They left without a fight in our sector but on the right and left they are still fighting, but out in open, no more trenches. The Germans have wonderful dugouts and pill boxes. Had a bunch of planes shoot us up with machine guns. Two bullets went through a box of my ammo.

❦

Sergeant Charles E. Ray of C Company recalls the events in his memoir:

"About that time the 313th Machine Gun Battalion was detached and sent into different fronts. At one time we were stationed at Verdun and fought at Dead Man's Hill.

Besides the Artois Sector we were rushed into the Meuse Argonne on two occasions. Most of our time was spent there from September 25 until the Armistice on November 11, 1918. The machine gunners were a short life. They were called the suicide squad and our Company was no exception. Our casualties were very, very heavy.

Perhaps one of the most horrible experiences I had was during the last days of the war. We were dug in on Dead Man's Hill where bones were thicker than stones. We were waiting for zero hour. Our watches were set to conform with one another. At 3:00 AM on 25 September the American artillery turned loose. They were setting hub to hub in back of us with the shells going over our heads. The skies lit up like a great fire in the background. It was a continuous flashing of fire as far as the eye could see. I was told the First Army was on our right and the Second was on our left. The Germans were not silent as their shells were bursting on all sides. All we could do was wait.

We lay by our machine guns waiting for zero which we knew would come at 5:30 AM. Smoke hung heavy from the bursting shells. Finally zero. We knew the infantrymen would start moving forward at the moment we started firing. We fired just over their heads. This was done by the trajectory of the bullet. Then we would have to elevate the gun to keep firing ahead of the men as they advanced and hoped they didn't move too fast and walk into our fire.

Then came the dawn and with it the German planes came over firing at everything they saw. Then we moved up to Mountfaucon with German planes swooping down on the roads with their machine guns firing, they would come in at tree top level making us a good target. When we moved through Mountfaucon, the infantry had been there and cleaned out all resistance but as we moved out of the town we found the road so littered with the dead and equipment, we could only get through by throwing them out of the way. In the distance I saw an observation balloon, they must have been watching us and directing their artillery as to where to fire. About this time, hell broke loose. They laid their shells right along this road blowing us to pieces. Of course we took to the fields but the shells followed us and many of our horses were killed or wounded. Some of them ran away going into shell holes and bringing other horses and limber in on top of them. The sky became filled with planes. The American and German planes were dogfighting by the dozens. I saw five planes come down at one look, all were not German. Then our tanks came in. It was a sight to see and few people ever saw it except in pictures. It's this thing soldiers do not talk about. Within five minutes I was blown over and three times by concussion of the bursting shells. I was stunned but I knew the machine guns must be taken out of the limbers.

Once while I was taking a machine gun from the members, I was on one side and a shell struck the wheel on the opposite side blowing the wheel to pieces. You will notice, I am only telling what happened to me, not the others who were going through the same thing nor of those who never came back. We finally got dug into a wooded area near the front where we stayed a few days. We were only a few hundred feet from where the Germans were dug in" (Ray 86).

The 80th Division was pressing their men hard to reach the objective of taking the Hindenburg Line. Although they advanced a significant distance, the objectives were not yet reached. The III Corps command sent the following message to all the Division commanders on September 27th, "Commander-in-Chief commands that Division commanders take forward positions and push troops energetically, and the Corps and Division commanders relieved of whatever rank who fails to show energy" (Stultz, 384).

The 320th Infantry were fighting an enemy counter-attack coming from the stronghold firmly held by the Germans in Brieulles-sur-Meuse. As the 1st and 2nd Battalions of the 320th Infantry advanced through Bois de le cote Lemont, they could only advance to the northern edge of these woods. Heavy artillery fire fell on the American troops. The terrain was such that the open slopes that rolled down from the woods to the low lands of the Meuse River made it difficult to advance without being overly exposed to enemy fire. The lands south of Brieulles were so fiercely defended as part of the Hindenburg Line that no American Division could advance through this position until the 5th Division finally succeeded in doing so on November 1, 1918.

❧

September 28, 1918- HAMILTON

Had a good night, except for the continuous roar of the guns. Got up to a good breakfast of hot coffee, bacon, bread and jam. No orders to move yet and no information about the war. I don't know whether or not we've won a great battle or not, but I guess we've given old Jerry an awful swat. Went souvenir hunting in the morning, and although I walked miles along the old German lines, found very little of interest. Their old front line where we are now must have been very lightly held because most of the dugouts hadn't been used in months. They are wonderful diggers these Huns, and they make themselves jolly comfortable whenever they are in a trench. Our Yanks would rather freeze, but old Fritz methodically sets to work and builds himself a hell of a great dugout, and makes a pretty good war out of it at all times.

The prisoners we have taken are of all ages and sizes, but don't seem bad physically, and certainly don't look underfed. They seem pretty glad to be well out of it, and you can't blame them a bit. I only saw three dead Germans on our whole walk. One was a very nice looking boy with a clean cut face, down on his back where he had fallen, not a mark on him, he looked asleep, not dead. Somebody in Germany is going to feel badly. A nice boy, not over seventeen, just cold mutton, Bah!

At three o'clock 'C Company' got orders to move up with the 2nd Battalion of the [317th] infantry to support their attack this evening. We packed up and moved out immediately. We marched half a mile joined our Battalion and marched out with them. We moved up four kilos through ground taken yesterday from the Boche, unpacked our limbers and hiked forward carrying our kit. It came on to rain about this time and turned as dark as pitch. We plodded on, slipping all over the place, falling into shell holes and at last reached our destination. The edge of a woods, dark as pitch and wet as the ocean.

After considerable palaver we got into position along the edge of the woods as best we could. The [317th] Infantry cannot attack because the woods are so dark. So we are just to hold the position for the night.

After getting the guns all set, the Captain and I found a little old shed in the wood and crawled into it. It kept the rain out although it afforded no cover from fire. The shelling began a little later and old Jerry plastered the wood without causation all night long. Nothing dropped very close, but a great deal dropped pretty close and it wasn't too jolly, and the fact that there were quite a few gas shells among them didn't help much. Everybody would yell 'Gas' and we would slap on our masks, and after a long pause would continuously sniff the air to see if all was clear. We had a dozen gas alarms in the night, and sleeping in a mask, although possible, is neither easy nor pleasant. On the whole it was a jolly bad night, my teeth were chattering at 4 o'clock, and that, in addition to the shell fire, kept our shack shaking like the well-known leaf.

September 28, 1918- KEAN

In a shell hole in what was German territory two days ago. I am well and there is very little that I can say. We took part in the present show, but didn't do much and so far have come out all right without casualties. However, we will probably have a much harder time later. Cox and their men didn't fare as well as we did.

We have seen several balloons of both sides go up in flames when attacked by the aeroplanes, it is quite a sight to see. The observers take to their parachutes.

The night of an attack is everything that one reads about it. The roads all covered with troops hurrying up towards the line, artillery in position, transport in seeming confusion. Finally, getting to one's position, the few artillery shells going over, then the counter battery work, and finally the barrage just put down, and then the infantry going forward with shells going and coming.

We came up starting at dusk and got clear of the transport by ourselves just as the moon came up. We got up to our positions, dug an emplacement, and at zero hour opened fire. Then we stopped, and after the fight had gone forward. We moved across a valley to a hillside where we have been for the past 30 hours. Trenches abound, and on a reconnaissance the other day, I worked probably the most shelled piece of ground in France. There isn't a spot that is not a shell hole, and I guess there isn't as much blood in the battle field in France as it has been. I am enclosing a red poppy. I picked them blooming peacefully, and a blue corn flower, or is it an Azalea, picked just outside my P.C. after the firing the other morning.

September 29, 1918 - HAMILTON

Morning came at last, cold and wet. Everybody is soaked through. I hear we will be relieved today and can't say I'd be sorry. We haven't seen much action, but the rest of the Division is pretty tired and need a rest. I hope they get it. Made some coffee over the canned heat and felt quite better. Nothing doing for some time except spasmodic shelling, and then orders to move out.

We moved back the way we came in last night, and in the daylight saw many evidences of the rapid retreat of Mr. Boche. Saw many dead Germans and lots of German machine guns, light and heavy artillery and all kinds of truck. We have certainly captured a lot of material. Saw lots of Yanks wounded, straggling back, and some mashed up boys being carried back on stretchers, the four bearers staggering under their heavy loads over the slippery trails. Saw the Infantry of our Division coming out of the line and they certainly are a mess. They drove the Germans at the point of bayonets for two days, gained all their objectives and then spent too much harder days digging in under heavy shell fire. They were a mess all right, but in action for the first time, they had proven their worth and now know that they can lick old Jerry anytime they try. It was a wonderful thing for our boys to be so successful on their first party, nothing can possibly stop them now. They are just like debutantes after a really successful coming out party, why the sky is the limit and although it is rather farfetched to speak of these dirty, unshaved, tired soldiers as debutantes, they are really just like big kids about it and the simile isn't as bad as it looks. My hat is off to them anyhow, they are all right.

We marched towards the wood a few kilos behind our position and after going a long way through the mud being shelled on the road and having a poor time generally, finally found that we had come to the wrong place and had to retrace our steps to get in some trenches. The trenches were full of men so we bivouacked in the open. Then when some big shells began to come over we got in the shell hole and Bobbie and Lin and I slept, all three of us in a place about big enough to put a wheelbarrow. We are getting pretty expert at sleeping any old place at all.

I've lost all track of days and dates, it's been just one long endless day for a week, although I've managed to keep this diary day by day. I've no idea when one day began and the other finished. I am tired and dirty beyond belief.

This morning we were run out of our nice shell hole by the Major who wanted a P.C. So we had to hunt another place and we finally found an old German dugout which is 'tres bon.' It is now 6:00 PM and I'm going right to bed, and hope to have a good sleep, although the chances are we will have to move again during the night.

Another day, and we are still in the trenches. Things are very quiet, no shelling, hardly at all. I can't remember doing a thing except shaving off my 4 day beard.

❧

On September 28, the 2nd Battalion of the 317th Infantry was attached to the 320th Infantry and was moving to the left flank of the 80th Division to establish a liaison with the 4th Division on their left. The Army's objectives were close, with the exception of the left flank. Support was needed in this area and the machine guns were moved to Bois de Septsarges.

By the end of the day the 80th Division reached Bois de la Cote de Laimont and were relieved by the 33rd Division. The 80th Division was ordered to move to the Mountfaucon area to be in readiness of supporting

177

the 37th Division who were facing a potential German counter attack. When word was given that the counter attack was not materializing, the 80th was then directed to move to Cuisy. On September 29, the 313th Machine Gun Battalion marched to a location about one kilometer southeast of Cuisy where 'C Company' rejoined the rest of the Battalion. They bivouacked in this location for three days.

September 28, 1918 – THOMAS

This is written from a German officer's dug out, on his paper, while his food is cooking. We won't see the paper for some time I guess, but you saw the show we put on yesterday. It must have been okay. I've had a wonderful, horrible, time but am okay up until now and my Company is intact to date. I can't tell how long it will be the same.

Last night I went out to find where we were, and from the map this morning, we must have been pretty well in the German lines. It is hard but wonderful. I haven't had my clothes off in four days and haven't shaved. I've slept about four hours. There on the ground and me in a lousy bed, but c'est la geurre. I've got a wonderful Company, they are so patient and responsive. I was scared to death of much shell fire at first, but will tell you of a horrible evening I put in some time.

September 28, 1918 - LEINHAUSER

Had a job building a road to our Battalion Dump in the morning. We got orders to help 317th and left for the line which was in Bois de Septsarges. We got there about 9:00 PM, raining like all and everybody is soaking wet. We mounted our guns and waited. I slept under a tree in the rain and got up soaking wet and hungry. We were taken out of line on Sunday the 29th and fed up. I've seen a lot of dead Germans and machine guns and other equipment left behind. We did some hard hiking over muddy roads and finally got fixed in our [-] for the night. It rained again.

◅❧

On the morning of September 30, the 80th Division passed final control of their fighting zone over to the 33rd Division for some much needed rest. Despite the slow movement of traffic that traversed the overflowing roads, the relief was completed by 2:30 PM that day.

Casualties for the dates of September 26-29, 1918 reported the 320th Infantry had 81 killed, 24 men died of wounds, and 253 were wounded. The 313th Machine Gun Battalion reported only 2 wounded (80th Division Summary of Operations).

September 30, 1918 - HAMILTON

We have done wonderfully well with our rations and have had plenty to eat, although the attack which was very remarkable, considering the state of the roads. Also, today we connected with our mail. I got five letters, Bobbie Stoddart got twelve. I don't know whether we are going to attack again or go out for a rest. I don't believe our horses can stand much more. Wish I could get a paper and see what has happened and whether the results of our efforts are worthwhile. We all feel as though we had done quite a thing, I suppose the official communiqué will say tersely 'Front N.T.R.' [nothing to report] and we thought we were raising particular Hell.

September 30, 1918 – KEAN

Since I wrote to you the day before yesterday I took the Company up, but wasn't in action and then came out again and we are now in ex-German system of trenches, occasionally getting a shell, just to keep us alive and awake. I don't know where or what we do from here. The food situation has been quite well done, as we have gotten rations pretty regularly and have had a least one good meal each day and sometimes more. In fact, the food has been much more plentiful than on many maneuvers. However, the rain and mud have not been very pleasant and this dug out is tres bon.

They tell a story of men the other night being asked to roll over and give someone else room, and he said, 'Hell no, I've just got this water warmed up.'

We have a nice German stove going and are warm and comfortable with a stire in store latter. Have accumulated quite a bit of junk from the Boche, some useful for the Company and some for the men, but nearly everything is too large to send over as a souvenir. Though I didn't get any of them, Cox and others did, and say that they captured beer, food and cigarettes that are very good.

They say the Boche stays by his machine gun until his last cartridge is gone or the Yanks are upon him and then cries 'kamerad.' Naturally the Yanks kamerad as he deserves. I saw several by their machine guns who had evidently done just that thing. Killed all he could, and then when overpowered, expected to be taken prisoners.

CHAPTER 9
'RISEN FROM THE DEAD'

The next engagement the Battalion faced against their adversary was not as fortunate as their few days in September. The enemy occupied the heights east and west of Romagne. The Division supported a new Corps mission of penetrating the hostile enemy positions between Cunel and the Meuse, advancing to capture the heights near Romagne-sur-Montfaucon. The frontlines were arranged with the 3rd Division on the left of the 80th Division and the 4th Division was on the right. The planned axis of advancement for the 80th Division ran through the villages of Septsarges, Nantillois, Cunel, Aincreville and Andevanne.

The 80th Division attacked the frontlines at the Bois des Ogons, a strong point held by the Germans located about half way between Nantillois and Cunel. The village of Nantillois had only recently been vacated by the Germans who held that location for about 4 years before it was taken by the 79th Division on September 28. The 80th Division was ordered to relieve the 79th Division in this town. It was here that the Battalion faced their most significant battle and greatest loss of life during the war, in the woods just north of Nantillois, the Bois des Ogons.

October 1, 1918 - KEAN

In an ex-German dug out. So far we haven't played a very important part in the battle. Fired a machine gun barrage to start off the show, and then have been beating it to various parts of the line to act as support. You see the attack was all made by the Brigade to which we are not attached. However, I suppose our turn will come soon.

I haven't seen it myself, but have it from pretty authentic sources, officers of this Division, that they captured machine guns with Boche chained to them. I think they were probably prisoners under sentence of court martial. [We] took machine gun crews with red crossed on their arms. Garretson [Leland Beekman Garretson 1880-1941] vouches for the last statement and says that the men questioned admitted he was part of a machine gun crew and tried to get out of it by saying after the fighting part of his duties was to look after the wounded. Garretson didn't shoot him but kept him a prisoner. They also have a habit of firing till their last shot is gone, or further opposition useless and having killed all they possibly can, they cry 'kamerad' and expect to be taken prisoner. However, they got fooled all right.

October 2, 1918 - THOMAS

We are still hard at it. We have moved several times since I last wrote you and have had some interesting experiences. Hope to get a real show in a few days. Our Division has been fine. My morale goes up and down with the weather. I will cable as soon as I come out and get a chance. Airplanes dropped newspapers to us yesterday afternoon and the news is really encouraging. I want to see the end. Excuse haste. Am well.

October 2, 1918 - HAMILTON

Bitterly cold, we had to huddle around the stove in our dug out. The stove smokes like billy-o. I suppose we will be going on again soon and I'd just as soon not.

The general situation looks a lot better. Bulgaria has yelled 'Kamerad' and is out of the war. The British have been going great guns around Cambrai and General Cronkhite says we may have peace by November. The German cause looks pretty hopeless and I don't see how they can stand up much longer against the increasing pressure of the Allies. I should not be surprised to find that they are much worse off than we imagine and we might see a general retreat this month along the whole front. I hope so.

War is certainly no fun at all. I don't see how anybody has stood four long years of it. I am not, I don't reckon, a particularly brave man. I am afraid of big dogs and burglars and tarantulas and precipices and all that sort of thing, but I must confess, of all the things that scare me, nothing compares with 'them big shells.' They certainly are rotten, bullets and such seem perfectly harmless in comparison and although I am 'a fearful man' as Hurree Babu said, I don't think I am alone in my feelings. Every time I set in a safe dug out and have something good to eat, I feel as if I would like to chase the whole German Army into the Rhine and every time a 6 inch shell sails over my head and bursts with a sickening 'Cosump' in the field beyond, I want to go home and sit on mothers lap and have her recite 'Little Orphan Annie' to me.

I find I'm not so bad about casualties as I thought. I don't remember ever seeing a dead person or a badly mashed man in my life before, and although there are things I'd rather see, Lord and Taylors show windows for instance, it isn't so bad, and I don't mind it as much as I expected. Dead Germans look much more attractive and live ones. I'll tell the world.

Uncle Alex [Alexander Torrance 1865-1950] writes that General Wright [William Mason Wright 1863-1943] is in command of the 3rd Corps, and as that is my Corps, I may have a chance to tell him that I am his second cousin once removed and would like a soft staff job. He has been at Cedar Ridge and never returned a 'Life of Frederick the Great' which he borrowed there.

Uncle Alex also wrote for me to live a good Christian life that everybody can be proud of. I've been thinking it over and I can't quite dope it out. A Christian life, I've almost forgotten what it's supposed to be. It seems as I remember it that the first thing you were to do was to love your enemies. Love your enemies! Great Scott, I can't do that and try to kill them at the same time. I don't hate them I admit, but love them! No, I can't do that, not so long as their machine gunners wear Red Cross brassards on their arms. Anyhow, I'm not going to turn the other cheek either, not so long as my pistol is loaded. As far as morals are concerned, although they have not much to do with Christianity, I lead a most exemplary life, partly because that's the sort of a cuss I am and partly because I have no option about it. Mine is neither more or less than anyone else's. As far as taking no thought for my life, or what I should eat or drink or put on, I must say I have little else on my mind except mail from home. No, I don't believe my life is too Christian. I am certainly not too proud of it myself, although I swear I can't see any way of improving the blooming thing.

~∽~

The 80th Division moved southeast of Cuisy to rest for about four days after being relieved by the 33rd Division in the last attack. The entire First Army went into another offensive attack on October 4 and the senior leaders of the Division had to scramble to put men into proper staging. Unfortunately, the haste in moving troops forward, coupled with a lack of inadequate preparations and lack of maps, proved quite detrimental to those men asked to carry out the attack.

The Division was given an objective that called for attacking the heavily fortified German positions in the Heights of Cunel. This sector was west of the Meuse River in north eastern France. The area around the village of Cunel provided the Germans with full observation of their enemy's approach. This defensive position was part of the Kriemhilde Stellung and a necessary strong point for the German Army to hold onto the Western Front. South of this position lay a well-defended patch of woods known as the Bois des Ogons. The Division had to pass through these woods in order to advance to their objective. The Division was placed into Nantillois with the 4th Division on their left, and the 3rd Division on their right. The approximate distance from Nantillois to Cunel was about 4.5 kilometers. The plans called for the Division to be placed on a line of departure in Nantillois using the road to Cierges on the left, and the road to Brieulles on the right. This sector was about two kilometers wide at the jump off line, but narrowed down to about one kilometer as they approached Cunel.

The 3rd Division held a defensive line just north of the village, well within the artillery range of the enemy. Movement in and around Nantillois was under constant German observation and bombardment.

The 80th Division's senior leaders received the III Corps Field Order on the morning of October 3 that directed them to be ready to attack the next day. The race was on to get battle plans to the subordinate officers who were to carry out the campaign. The officers had to complete a reconnaissance of the area, bring up supplies and ammunition, position the troops into their jump off sectors, feed the men and then be in a position to wait for the final word on H-Hour. Only a few of these ideal planning conditions occurred. The most significant breakdown happened in the time it took for the Brigade and Regimental commanders to receive the details of the attack.

The Division received the III Corps Field Order No. 22 in the morning of October 3. The Officers were gathering in Cuisy in anticipation of the conference, but also knew that it would be necessary to reconnoiter the sectors north of Nantillois, an area that was currently being held by the 3rd Division.

The plans called for two infantry regiments to lead the attack on the Bois des Ogons. Company A of the 313th Machine Gun Battalion was attached to the 1st Battalion, 317th Infantry who positioned on the right side of the attack. Company B was attached to 3rd Battalion, 318th Infantry who attacked on the left.

On October 3, 1918, the 80th Division headquarters were located near Cuisy. That morning the Division received a field order instructing them to attack on the morning of October 4 with the 3rd Division on their left and the 4th Division on their right. The orders outlined the specific objectives and Division boundaries. The 159th Brigade commander received his orders, and in turn instructed the Regimental commanders of the 317th and 318th Infantry that they would attack in the morning.

It wasn't until 1:00 PM that afternoon that the verbal orders were communicated outlining the attack. Major Jennings Wise (1881-1968) and Major Henry Burdick (1878-1953), then occupying Hill 295, south of Nantillois, headed to Cuisy to meet with Colonel Ulysses Worrilow (1866-1930) who was just given his orders. Majors Wise and Burdick were the senior officers of the 318th Infantry, and Colonel Worrilow was the Regimental Commander of the 318th Infantry. Worrilow ordered his Majors to reconnoiter the front lines just north of Nantillois and then return back to Cuisy by 5:00 PM where formal orders of the attack were to be given at the headquarters of the 4th Division. The distance between Nantillois and Cuisy was about 5.5 kilometers. Major Wise, already knowing the disposition of these front lines expressed to both Colonel Worrilow and General George Jamerson (1869-1960) that a frontal attack would only be successful if proper artillery was placed on the flanks of the woods.

Major Huidekoper joined Majors Wise and Burdick that afternoon and headed to Nantillois to complete their reconnaissance of the area. The roads to Nantillois were congested moving men and supplies into the forward sector in preparation for the attack. The three officers attempted to take a short cut across a ridge east of Montfaucon-Nantillois road, in hopes of finding a faster route back to Nantillois. Unfortunately, this new route only added to their delay in afternoon preparations. While on route north, the shelling continued and a heavy shell burst near the officers, knocking Burdick and Huidekoper down to the ground. The forgiving ground absorbed most of the impact preventing the men from being seriously wounded or killed. They continued on their way to Nantillois recognizing that the path they took was too treacherous to cross in broad daylight with troops in the open. Wise eventually left the two officers in Nantillois and headed back to Cuisy for his conference.

Major Wise returned to Cuisy about 5:00 PM to receive his formal orders from Colonel Worrilow. He discovered that the 4th Division Headquarters were abandoned due to the recent shelling of the area. He came upon General Jamerson who told him to expect to attack in the morning. Wise pleaded with his superior to give him proper artillery support on the flanks of his advancing units in order to give him any chance of success.

As dusk approached, Wise found Worrilow waiting impatiently and gave him orders to relieve two companies of the 4th Infantry then holding the line at Nantillois. The relief was to occur by midnight, a near impossible task at such a late hour. Wise also discovered that his troops had not been rested during the day, but instead had been marched from one location to another and had to be rushed north again to be in position for a morning attack. These were hardly fresh troops for an impending attack.

Wise assembled his Battalion officers, distributed maps and directed them to prepare for an evening hike back to Nantillois. All units were ordered to be in position by 4:30 AM on D-Day. As evening approached, H-Hour was still not known by these officers.

Alfred Charles Affantranger (1895-1992) was the Sergeant Major in the Headquarters Battalion. While he was only 23 years old at the time, he was responsible for maintaining the Battalion's records. This assignment likely came from his previous job working as a clerk for Erie Railroad when he was drafted into the Army.

Affantranger recorded the following on October 3, "At 6:00 PM Company A was attached to the 1st Battalion of the 317th Infantry. Joined same at point 500 yards west of Septsarges on Septsarges-Montfaucon road. Company B attached to 3rd Battalion of the 318th Infantry joining them on road at edge of bivouac. Remaining Machine Gun Battalion less two above companies marched to Fayel Farm and bivouacked per verbal orders Commanding General" (Affantranger 7).

∽

After dusk, Lieutenant Colonel Charles Keller (1878-1961), 317th Infantry, set out on a course from Cuisy to Nantillois leading the 1st and 2nd Battalions of his Infantry Regiment. Colonel Howard Perry (1868-1945) was the senior officer of the 317th Infantry and led the 3rd Battalion to a position just east of Montfaucon, near Fayel Farm. The remaining companies of the 313th Machine Gun Battalion, also ordered to be part of the Brigade Reserve, were staged near a trench called Trench des Fainaentes, about 1 kilometer east of Montfaucon. Just before 8:00 PM, Keller left his two Battalions and headed for the conference where he was supposed to receive more detailed orders for the attack in the morning.

During the early hours of October 4, Colonel Worrilow established the 318th Regimental command post about 300 meters south of the jump-off line in Nantillois. He received formal details of the attack stating that H-Hour was 05:30 AM and that a preparatory barrage was going to precede the attack by 20 minutes.

Major Wise successfully guided his exhausted men into the railway yard in Nantillois after hours of difficult hiking that evening to get to the jump off line. He gave orders to his company officers to place the men in position at the line while he searched for the Regimental command post. While in the railway yard he was given alarming news from his liaison officer. He was told that an officer of the 4th Infantry, 3rd Division had no orders for an attack that morning. Wise quickly realized that the 318th was about to go into an attack with no protection on their left flank.

Meanwhile, Lieutenant Colonel Keller, who just returned from his conference, came back to the location where he left his two Battalions. It was 4:00 AM and both Battalions were gone. Major William Clifford (1875-1962), 317th Infantry, knew he had to be in Nantillois at the jump-off line at 4:30 AM, so he left the area without Keller. Major Paulus Glass (1886-1945), also with the 317th Infantry, moved his 1st Battalion up to a staging area on Hill 295 in a support position for the drive. Keller set off to find the two Battalions and came upon Major Glass at Hill 295. There he found Major Glass with the 1st Battalion, and also Major Clifford, but without his 2nd Battalion. Clifford explained to Keller that when 2:00 AM arrived he felt uneasy with the passing of time, and knowing that the 2nd Battalion was going to lead the first wave of the attack, Clifford decided to send his Battalion forward to the jump-off line under the command of Captain William Frazier (1888-1973).

Keller and Clifford quickly headed north for the jump-off line located on Brieulles Road. When the two officers arrived, Captain Frazier and the 2nd Battalion were not in position. The attack was about to begin and an entire Battalion was missing from the line.

At about 5:00 AM Keller rushed back to Hill 295 were he left Major Glass. He ordered Glass to quickly advance his 1st Battalion to take the place of the 2nd Battalion in the first wave of the attack. Glass had to travel 3 kilometers to the north in order to be in position with H-Hour rapidly approaching.

To help illustrate what was about to occur that morning, it may be helpful to use a football analogy and visualize the battlefield as three football fields positioned next to each other. The 80th Division occupied the field in the middle, the 3rd Division occupied the field on the left, and the 4th Division was on the field to the right. The 80th Division planned to send two Regiments down the middle of the field, side by side, in two waves. The 317th and 318th Infantry Regiments were going to enter this middle field at their own end zone and move forward through the Bois des Ogons, or the 50 yard line. Hill 274 was located at their own 20 yard line on this imaginary field. The Heights of Cunel was the end zone at the opposite side of the field. When the Infantry Regiments took the field, the 318th occupied the left half of their own end zone ready to push forward. They looked to their right, expecting to see the 317th Infantry taking the right half of the field, but to their surprise, that side of the end zone was empty. There were no troops in position.

The 318th Infantry then looked to their left, and saw the 3rd Division in position, but these troops were not ready to attack. They had not received orders. This was the predicament left to Major Wise on the morning of the attack.

Wise needed to move his men down the field toward the 50 yard line without support on either side. He knew that there was nothing to stop the enemy on his left from leaving their field of play and getting into his backfield. If he got too far ahead of the others, it would leave an open flank and allow the enemy to come and envelope his advancing men, a common military strategy taught to young officers.

The 80th Division command was of course expecting that all of the American Army is going to occupy and advance at the same time. However, if this did not happen, all Regiments had been ordered to advance forward without regard to whether or not their flank positions were also advancing.

At 5:35 AM a barrage began and artillery was put down on Hill 266 to the left edge of the 80th Division's sector. The barrage rained down across the zone to the lower edge of the Bois des Ogons, more than 1 kilometer north of the line of departure. The barrage lasted from 5:25 AM until 8:15 AM that morning.

At 5:40 AM, Companies F and G of the 318th Infantry left the jump-off line as the first wave of the Battalion and headed toward Hill 274. Despite the fact that the Regiments to their right and left were not in position to advance, Major Wise ordered the men forward so they did not lose the cover of the rolling barrage. They followed four French tanks that were sent forward as part of the initial attack. At the same time, the German Army, knowing that the Americans were about to advance toward them, also put down a barrage of their own. The German barrage fell directly on the area where the American Army was advancing, north of Nantillois and south of Hill 274. The enemy bombardment inflicted multiple casualties at the start of the attack. However, the men were given orders not to stop to succor the wounded. They were told that litter bearers would come from the rear to aid any men that would fall during the advance.

Within 600 yards of leaving the departure line in Nantillois, a platoon from F Company was overrun by a German listening post located in a pit that concealed their presence. Listening posts were common for both sides as they became an effective means of learning about troop activity and could report information back to the rear command. This German listening post could have provided the information necessary to place the well-timed and accurate barrage that fell on the advancing Army. Within yards of leaving the jump-off line, an alert was sounded. Gas! Gas! Masks were donned as the men advanced forward under the heavy fire.

When the four tanks crested Hill 274, the Germans pounded them with artillery and machine gun fire. The tanks were fully exposed on the northern slope of the hill. After the lead tank was hit, the other three tanks retreated back to Nantillois. As the tanks moved back, the Germans continued to place artillery fire on these moving targets, which also brought fire down upon the rear companies that were moving up into their support positions.

At 7:00 AM, Company D of the 313th Machine Gun Battalion marched through Montfaucon towards the front lines under a continuous barrage of heavy shell fire. By 7:35 AM the concerns that Major Wise expressed the day earlier to both Colonel Worrilow and General Jamerson, were coming true. Wise and the 318th were out front and had no protection on their left or right. The Regiment was proceeding down the northern slope toward to woods where it came into a swale just below the edge of the Bois des Ogons. The advance did not come easy. The 318th suffered multiple casualties. A portion of one platoon made it into the woods, but the majority of the men were trapped in the swale south of the woods and were being slaughtered by enemy machine guns from the flanks. The men could not remain in this swale for long or they would have faced ultimate annihilation from their flank. They had to either advance into the woods or fall back to the positions from where they came. Unable to maintain a position of any substance in the woods, and finding no cover in the lower swale, the 318th found it necessary to withdraw back to the cover of Hill 274 from where they came.

The 2nd Battalion, 317th Infantry, who was lost early in the morning of the attack, mistakenly made their way far left of the 80th Division's sector. Captain Frazier, discovering his error, believed that he was behind the 4th Infantry in the 3rd Division's sector. Instead of turning his Battalion to the right and heading into the area now occupied by the 2nd Battalion, 318th Infantry, Captain Frazier took his Battalion back to Nantillois. During his withdraw to that area, Frazier was seriously wounded and had to be relieved by Captain John James.

Escaping the slaughter in the swale, the 2nd Battalion, 318th Infantry, withdrew to the cover of Hill 274. The troops were meeting up with the other companies that were also moving up in the second wave. There were four companies mingled together on this southern slope. This area between Hill 274 and Nantillois was crowded with men taking cover and presented an opportune target for enemy aircraft flying above unopposed. The constant artillery and gas attacks made communications difficult with the rear command. Runners had trouble getting through and wire communications were temporarily lost.

After the rolling barrage ended, the left flank took heavy machine gun fire, while gas and shelling continued to fall on the Battalions. German airplanes directed fire upon the troops that held a line stretching only about 500 yards, with the left flank hugging the Cunel-Nantillois road. The Regimental commander advised them to dig in and hold Hill 274, and repeated warnings to watch their left flank.

The crest of the hill was difficult to hold. Constant artillery barrage and sporadic communication lines required the 318th Infantry to withdraw further back down the southern slope of Hill 274 to area of the 'pit' from where F Company was first attacked. The wounded were also making their way to the rear and began gathering in the refuge of this ditch. This crowding fixed the attention of hostile airplanes that brought down more machine-gun fire on the assembled casualties. The continued strafing of the attacking planes allowed the German artillery to pinpoint the location of the retreating wounded bringing down even more misery on the troops.

By noon, General Jamerson deployed anti-Aircraft, gas and flame units of the First Army to assist in holding Hill 274. Unfortunately, the activity created in deploying these specialized units, brought down an unrelenting barrage on the rear crest of the hill, making their presence ineffective. In the lulls of the barrage, the wounded were carried back to the rear while ammunition was brought forward. The two Companies of the 313th Machine Gun Battalion, Companies C and D, who were held in reserves near Montfaucon were called to advance to the front lines for support. At 1:00 PM, Company C took up positions astride the Cunel Nantillois Road to cover the left flank of the brigade.

October 4, 1918 - AFFANTRANGER

The Battalion, less Companies A and B, took up position in support one kilometer southwest of Nantillois. We marched at 7:30 AM per verbal orders. It was at this point that First Lieutenant Joseph Harold Parsons [1894-1918] was killed, Rosella Wilson's husband [Rosella

Wilson 1895-1975]. He was one of the best friends the fellows in the Battalion had among the officers and he was certainly one great fellow. Everyone misses him. He was the dentist for the Battalion and really had no business up there where he was, but went along with the Battalion Surgeon to help out all he could in dressing wounds, etc.

PARSONS

The Battalion was ordered to proceed from Montfaucon along the Montfaucon-Nantillois Road and to remain in the valley to the left of the road until further orders were received. This road was being heavily shelled with high explosive and mustard gas shells along with the valley that ran into it. The Battalion took cover in the trenches available in this area. Lieutenant Parsons took cover with Dr. Jarman [Bernard Lipscomb Jarman 1889-1962] in broken shallow trenches after seeing that the men of the Medical Detachment were undercover, and it was in one of those shallow trenches that Lieutenant Parsons received a slight wound about 6 inches above his right knee, due to a small piece of shrapnel hitting him. Lieutenant Jarman at once went to him, dressed his wound and assisted him to the rear in the direction of the road, when, due to the heavy shelling, they were obliged to seek shelter in a shallow broken trench about 40 feet from where Lieutenant Parsons was injured. After remaining in this trench with Lieutenant Parsons for a short time, due to the crowded condition, Lieutenant Jarman moved to a shallow broken trench about 25 feet below him. More gas made its appearance and after putting their masks on, in a few minutes, a high explosive shell burst near Lieutenant Parsons and killed him almost instantly. Lieutenant Jarman ran to him at once and removed his gas mask and found a penetrating wound just about an inch and a half from the external angle of his left eye, another penetrating wound about 1 inch above the angle of his lower jaw. Further examination revealed several penetrating wounds directly over his heart. Lieutenant Parsons groaned only once and his pulse was barely perceptible when Lieutenant Jarman reached him. It was a great loss to the Battalion and was felt by every man in the outfit (Affantranger 7).

An account of these events was also recorded in a letter written by Dr. Bernard Jarman to his father, James E. Jarman, thirty one years after the war had ended. At the time of the battle Dr. Jarman was the Field Surgeon attached to the 313th Machine Gun Battalion, Medical Company:

JARMAN

"While dating this letter October 4th, I am carried back 31 years, for it was October 4, 1918 that I suppose I went through one of the most trying days that my young life had to that time experienced. We were at the war front and first my dentist was injured by being shot through the knee. I fixed him up and then I stooped down in a shallow trench partly filled with water contaminated with mustard gas, an enlisted man was on each side of me. A little post was on the edge of this trench for telephone wires. At first I got behind it but for some reason that I will never know, I moved up just a foot. Then the man below me moved up to where I had been, thus we three were also close together that we just about touched. Then a shell hit about 2 feet from us making a large hole and fragments of steel scattered in every direction when the shell exploded. The man behind the post, partly protected as he thought, was instantly killed. Had I not moved up I guess this fate would have been my fate, it was just that distance, of less than 2 feet, which has me here today. I have the man's name [Michael J Konick 1895-1918] in my book at home made up of tags. One tag you put on the man and the carbon copy was kept in the book.

Just after this happened, Parsons my dentist was injured as I reported. I lay in a trench with him but left to fix up another injured man, and when I returned, something made me think that if I got beside him that maybe both of us would get it from a direct hit, so I lay down in a trench about 6 inches deep and about 20 feet below him. In a few minutes a shell made a direct hit and he was killed instantly. I tagged him as killed so no other medical officer would have to stop to administer first aid, thinking that he was only unconscious.

Another one of our men had and eye just about shot out and I later saw this man at Walter Reed Hospital when I was on duty there in 1920. He was being repaired so that he could wear an artificial eye. His name was DeMora [Augusto Demauri 1889-1977], a little Italian boy, who was afraid of nothing and he was smiling when I saw him both times as I recall.

After this day I took my men and went further up towards the front and we were under gunfire most of the night along with gas. I do not recall getting any sleep that night for although I had the night divided up, having one man watch for an hour at a time, I was afraid to trust any of them as I feared they would fall asleep due to the fatigue and we might all get gas which would have ended it all for us all.

Morning came and we were relieved and marched back to the rear about 2 miles, and while hunting for a place to sleep I heard a messenger going around telling all officers to report to our headquarters and this I did. We were to take as many men as we could from those we had left and go to the front again. I found some of my men and decided to take my best four with me. Of those I picked I could not find my best man as he was hunting for something to eat, so I took Bell [George Frederick Bell 1887-1984], Lassiter [David Allen Lassiter 1889-1960], and Jahraus [William George Jahraus 1896-1986]. It was less trouble to take care of three than four. Bell and Lassiter lay in one trench about 6 feet long, 3 feet wide and 3 feet deep. Jahraus and I lay in another such trench about 10 feet from the others. It was on the top of an elevation that the Germans had recently been driven from so they knew exactly its layout and they knew that our troops had to follow that path. As we neared this place we passed all sorts of equipment discarded by the Germans in their hurried retreat. Men were lying dead all along the way. We made our way through the mud and rain and the darkness of the night, up this hill, and every so often the Germans shot a flare up in the heavens. It would land, and while coming down, made a blaze that made the heavens as bright as day. Then they could take pictures or their planes could detect what was going on. When these flares were used we would all fall to the ground on our faces so that we could not be seen and we remained perfectly still until they burned out, after which we would proceed toward our goal. Having reached these trenches, the gunfire was so accurate that one shell would fall near us, the next a little closer, and as luck had it, the next would go beyond us, so we stayed in this one spot for three days and three nights.

During this time we had some stale hard bread and we cut the crust off as we were afraid to eat the outside as it had been exposed to mustard gas. Mustard gas, while called a gas, is really a fog, like mist, and it settles on things and is absorbed, and then when one gets in contact with it, it penetrates and in a few days you may have a deep burn. Such burns are deep and black as if the area had been charred by an electric shock. I got a little burn which only caused my skin to peel off when I lay in the water in that trench where the man was killed behind the post. Thus, you can see why October 4th makes me recall the events of 31 years ago" (Jarman).

᪥

Lieutenant William Ballard Preston (1888-1959) of Company A, 313th Machine Gun Battalion, sent this message to Major Huidekoper, "Battalion consolidating. Badly in need of ammunition. Send to Regimental P.C. situated Nantillois. Lt. Mackey [Sidney Augustus Mackey 1888-1959] severely wounded. 1st Platoon badly shot up, out of action, reorganizing here. No casualties in 3rd Platoon. 2nd Platoon not heard from" (Headquarters Correspondence).

George Victor Cooke (1892-1918) and John Frances Coakley (1890-1918), both from A Company, were killed on the first day of fighting. Among the severely wounded in Company A was Private Walter Blanchard Shaw (1894-1961) who was shot in the neck and lost his right arm during this battle.

John Lezuhovsky (-1918) of B Company was also killed on this first day of fighting and John Joseph Herzing (1895-1918), also of B Company, was severely wounded and succumbed to his wounds ten days later.

First Sergeant Alexander Duncan MacWilliam Sr. (1891-1966), Company B, observed one of his men tangled in barbed wire that afternoon. Putting himself at risk, MacWilliam "went to the aid of his wounded comrade and brought him to a place of safety, his route being subjected to a concentrated artillery bombardment. Concealing the fact that he was severely wounded; Sergeant MacWilliam remained on duty until the afternoon of the

MacWILLIAM

following day" (War Department, General Order No. 35, 1919). For this selfless act, MacWilliam later became the highest decorated member of the 313th Machine Gun Battalion when he was bestowed with the Distinguished Service Cross.

Two other members of the Battalion were cited by the Commanding General of the A.E.F. for actions take that afternoon as they each distinguished themselves by gallantry in action.

Captain Harry Lee Maynard Jr. (1888-1954) of B Company, and First Sergeant Frank Ferdinand Fee (1884-1934) of C Company were both severely gassed on October 4th, but both men refused to be evacuated to the rear and continued to fight with their men. Recognized for their actions, the citation called for the placement of a silver star on the suspension ribbon of their Victory Medal.

By 3:00 PM, Company A of the Machine Gun Battalion was relieved from duty with the 317th Infantry and marched to positions occupied the previous night on Septsarges Montfaucon Road. Company D moved from Fayel Farm on October 4 to support the rest of the Battalion who were supporting the attack. Unfortunately, their position would not provide cover from incoming artillery shelling and the company was hit by incoming mustard gas. By 6:00 PM that day, D Company had to return to Fayel Farm having suffered a considerable amount of casualties from gas. Over eighty members of Company D had to be treated by medical staff as a result of the gas.

Company C was ordered to support the left flank of the Division. In this same vicinity, a patrol of the 318th Infantry ventured across the Nantillois-Cunel road only to find that the sector was still subjected to strong enemy defenses. Repeated warnings from Colonel Worrilow to "watch your left" was sound advice for the Regiment (Wise 207). However, word of the impending danger to the left flank was not emphasized enough to the Brigade Reserve command as they moved forward that afternoon. The historian for the 313th Field Artillery writes, "A new attack was ordered by the Division commander for the afternoon of the 4th. A rolling barrage was executed through the Bois des Ogons at 5:30 PM. B Battery delivered its barrage from its forward position. The battery was subjected to harassing fire and later in the day was adjusted upon by an airplane" (Crowell 51).

H-Hour was recorded as 5:30 PM by the historian of the field artillery and is an important detail when reviewing the events that occur on this date for the Battalion. Company C was sent forward along the Nantillois-Cunel road and was lured into a killing field. The Germans were patient at drawing an advancing army forward into a ravine or a path that appeared to be a safe avenue for advancement. However, hidden from sight, the Germans often set up their machine gun nests on each side of a ravine, and when the front of an advancing patrol hit a patch of barbed wire or other obstruction, the German pillboxes would open fire on the entire platoon, particularly those who were trapped up front. The harrowing events that occurred on the afternoon of October 4 have been recalled by both Lieutenant Hamilton and Sergeant Ray in their personal writings.

October 3-6, 1918 - HAMILTON

This day has lasted for 96 hours more or less. On October 3rd we got orders just as we were preparing to go to bed to go into the attack. I was not so damn pleased. When you've got your mind all set for the hay, you hate like thunder, and when I say you hate like thunder, I mean every word of it, to have to go into an attack of any kind. Anyhow we packed and moved up into position just behind the front line. We bivouacked on the ground and got a little sleep, but as it drizzled a little and we were shelled a little, and were scared a little, sleep was not too good. Our barrage came down early and shortly after that we started forward. This warfare is quite open and we moved along the roads without transport. We went through [censored] which we took a couple of days ago and God knows how they did it because it sits way upon a hill and looks absolutely impregnable. However, the Yanks took it and today when we went through it, the place was a mess. Oh, before I go on, I'd like to say that yesterday Lin and I had a look at the German lines in the distance and decided that they only had one piece of artillery which they probably moved from place to place and no infantry at all. 'Why they had all gone back to the Rhine,' said Lin, and I agreed with him. Well, we were wrong, as subsequent events will show. We parked our transport much further forward than was safe, the Adjutant came running up shortly shouting above the roar of the guns 'Spread that transport out, the place is being shelled.' I ran over to the Limbers and told them to scatter out and the words were barely out of my mouth before a big shell hit within 20 yards of me, bowling one of my sergeants completely over twice and got up unhurt. The transport scattered all right and went in all directions like chickens in front of an automobile and had hardly moved away before a shell dropped in the exact place they were. I went and told the Captain [Kean], 'They are all scattered Sir.' He answered 'I'm hit.' He certainly looked it. I think he thought he was killed, but it was the best wound I ever saw. A piece of the shell that bowled over my sergeant had gone in the point of his shoulder and had inflicted the incest blight that ever a man hoped for. We tied him up and laid him in a trench and later he went off to the dressing station. After that the shelling got worse and we had to get down. I had a little bit of a trench and was snug as the proverbial bug.

I went out some time later and went around to see how the men were getting on. They were scattered around in shell holes and were getting on all right, although the shelling was hot. I saw one man lying down and thought for a second it was good old Lin. My heart stood still and I hardly dared look at him. He was quite dead, horribly mashed by a shell, but thank God it was not Leinhauser. It was the battalion dentist, Lt. Parsons, and what he was doing going over the top God knows. It was hard luck too, he had been hit in the leg, had that tied up, and crawling into a trench and had been hit by a shell and killed instantly. A married man too.

Incidentally, I almost got it myself a couple of times and twice flattened myself into the grass while the deadly ground shrapnel raked up the dirt around me. We stayed there all morning and finally got orders to move forward. I got the company together and moved forward. Just as we started, a shell sailed over our head and burst 200 yards beyond. I knew instinctively that the next would be shorter and hurried them all I could and just barely got the tail of the column clear of the place before the next one came in with a crash just where we had been. We moved up about one kilo without being shelled much and dug ourselves in some 500 yards in front of the German front lines. We were in a wood and had one infantry in front of us. We barely got ourselves out when the devil went loose in the woods. Each man had dug a little trench for himself just big enough to lie down in. I had one big enough for two and lay in a shallow hole with Bobbie Stoddart for 24 hours under the German barrage. I don't remember ever having such a bad time. The shells hit everywhere but right on my hole – and by George it was bad. Bang! Whang! Zip! Crash! Pow! Zow! Blooie! They would let up for a minute and you would take a deep breath and then they would start again. Towards evening I went forward to connect up with our infantry and had not gone 50 yards before they pinned me to earth with enough shells to annihilate the British Army. I lay flat for half an hour and when they let up I started out again and had not gone another fifty yards when they began it again. I finally got out to the edge of the woods and was promptly sniped at by the Germans, but they were poor shots and missed both times. I finally got back to my hole and spent a rotten night under continuous shell fire. The night ended in a furious barrage and then quiet while both sides had some breakfast. We had wonderful luck and only had four men hit. I don't see how it was possible, theoretically nothing could live under fire like that, but we did and the only cover we had was these six by three by two holes. I moved my guns later as I got my order saying that I was responsible for the left flank of the Division and a different disposition was necessary. I also moved my headquarters and got into a half destroyed German dug out. It wouldn't have stopped anything but it had head cover and was splinter proof and increased my morale a lot. I see now why the ostrich puts its head in the sand, to increase its morale. Believe me, however, we got shelled all right and it's a wonder we didn't get blown in, but we didn't.

At five minutes to five I got an order to send four guns forward with the infantry who would attack at five o'clock. I ran all the way to my most advanced guns and told them they must leave at once. I hurried them all I could to allow them to get through before the counter barrage came down. Our barrage was to have started at five but there was so much shelling going on that you couldn't tell what was barrage and what wasn't. I saw them go forward over the ridge and as they went I wished them good luck, little knowing what was in store for them. They topped the crest and disappeared and then I heard the German machine guns open. I didn't know what they were shooting at but I felt it must be my men and I couldn't understand it because if the infantry had gone forward at five, there should not have been any machine guns there. I went back and told Lin. 'Good God man,' said he, 'that order said 5:30 not 5:00!'

I had given the order to Gil [Gilbert Thorne] so I couldn't tell for sure, but the cold sweat broke out on me. I had sent them over before our own infantry! I had made a most terrible mistake. I had sent a whole platoon to certain death through misreading an order. Good Christ in Heaven what am I to do. They have gone now, I can't possibly stop them. Lin is never wrong, he saw the order and said it said five thirty. Oh God, I was sick. I waited in anguish for 5:30 to see if the barrage came down, then sure enough, the artillery fire double at 5:30 and at six was a continuous roar. Just after six I saw the German S.O.S. lights go up and I knew that the mistake was made. A thousand thoughts flashed through my mind, I had sent a whole platoon to perdition. I would commit suicide. No, not that, I would resign my commission and enlist. No, that wouldn't do either. Then I thought, well maybe the order said 5 o'clock after all, and that would clear me, and then I thought that Gilbert who had the order would probably be killed and I'd never know whether I had made the mistake or not. All this time orders were coming in and things had to be attended to and I had to force my tormented mind to think about the rest of the Company. A lot of letters came in from Gilbert's fiancé and that didn't make matters any better. It was terrible. Finally, a wild eyed runner came in to say that the platoon had advanced to within 100 yards of the German lines and then had had a dozen machine guns open on them. He said he crawled on his hands and knees and the rest of the platoon had been wiped out. He had seen Gilbert go down and believed he had been killed. It was the worst possible news. I am going and I think, what can I say to Gils girl, how can I ever stay in the Army, how can I ever look anyone in the eye again, and all the time I have to think about tomorrows advance.

Finally, in comes Gilbert himself, risen from the dead. He was crying like a baby and confirmed what the previous runner had said, they walked directly into a machine gun nest and only three managed to crawl out again on their hands and knees. Gilbert had been in charge of the platoon.

The Major was there. 'Have you the order?' he asked. 'Yes,' sobbed Gilbert, and he held out a crumpled piece of paper. The Major took it and read it, he had signed it, he handed it to me without a word. I swear my hand shook and I hardly dared look at it. It read as follows, 'The infantry will attack at 5:00 P.M. etc.'

My heart leaped into my throat. The mistake was not mine. I almost broke down, the strain had been horrible. The miracle came later; the platoon had not been wiped out. Practically all of them had managed to crawl back. Two were killed [Walter E. Stuhlfaut 1894-1918 and Max McConnell Caldwell 1892-1918], five unaccounted for, seven wounded and twenty untouched. I don't understand it. It was broad daylight and the Germans let them get within a hundred yards and there was no cover at all. It was a miracle and that's all there was to it.

The next day nothing much happened. The infantry attack of last night was successful and we expected to follow them up all day and lead many conflicting orders and rumors. The day finally passed without our moving. The shelling was terrific all day. The Boche got flank fire on us from across the river and put down all he had. His artillery is marvelous, he puts them just where he wants 'em and it was most unpleasant. Our 'bivvy' would not stand a direct hit and it seemed only a question of time before he got one. The strain of waiting makes you want to go to sleep the minute the shells stop. He used a bit of gas on us and it wasn't nice. The next morning we were taken out and nobody was sorry. I think we have had as much concentrated Hell in these three days as is possible. We came back the way we came in, and the very same trenches [Trench des Fainaentes] that we left a few days ago. We went back to our same old dug out and went to bed. We were all dead tired. Spent one night there and the next morning moved back three miles, almost out of shell fire, and its great relief. I don't know whether we are going in again or out for a rest. The main thing is we are now out. We have been in the thick of it since the First Army attacked on September 26 and I think today is about the ninth of October, almost two weeks. We are pretty tired, the men are in rags and we've had quite a few casualties. I can't write down a lot more on account of the censor and a lot more because I am so tired and fed up. I don't see why I am alive at all. Our infantry has done wonders and some of our green divisions have fought like veterans in this most difficult sort of country. All woods and swamps and machine gun nests and fighting in the open against heavy artillery. I was quite wrong about the Hun, there are plenty of them left and their tactics are admirable. They know the game better than we do, although man for man we can lick the spots out of them. Our engineers have built roads and bridges in marvelous fashion. They had to do most of the work under shell fire and much of our success is due to them. Our rations have gotten up without fail and the weather has been in our favor too. Our Division has certainly made good and I hope will now be taken out for a rest, but if we have to go in again, I reckon it won't kill us and we'll drive the Hun some more.

I have been promoted Captain, and as Captain Kean was wounded, I am in charge of 'C Company.' I shall begin to keep this diary regularly again as soon as I get caught up on sleep, which is not yet.

❧

Charles E. Ray recalls the events of the Bois de Ogons in his memoir:

"On October 4th, our Platoon received orders to go over the top at 5:00 that night. We were to go to the top of the hill in a diagonal direction and fall in behind the first wave of infantry. The sun was still in the sky when we pulled out. The front was quiet. We came to the point where the infantry was supposed to be. Lieutenant [Gilbert] Thorne of New York and I were at the head of the column. At this point I said, 'This don't look good.'

We were moving down a sloping hill and now were in full site of where the Germans were supposed to be in the wooded area ahead. The lieutenant said, 'I think they have retreated and the infantry has already gone into the wood.' Our men carrying machine guns, tripods, and ammunition still moved forward, but not a shell was fired. We were within a few yards of the woods when the machine guns opened up. The flashing fire of guns seemed only a few feet away. They took the troop from the back to the front. The entire group went down like one man. I dived for cover but it was too shallow and I felt a bullet hit my helmet and another went through my coat sleeve. It was then that I broke and ran for a hedge only a few feet away. I was only carrying a light pack pistol and field map case so I traveled fast with the bullets plowing up the earth around my feet as I ran, going over the hedge head first. I practically landed in a shallow bivvy and hugged the ground face down with my feet sticking up. They kept their guns searching up and down the hedge because they knew some others were back there. Strange as it may seem, Lieutenant Thorne and I at the head of the column both came back. The Germans in some way must have called for the artillery help for about this time the shells began to rain down on us and the American artillery opened up, so we were caught between the two.

Apparently we were far enough away from the American artillery to miss us, and too close to the German line to get us, but big chunks of earth rolled down on us. As things quieted down, I wondered how to get out of this. From where I lay, I could see two of our men getting ready to make a run for it. They were heading for a small gulley and protected from view by the hedge. Just as they reached the gulley, I noticed machine gunfire coming from an abandoned tank and it looked right up the gulley. They both went down like one. It was Condon [Daniel M. Condon 1889-1954] and Stuhlfaut [Walter E. Stuhlfaut 1894-1918], both from Erie PA. I met Condon years later and he told me they were hit, he with about a dozen bullets in his right arm. He played possum and later crawled out after darkness. Stuhlfaut, he said, was badly wounded and started to move and they killed him with another burst of fire. That is when I decided to stay put until dark. We were close enough the Germans to hear them talk, so there was the thought of them coming over to take us prisoners or stick a bayonet in our back. Darkness finally came and as it did I unsnapped my pack containing hard rations and all. I only took with me my pistol, field glasses, first aid kit, and map case, leaving the rest in the bivvy. First I crawled along the hedge and the first living soldier I came to was Discipio [Joseph Discipio 1887-1965] of Pittsburgh PA. I said to him in a whisper, 'Come on, let's get out of here.' He only said, 'I'm riddled with bullets, just let me lay here and die.'

Next I came to Berchtold [Fred Andrew Berchtold 1892-1969] of Erie PA. Though he was badly wounded with a bullet or bullets through both hips, he was anxious to go. He stood up, put an arm around my shoulder and we started to walk out. We had not gone far when the Germans started shooting up flares. It was light as day and they spotted us and again opened fire, so from then on we crawled and laid low when the flares went up. We were getting near the crest of the hill when we heard our troops coming forward. I knew this was a dangerous situation, as they could only take us for Germans coming from that direction. We took cover in a shell hole and waited for them to pass. By this time, Berchtold had become weak from loss of blood. We decided it better for me to go back and get stretcher bearers. I marked the spot by a small maple tree nearby so I could find it. I went for the rear. The flares would go up and blind you. I would only come out of one shell hole to fall into another. Finally, I found the first aid station and got in touch with the officer in charge telling him what had happened and asked for the stretcher bearers to go back with me and pick up Berchtold and others. He refused, saying it would be suicide to send men out there under this heavy fire. The next morning at the first aid station I learned that Berchtold had crawled in during the night and was sent to the base hospital. I believe there was one other badly wounded soldier named Shields [Gordon Matthew Shields 1887-1928] who crawled in that night. Outside the first aid station, dead were ricked up just like cord wood, and the fields were completely covered with the dead. I have never learned what happened that could have sent our platoon into that front without any protection. The only explanation I was ever given was that the infantry got word to hold until 7:00 PM and that the runner or messenger got killed on the way to our headquarters. Anyhow the platoon was wiped out, except for perhaps half a dozen or so. I never have heard how many were left" (Ray 88).

※

It may be inferred that Sergeant Ray was unaware of the incorrect field order apparently given to Lieutenant Thorne that read 5:00 when it should have read 5:30, according to Hamilton's account of the events. Although Hamilton does not state the officer by name, Major Huidekoper was the only ranking Major in the Machine Gun Battalion chain of command.

Errors such as this would not have been uncommon with the great amount of fatigue and stress placed on the officers at that time. Major Huidekoper had nearly been killed himself by a shell less than 24 hours earlier when he was with Major Wise. The opportunity to rest or the capacity to concentrate under the constant bombardment would have tested anyone's ability for sound judgment and precise decision making. The officers were being pushed to their limits and the Command above was not going to listen to excuses. Major General Robert Lee Bullard (1861-1947), commanding the III Corps, said to his officers before the battle, "I had heard division, brigade, and regimental commanders excuse their failings to continue the advance by blaming the units on their right or left for failing to come forward with them...take no such excuse...each of your division maintains its reserves for the very purpose of protecting its flanks" (Lengel

90). This was the pressure being put on Huidekoper from his command. His men were the flanks and his men were the reserves.

Private Young of the 318th Infantry recalls the pressure experienced by the officers during these days in the line. "Orders, orders, orders, where are they coming from? No one seemed to know what they were doing in all the confusion. All the officers had a worried look on their faces, because the men were getting shot to pieces. Did General Headquarters know what was going on in here? We were looking for a counter attack any time after all this shelling. 'Orders, orders,' I said to myself, 'and they don't mean anything. If this isn't a mess I've never been in one. Don't let anyone tell you a commission office has it soft on the lines, far from it.' I actually felt sorry for them, they were catching hell coming and going" (Young).

Sergeant Ray's search to understand these happenings may partially be understood by examining the history of other units involved in this battle. When the 313th Machine Gun Battalion met heavy resistance on the afternoon of October 4 descending the hill near the Nantillois-Cunel road, it is evident that the sector between the two Divisions was still heavily occupied by German machine gun nests. The 3rd Division historian chronicled these conditions by illustrating the heavily fortified flank that would have harassed the 80th Division's attempts to advance. "At the appointed hour, our artillery [3rd Division] put over a rolling barrage, and the First Battalion [4th Infantry], accompanied by tanks, went forward in attack, jumping off at Cierges-Nantillois Road, and pushing the enemy line in the direction of Cunel. This battalion took Woods 286, reaching their northern edge in good shape, although subjected to terrific artillery and machine gun fire, the artillery fire from east of the Meuse particularly working havoc with our trips. The battalion then advanced in attack on Woods 250. This attack had been made across an open hill for a distance of 1200 meters. The tanks, in the meantime, had swept around this wood, missing the many machine guns concealed in it, due to the fact that the German machine gunners did not open on them, and had proceeded toward Cunel. While the First Battalion was advancing across the open space, it was met by such intense machine gun fire that it was unable to complete the crossing. Such heavy casualties had been suffered that it was deemed advisable to have the Second Battalion leapfrog the First Battalion and storm Woods 250. The Second Battalion went through the First

Battalion at 11 AM October 4th, and repeated attempts were made to take the woods by infiltrating, in small groups, close enough to the German positions to capture them by storm. However, the Germans evidently had a large number of machine guns in these woods, ideally placed and strongly entrenched, so that they were able to put down almost an impassable band of machine gun fire. It was clear that these positions could not be taken in daylight without incurring enormous losses" (Hemenway 69).

Further knowledge can be gained from what Worrilow and Wise were attempting to convey up the chain of command. The left flank was not secure. The 318th Infantry established a patrol of about 20 men and attempted to make liaison with the 4th Infantry on their left. Reports were coming in that the 4th Infantry had reached Cunel, which would have put them about 4 kilometers beyond Hill 274. The 318th's patrol crossed the Nantillois-Cunel Road and was in the 4th Infantry sector when they were met by heavy machine gun fire. The 3rd Division did not advance as far forward as the 318th Infantry on that day as was erroneously reported. The 313th Machine Gun Battalion was thus misinformed as to the position of the 4th Infantry. Wise recalls, "Soon a furious fire breaks out on the left. Instinctively the men take to their pits, prepared to meet a counter attack. The fire dies down. Later it is learned that the 'higher-ups' would not believe the Colonel. A machine gun battalion [C Company, 313th MGB] had been taken from brigade reserve and sent forward along the Nantillois-Cunel road. On reaching the ridge beyond Nantillois, it had come under a heavy fire from the front. So Hatfield's patrols [318th Infantry] must have been right after all. 'Watch your left,' the Colonel cautions over and over. The very silence of the hostile guns is ominous" (Wise 207).

⋘

During these few days in October, the Battalion suffered their highest rate of casualty deaths during the war, including the following members of C Company, Sergeant John E. Christenson (1892-1918), Corporal Mark McCann (1891-1918), Corporal John Eliason Conway (1886-1918), and Private First Class Frederick Arnold Warmbrodt (1894-1918).

Private First Class Curtis Alexander Dye (1890-1918), and Private Joseph Francis Cusic (1896-1918), both from B Company, were killed in Bois de Beuge, just west of Nantillois.

The bodies of John Conway and Curtis Dye were buried on the battlefield in a temporary gravesite on October 11, 1918. Unfortunately, the location of their remains is not known today. In 1928, in an effort to try and locate the remains, the Graves Registration Service (GRS) asked Chaplain Charles C. Merrill (1883-1971) to indicate on a map where he remembered having their bodies buried. Merrill indicated a location on a hand drawn map west of Nantillois, but after an extensive search, the GRS was unable to locate their remains. Conway and Dye are just two of the five men from the 313th Machine Gun Battalion currently listed as an 'open case' for the Doughboy MIA Project headed by historian and author Robert Laplander. The other three men from this Battalion who are included in the Doughboy MIA database are Joesph F. Cusic, George W. Marshall, and Louie E. Seifert.

CHAPTER 10
CAPTURING THE WOODS

I n the early morning hours of October 5, Major Charles M. Sweeny (1882-1963), 1st Battalion, 318th Infantry was on course to attempt a right flank attack of the Bois des Ogons. His troops proceeded east into the 4th Division sector and attacked a hostile position found in the Bois des Fays. These woods were not mopped up by the 4th Division and his battalion had a difficult time trying to execute the right flank maneuver.

Sweeny's battalion successfully fought through hostile machine gun nests still occupying these woods, but even after moving closer to the intended target, the continuous artillery fire pinned them to the western edge of the Bois des Fays. They remained in the woods until they were relieved the next day by a battalion of the Fourth Division.

After a difficult evening and little to no sleep, troops from Major Montague's Battalion were able to proceed under the cover of darkness and infiltrate the southern edge of the woods. They remained in that position until the morning of October 5 when another attempt was made to attack the Bois de Ogons.

At 5:30 AM a company of the 313th Machine Gun Battalion was ordered to cover the 318th Infantry with a long range fire for the planned attack. Orders were also given for an early morning artillery barrage to be placed on Ferme de la Madeleine and points north of the Bois de Ogons. This enemy sector near the farm was supporting the Germans who were still in the woods, and this area around the farm provided them a place in which they could fall back.

Wise still held his position on Hill 274 covering the left flank, while Burdick's 3rd Battalion supported Montague's attacking battalions. Both sides fought hard to control this small patch of woods. The men were being pushed by their command to take the woods, and had been under pressure for hours. The chain of command was not going to accept defeat in this sector as evidenced by the scolding that General Bullard gave Major General Cronkhite on the necessity to press the troops to take more ground. "Give it up and you are a goner. You'll lose your command in twenty-four hours. Make one more attack. This time you'll take the wood and throw the enemy out" (Ferrell 102).

Despite the continued pressure, the woods could not be taken that morning. Major James Montague (1893-1987) withdrew his men from the woods and pulled back to the slope of Hill 274 after yet another attempted push on the Bois des Ogons failed to materialize.

While reorganizing his line, three French tanks from the previous day's battle arrived back on scene to take yet another crack at attacking these ominous woods. The tanks crested the slope and were pummeled once again in plain view on the exposed slope. Moments later, the occupants of one tank abandoned their machine after having it wrecked by the hindering shells. The other two tanks turned around and headed back to Nantillois. The French crew exited the destroyed tank and retreated back on foot. A sergeant from Company K, believing these men to be German and rushing their position, hurled grenades at the men. This story is later retold by Hamilton.

On October 5, the 4th Division was ordered to assist the 80th Division by infiltrating the western edges of the Bois de Fays and the Bois de Malaumont. Meanwhile, the 3rd Division was on the southwest corner of the Bois des Ogons in the woods of Hill 250 attempting to mop up the remaining machine gun nests. After hours of fighting, orders came from the Machine Gun Battalion that Company B was relieved from duty with the 3rd Battalion, 318th Infantry and ordered to rejoin the command at Fayel Farm. Company A also rejoined the command at the same place (Affantranger 8).

At 2:07 PM, General Bullard sent this message to General Cronkhite, "Give orders for Jamerson to reorganize at once for another effort. Give him a barrage and let him follow it closely and take another attack this afternoon, at an hour to be fixed by you. Organize a good barrage for him" (Stultz 441).

The men of the 313th Machine Gun Battalion who had moved back to the area near Septsarges during the day were ordered to return back to the fight. During the small period of rest, Private Devir discovered just how badly the 313th had been shot up just hours earlier. "There it is learned that many of the boys are wounded, killed and gassed. 4:30 PM we are ordered back into the line. Only four squads can be mustered together and these are sent above Montfaucon. After getting to the hill, orders are changed and gun teams put up guns for breakthrough defense along with the 3rd Division" (Devir 27). It was during these attacks that the Battalion lost three more men; Private Floyd William Seely (1896-1918) and Bugler Clyde Frederick Jones (1888-1918) of A Company were killed along with Private Sydney Howard Reiter (1893-1918) of B Company.

"By 5:30 PM Companies A, B and D marched from Fayel Farm to Bois de Beuge and took up positions for a defense in depth of the left flank of the Brigade. Four guns in triangular woods north of the Bois de Beuge, seven guns 100 yards south east of the above woods, four guns on the northern edge of Bois de Beuge and 12 guns astride the Nantillois-Cunel road covering all of Hill 274 and approaches from north and west" (Affantranger 8).

At 6:00 PM a barrage was set down south of Bois des Ogons and rolled north through the woods to hold a line just north of the edge of the woods. Major Montague led his men across the swale and into the woods following the rolling barrage. Wise and Burdick's Battalions of the 318th were to follow in support, but were not to abandon Hill 274 without out orders. The two waves of the 2nd and 3rd Battalions were slightly delayed behind the crest of the hill as the enemy set down their own counter barrage. Although Wise and Burdick were held back on the slope, Montague was able to get past the death swale and enter the woods.

At 7:15 PM Wise sent a message to Worrilow that Montague entered woods in good order and by 8:45 PM Montague and his men gained their objective and were digging in for the final fight. By 10:00 PM on October 5 the Bois des Ogons was finally controlled by the American Army.

The memoir of Charles E. Ray describes the evening after the Division captured the woods: "The following night Major Huidekoper of Meadville sent word for me to take a detail of men and go out where we had been and pick up what machine guns we could find where the men had been killed.

He said they were needed. I took the detail from the infantry. We crawled out under the cover of darkness and recovered four machine guns, I believe. The front was quiet and I learned later that the Germans had retreated the night before so we were in no danger. However, when we got the machine guns in the light, every one of them had the water jackets full of bullet holes, so they were of no use.

A few days later we were relieved and sent back to recuperate in a wooded area several miles back of the lines and have our units refilled by new soldiers. We had been back but a few days when I along with Lieutenant Leinhauser of Philadelphia were sent to the front for laying out machine gun and emplacements. We went by pickup truck in broad daylight, crawled out and laid out the emplacements with steaks and came back without a shot being fired. I learned later we had been in plain view of the Germans, but apparently they chose to hold their fire rather than give away their location" (Ray 90).

❧

The Division was briefly relieved after its battle in the Bois des Ogons and was sent to rest in nearby Cuisy. The brutality of the events that took place taking these woods cannot be understated when looking at the sheer number of casualties suffered by the 80th Division for the period of October 4 to 8, 1918. The total casualties suffered for the 80th Division exceeded 1,800. The 318th Infantry suffered the largest losses with 83 killed, 33 died of wounds and 595 wounded. The Division's official records report casualties for the 313th Machine Gun Battalion for these five days as 14 men killed, 7 died of wounds, and 178 wounded.

While being the worst action the 313th Machine Gun Battalion experienced to date the letters written back home to the family at that time did not reiterate what the men had just experienced. The Battalion continued to rest outside Cuisy until October 8 when they were ordered to move to Bois de Malancourt for another two days. Major Huidekoper made this brief observation in his operations report about the battle: "Outside of the fact that the guns of this Battalion could have effectively stopped any attack developing on our left flank, the results obtained by use of machine guns were practically nil. The conditions existed at the time of attack where such that machine guns could be of little use in aiding infantry attack" (Headquarters Correspondence).

First Sergeant Affantranger reiterated these observations about the prior events that match the comments of Major Huidekoper, but Affantranger added these words when writing home to his family:

"To just read the above you would think that it was very easy and not very exciting, but all of this time the big German shells were hitting within 5 to 100 yards of the one they didn't hit. No nights were safe, gas masks were in continual use, and Battalion suffered considerable casualties, amounting to about 300. When companies were attached to infantry regiments it was while the infantry regiments were attacking and going over the top. A Machine Gun Battalion is very seldom used as a unit, but is split up, one company to each Infantry Regiment and two companies in reserve. They always held positions to stop counterattack (Affantranger 8).

∽

October 9, 1918 – THOMAS

I don't know when this note will leave, but it's on its way. Just to let you know I am well. We are still in and not much the worse for wear. Will write you a long letter and soon as I have time. With love to all.

October 10, 1918 - HAMILTON.

After 14 hours sleep I feel darn good. The weather is lovely, the Boche is reported in full retreat and from the number of prisoners that came through here yesterday, he is certainly getting it hot if nothing else. We expect to go back into it again sometime today. I am sorry I hoped we would be relieved but apparently there is no rest for the weary. We are winning the war and it is of utmost importance that we follow up our success and I reckon it is far more unpleasant for Jerry than for us. There isn't much glory in war, just dirt and dead horses and cold and stretcher bearers and misery, but I am fed up this morning.

Last evening saw old Jerry bring down one of our observation balloons. He certainly did a neat job. The balloon was only a few hundred yards away from us and we saw the thing very plainly. The Jerry was way up high and in spite of the 'Ardennes,' dove right for the balloon. He came down like a king fisher until only a hundred feet above the balloon, flattened out, let loose his machine gun and was up and off again in about 30 seconds. The two observers lost no time in getting out and came on down in their parachutes. For fully half a minute the balloon gave no sign of being hit, then suddenly a tiny puff of smoke and then a burst of flame and 10 seconds later the balloon was entirely gone. Just a cloud of black smoke showing where she had been. The Jerry immediately paid for his fun by being shot down by a Yank battle plane who went after him. We see planes by the hundred and any amount of air flights, also lots of balloons brought down. It is all jolly exciting, I'd give a lot to be in the air service. I think we have the edge in the air but it seems a pretty even thing and both sides lose plenty of aircraft.

Two years ago these boys were howling for war and it was the President who was howling peace at any price. Now it's just the other way around. I guess it's always been like this, the tired, hungry, dirty, fed up soldier at the front is the last person in the world that wants to fight. It's the politicians and press and just the general hysterical public that shout for blood so long as it's somebody else's, but I say I am fed up today. I don't care who licks Germany, so long as they will let me rest one more night. I think we will have peace however before snow flies and we'll go back to our wives and our napkins, our sports and our double beds, our flower gardens and books and pray God that our children won't have to fight the Hun again because it is the poorest sport I know of.

❧

On October 10 the Battalion moved again south and set up a bivouac spread out in two locations of the Bois de Cumières and Forêt de Hesse. They rested there for five days.

October 10, 1918 - HAMILTON

After a day of unrest, expecting every minute to get orders to move up, night finally came without them and we curled up in our blankets hoping for the best. The company was bivouacked in the old German front line of two years ago and it is the most frightful snarl barbed wire and old shell holes and tangled underbrush. I don't know how we would have been able to extricate the Company had orders come, and every time a twig cracked outside my tent I jumped expecting to hear and orderly say, 'The Battalion will march out in one hour.' However, the night passed and morning came and I was still in my blankets praising God.

October 10, 1918 – HOLLAND

I suppose you have begun to think I wasn't going to write. I have received several letters from you and Marie but really I haven't had any chance to write. I am well and alright in every way. I received all your mail okay and I am glad to know you got the money alright. I am not any fatter or poor as I know of, just the same Ben. Yes, I am still figuring on that Christmas. Don't worry about me. I am only one in this big war, and no doubt, I have just a good a chance as anyone. I will write more when I get a better chance.

October 11, 1918 - HAMILTON

Nothing doing all day. We are having a most remarkable mess. Yesterday donuts, lots of 'em. The kind mother used to make, and today for dinner, apple pie, all this in a forward area, under shell fire, theoretically anyhow. It certainly is fine, our American rations are perfectly splendid and our mess sergeant a wonder. In the field like this the company officers mess with the men and take it as it comes out of the pot, and it certainly is darn good food.

We got orders to move and at four o'clock and moved back 4 kilos to another wood, pitch dark when we got in, so we flapped down and went to sleep. I found an old French dugout and got into and I'll bet I have cooties directly, but it was quite warm. The men all set in less time than it takes to tell it. They make and break camp any time, any place, anywhere without confusion or delay, they are good soldiers.

October 12, 1918 – KEAN

In an Evacuation Hospital. Unfortunately, last Friday the 4th, I connected with a piece of shell. It hit me right on the front of the shoulder just in the center of the [sleeve picture drawn]. They cut it out by slicing my shoulder up so that a bird's eye view of my shoulder now looks like this [drawn picture]. Nice and red and quite a hole. They found the piece, as having gotten it from the nurse this size, as I have it and I am drawing you the outline of it [drawn picture]. It was up against my collar bone, having taken a corner off the bone and broke the collar bone. However, the arm and shoulder are O.K. and when the hole, which looks big, fills up and the bone [-] I should be as good as ever. The only trouble now is that it is difficult to get the bone to [-] when they have to remove the dressing every day to dress the wound. This hospital unit comes from Portland, Oregon and I am getting very good care and getting along finely.

One of the nurses, who has a wounded brother-in-law in the bed across the aisle took after Gunther Hoyt Corbett's children summer before last. I am trying to write Mamma a long letter but not succeeding very well as it isn't particularly comfortable sitting up as they insist on hanging my arm on the bum shoulder and its weight makes the whole business ache until I lie down. However, when prone nothing bothers me. I have been doing nothing but eating and sleep.

October 14, 1918 - HAMILTON

And orderly routed me out of bed last night to say that we would march out at 7:00 AM. So we got off at that time and came 20 slippery difficult miles to another wood and camped again. The men are very tired.

October 15, 1918 - HAMILTON

Got off to another early start and marched another 15 miles in the rain to here and actually went into billets [Ippécourt France]. The men are going under a roof for the first time in almost 2 months. They certainly appreciated it. I'll bet some of them haven't been dry through and that time and there is remarkable little sickness considering. We need new clothes like the Deuce, hardly a man in the company has a seat to his breeches and their toes are coming out of their shoes. This sort of a party certainly plays Hell with your lingerie.

I have a good place with an open fire and a red plush chair, but the French Madame of bent back and terrible age is lacking and I miss her sadly. We have a plan in our Company to get an old French woman to carry the men's packs on the road. If it's a big platoon probably a woman of about 95, quite a young woman would do. These certainly can carry practically anything and when they go by carrying two huge bundles of faggots on her head and a sack of potatoes on their back and wheeling a wheel barrow full of bricks into the bargain you can see our Army pack mules blush, I know for I've seen it.

⚜

The Battalion packed up and moved south to Ippécourt on October 15. They rested one night and then moved on to Villotte where they remained until October 24. The Division was preparing to enter into the Third Phase of the battle that took place west of the Meuse River. "The stay at Villotte was spent in drawing new equipment and drilling, using the experience of the past engagement for discovering the weak points" (Affantranger 9).

As plans were put into place, the Battalion turned in the Vickers Machine Gun and was issued the Browning Heavy Machine Gun. During this rest period, the guns were put into practice firing 2,000 rounds each before the Battalion could take them into the Third Phase of the battle.

October 17, 1918 - HAMILTON

My promotion to Captain came through during the attack. The order came through to me half an hour after Captain Kean was hit and I accepted my commission as a Captain in the U.S. Army sitting in the bottom of a trench under shell fire which may have been quite romantic, promoted on the field of battle and all that sort of thing, but I must say, I wasn't so darn pleased and later during the bloody attacks on the Bois de [Ogons] was still less pleased and would have traded jobs at any time with the meanest Buck Private in the Company. And after all, it was just a coincidence having it come through that way. It might just as easily have happened when I was in my rubber bath tub the night before last. As I've said before, promotion is all luck and goes by no logical sequence whatever. I am the only man in the Battalion who has been promoted twice, showing the great advantage of starting at the bottom.

October 17, 1918 - KEAN

Base Hospital No. 6. Just a line to say I am getting along nicely. Still in bed and only have one hand, but this business takes some time as it is not like a simple little rifle or machine gun bullet. I was evacuated from my last hospital to this one the day before yesterday. We traveled for 36 hours in a hospital train, quite comfortable I assure you, and then ended up here which is where I started from last June. This hospital is in a large château, as far as I have been able to make out in the short time I have been here and the unit is from the Massachusetts General Hospital.

October 18, 1918 - HOLLAND

Really, it's hard to write when one doesn't have any news, but if I was home, I could talk you to death. Experience makes perfect, and believe me, the boys that are over here sure knows what a home means.

Not to be bragging, but skinny Ben come in on the home heat, I don't even see a sick minute. I have been wet, cold, and sleep on the wet ground. Well, everything one could imagine, and it didn't even bother me a bit. I saw Wilbur Myers [Wilbur Richard Myers 1895-1979] today, and he said he had been looking for me for a long time. He thought I had been transferred. He is in the same Battalion as I. He said he saw Archie Hunt [Archie Sylvester Hunt 1895-1951] and he was looking for me, you know, from Atlantic [Atlantic Street, Union City, PA]. I would have liked to of saw Archie. Are John or Paul Kelly in the Army, or do you know? I don't think the Peace Talks will amount to anything, do you? They ought not to give them any show whatever, chase them off the earth is my idea.

I will soon have a service stripe. Every six months for Foreign Service, we get a stripe on our sleeve. I will be satisfied with one. I smoke cigarettes, but don't tell father. Bull Durham, that's about all we get, and one has to do something to kill time. I have a good supply, eight or ten packs now. For dinner we have beef steaks, donuts, mashed potatoes, tomatoes, gravy, coffee, good bread, and syrup. I have a big steak and bread for lunch. Before I go to bed we sure can't kick on the feed really better than Camp Lee.

October 18-20, 1918 - HAMILTON

Captain Thomas and I went to [censored] today. The 1st Division was there, and I again just missed Tante [Ethel Creighton Torrance 1876-1975] who had gone the day before to Paris and was expected back soon. I am certainly having bad luck to have missed her twice by one day when you consider what a big place France is. However, we are now both in the First Army, she in the First Corps [YMCA] and I in the Third Corps, and we certainly will see each other before long. [Censored] is full of Yank officers and men mostly out of the 1st Division who are billeted there and they certainly are a very nice looking lot of men. I bought a few things I need, saw Ham Lynch [Hampton Simpson Lynch 1892-1941] of the old 'D Troop' and came home here again bumping over the roads on a flat tire, which we were too lazy to fix.

Today is the 20th and I've rather lost count of the time. Yesterday the 19th, nothing happened but an inspection which was very highly unsatisfactory, but I didn't expect much more, we have a long way to go before our men are really 1st class, particularly as they have keep taking away all of our good N.C.O's for the Officers Training Course. We will have a memorial service today for the men of the Battalion who have been killed in battle. Then I shall go to tea with a Red Cross nurse from Boston. Tomorrow we begin work again and in one short week we will try to pull ourselves together for the next push. It's going to be a hard one too, so I am only going to have one Lieutenant available for duty with the Company instead of five. The tea party will probably fall through but I hope it doesn't because I haven't spoken to an American girl since leaving America, except Mabel Gardner who I saw for two minutes at Tavisy.

We had our memorial service this afternoon. The Battalion lined up in the rain in a hollow square and one of the Divisional Chaplains went through the service which consisted of a couple of hymns, a short prayer and a sermon. It isn't easy to do well with a 50% Catholic congregation and Episcopal hymns and singing was not too good. The sermon was rotten. I could have done it much better myself. Think of talking to a lot of tough machine gunners from Erie, PA about Oliver Goldsmith's Vicar of Wakefield, or about Rupert Brooke or about any sort of foolishness like that. It might be alright to give to Debutantes around a New York tea table, but not to a lot of soldiers standing with bowed heads in the rain to commemorate their dead comrades. He should have spoken simple words and very short, instead he used long words and spoke at length. He should have known better.

My Red Cross tea did not come off because I got orders that kept me here it does not matter much. Romance is for the time being quite

219

dead. I would like to talk to the girl but I know that I have nothing to say. I believe I must be getting old. The war does not make people old. Major Chaytor [Sir Edward Walter Clervaux Chaytor 1868-1939] who I was with for some time in the New Zealand trenches seemed like an old man. I would have guessed at least 35 or 36, yet he was 10 years younger than that. It was the same with Major Ingalls a great big burly mature fellow who you would take for over thirty was just twenty three. They had been out four years through Gallipoli and Egypt and in almost every fight in France and I suppose it is no wonder they seem old.

I've seen lots of others too, they are old and tired before they are 25, and it is an awful pity. Gas is responsible for a lot of it. Everybody gets more for less gas in them, you can't avoid it and he plays the deuce with your lungs and heart. We all got some in the last attack. I got more than a lung full myself and I've been beastly short of wind, and I suppose there are but few men who didn't get a little, and so it goes on, you get a little every time you get into a big attack and it's no good, it is very 'pas bon.' The mask is perfect protection but there is as much about that you can't help picking up a little here and there when the mask is off. Mustard gas is the worst. It is horribly poisonous and almost odorless and while most other gases dissipate very quickly, it clings to everything it touches - grass, leaves, water, the ground itself and it is possible to get the most horrible burns by sitting or kneeling in a place where gas has been, and the worst part of it is that you don't know it at the time. The burns don't come out for hours afterwards. It is certainly the invention of the Devil himself and does a lot to make the war unpleasant.

I don't remember speaking about the aerial activity in the last fight, but it is unbelievable, you see planes literally by the hundred and you see lots brought down. I saw three German planes brought down in a half-an-hour. One came crashing down on top of a hill about 1000 yards away. It stood on its nose with its tail in the air, we could see it very plainly on the skyline, and immediately and enormous crowd of Yanks gathered around looking for souvenirs, the worst darn fool thing I ever saw, there must have been a thousand in a crowd right on top of this hill, in the middle of the attack and in plain view of the Germans. The Germans immediately broke up the party by putting about 10 shells into the group which rather scattered them. Your Yank soldier is certainly an insatiable souvenir hunter.

I've seen very few air battles, most of the planes are brought down by either 'Archies' or by machine gun fire. That is the life however; the air service has it over this kind of thing 40 ways to 1. I certainly am fed up with marching on my flat feet, I'd rather fly.

I saw lots of tanks used, and they are great. I don't believe the French are as good on tanks as the British. In one place a tank went forward alone and for some unknown reason stopped and about five Frenchmen got out and crawled into a shell hole. An American platoon coming up behind saw the blue uniform and mistook it for the field gray. So the Sergeant hurled a grenade which landed very close. The lieutenant [Robert Higgins 1894-1969] was about to hurl another when he realized that they were French. He was trying to get the pin back in his grenade when one of the French stepped out and waved his hand. 'Pretty hot up that way?' said the lieutenant fumbling with his bomb. 'Wee' said the Poilu not having the least idea that the first bomb which had incidentally wounded one of them had been thrown by a Yank.

October 19, 1918 – THOMAS

I haven't had a chance to sit down and write you a letter for almost a month, but will try to do so tonight. We are back in reserve, that is about 20 miles back from the lines, we are where only occasionally we can hear the guns and you haven't an idea of what a wonderful thing the quiet is. It lets your nerves get easy and you feel all well again. I was three weeks without a bath, and without a change of anything but socks. I don't know when we will go back, but imagine in about a week. I lost a large bunch of my company in the last fight but our only part was support. We hope to get a chance to kill a few Boche this next trip.

I'll admit I don't like the big guns much. They are the best argument for peace I know of, but we are all anxious to go to it and give the old Boche our continuous round until his heart is broken, and it is pretty badly bent now. Jimmy got right badly gassed and half of my life is taken away from me. There is some talk that he won't come back but I hope that is not true and look for him every day. War is not very nice, but at other times it isn't so bad. I am just about as I thought I would be. I think about my company naturally more than I do myself and it makes it a lot easier. We are drilling pretty hard now and will be ready in a week.

You can't spend much money up here and I am saving practically all I make. Leaves have started for the men, and I hope will continue. I don't think we will get any till the war is over. Right now it looks like it might be over by Thanksgiving or might go on indefinitely. I think it is one of the two things. It is funny to think that the next few weeks will be the most wonderful in history probably. The Canadians all said that the day would come when we would all drive the heart out of the Hun and that is what is happening. It's a hard fight in here though, and one that will leave its mark on a lot of us I guess.

I'm the senior Captain in the Battalion just at present. John Kean got hit by a piece of shrapnel. Not badly, but enough to put him out for a while. The country is certainly doing wonderful things, isn't it? It is the only way. I saw a fresh bunch of Hun prisoners coming in today. They are a tired looking lot now. It is evident that they are holding out promises of an early peace to them. I don't see how it can come though and don't know that I care so much to see it unless it is an unconditional surrender. I'll tell you all about it one of these days, in the meantime, it is what I want to be doing and it won't be bad in the long run. I would like to be with the bunch going into Belgium. It must be wonderful to be going into Hills. There is a bunch of mail in tonight and will all in probability get some either now or in the morning so will get some mail anyway. I don't need anything at all so don't bother. You can send what you feel like in the Christmas boxes. I hope my watch got home safely. I suppose I will hear tonight. Love to all. Maybe we will hear good news shortly.

❧

The Battalion left Vilotte on October 24 at about 8:30 AM for Le Neufour, arriving there about Noon the same day and bivouacked in the woods near Les Islettes. Twenty eight new replacements augmented the strength of the Battalion. The time spent here was devoted to signal school, learning to shoot the Browning machine gun and target practice.

October 24, 1918 – KEAN

Well my arm is out of its sling, and the hole is closing up and it is not perfectly comfortable when I sit up, so I think I will write you a long letter, and tear up the one I started on the October 8th that I wasn't able to finish.

After a day or so in that dug out, or to be exact, after staying there from September 29th 10:00 PM to September 30th 9:00 PM, we moved, and the Division went over the top again. My command post was in the Brigade reserves and about 7:30 AM on October 4th our Major directed me to take my Company and the other Company in machine gun reserves forward about three kilometers. I got them safely up into a field, on the back of a hill, without loss and was standing in a shallow trench about 9:15 looking around to see if I couldn't find a better place for the men and the transport when something hit me on the shoulder and knocked me down to my knees.

My Lieutenants asked if I was all right, and I said I guess so, as my shoulder felt as though I had received a bad kick in a fast ball game. I thought I had been hit by a rock, or some earth thrown up by a shell. In three or four minutes one of my Lieutenants came over to me looked at me and announced that I had a hole in my sleeve. I still didn't believe that the skin had been broken, but we decided to look, and when he got my coat off we discovered 'beau corp,' blood on the shirt, so he got ahold of a hospital corps orderly, who bandaged me up. I started to walk back to the rear, as my arm was so stiff, I wasn't much good and we weren't doing anything anyhow. At this time I was at least three kilometers from the front line, and I was the first casualty from my Company, with the exception of the two men who were killed on the Somme, rather ridiculous. I was also the 4th casualty in the Battalion as far as I know, as we had been very lucky.

It was quite a sight that morning, exactly like a moving picture, a drawing or painting of a battle, lots of aeroplanes, shells bursting all around, artillery and their [limbers] behind every fold of ground, and small columns of infantry moving over the bare hills. All in the open and all one grand jamourer.

I walked back to where I started from and told the Major we had gotten to where he wanted us and that I had been hit. He send an orderly with me, though I demurred, to where I knew I could get an ambulance. I don't know here the thought of where I would go, but I got to the aid station OK and they shot me with A.T.S. [anti tetanus serum]. Then I climbed on the front seat of an ambulance, and got a three hour ride to an evacuation hospital. There they gave me a cigarette, a cup of chocolate, re-dressed my hole, painted it with iodine, took off my clothes, and put me to bed. By the way, that has been my last acquaintance with clothes. The next morning at 3:00 AM they loaded me on a stretcher and put on me on a train. It was a very nice Red Cross hospital train that was built in England. They moved me south to Base Hospital Number 46 which is another evacuation hospital. I arrived there at 3:00 PM. That night, at about 9:30 PM, they put me to sleep, sliced my shoulder, and took out the piece of shell. I rather enjoyed the etherization. They told me a piece of clavicle, collar bone, or something, had been chipped off. They tied my arm up tight, which made it rather uncomfortable. As I told you before, that hospital was a Portland, Oregon unit and the surgeon who operated on me was Major Joyce [Dr. Thomas Martin Joyce 1885-1947]. I considered that hospital an excellent one on every way and they certainly took good care of me. There was a commissary there and one could get chocolates and cigarettes a plenty, also lots to eat; the first place, except the debarkation camp that I had been able to get them. The Red Cross, which does everything for you as soon as you get in a hospital, presented me with a bag containing the writing paper, socks, slippers, tooth brush, comb, razor, shaving brush, shaving soap, and handkerchiefs.

From Saturday PM until a week from the next Tuesday, at about 6:00 AM when they loaded me on another train, just like the other one, and after traveling about 36 hours, we arrived at Base Hospital No. 6, Bordeaux about 10:00 PM. As the place was crowded, another fellow and I had a room together in the medical ward. The room had a nice fire place, and you can imagine, that it was nice to have a fire, lots to eat, candy, cigarettes and a bed. Now, however, I am in the surgical ward as they keep moving us about and soon I will be out entirely. They took an x-ray of my shoulder the other day and said that except for a piece being off 'the something', it is all right. So they unstrapped my arm and I am gradually getting the stiffness out of it. The hole is almost beginning to heal up and when it does, I will be out, and then I hope back to the

Company. I guess it will take at least a couple of weeks before I get out of here, and then perhaps a week more to find my Company, if I am lucky enough to get back to it. They are funny about those things sometimes. They send you back right off to your own Division and then sometimes they don't.

October 28, 1918 – LEINHAUSER

Left for Saint Juvin to lay out barrage positions. Everything was quite on the front. Met my brother Frank [Frank J. Leinhauser 1894-1954] at Fléville.

On October 29 the Battalion was ordered to be placed into position on October 31 and ready to fire a barrage. The infantry officers had been making reconnaissance missions to the area in the days proceeding, in order to prepare for the upcoming offensive. In this engagement the 80th Division did not use their own artillery. Instead, they were supported by the 82nd Division, 157th Field Artillery Brigade. Attached to this Brigade was the 320th Field Artillery Regiment. They too were moving their battery forward between October 26-30th to prepare for the November 1st Offensive. In the small village of Fléville, Otto Leinhauser of the Battalion had a chance meeting with his brother Frank Leinhauser who was attached to the 320th Field Artillery.

The points occupied by the Division included the road between Saint Juvin and Sommerance, and areas west of the road between Fléville and Sommerance. During the preparation and staging, these locations were under continuous shell fire from the enemy in terms of both high explosive shells and gas shells. It was in this part of France that Lieutenant Leinhauser of the Battalion was wounded.

October 29, 1918 – LEINHAUSER

Don't move until further orders. Got wounded. Went to evacuation Hospital 116 and got operated on. Had ether, some sensation. Awoke at 8:00 AM.

Leinhauser mentioned in his journal on October 28 that he was laying out the machine gun positions near Saint Juvin, but his entry the next day suggests that he was in a position awaiting further orders. The circumstances of how he was wounded are unclear. Lieutenant Hamilton wrote home that Leinhauser "blew himself up with the detonator of an aerial torpedo" (Hamilton December 21, 1918). Leinhauser's wound may have occurred as a result of an accident.

After Leinhauser was injured, he was evacuated to a field hospital and then loaded onto a train and sent to Paris where he was operated on at Hospital No. 3, a Red Cross Military Hospital. Leinhauser wrote that he considered his wound 'slight' and that he was "feeling fine" (Leinhauser October 31, 1918). He was happy with the treatment he received by the doctors and nurses at this hospital and was able to write a letter home to his wife the same day of the surgery. Leinhauser returned back to the Battalion after about 50 days of rest. Fortunately, Leinhauser was able to write home to his wife about his condition due to the delay in the delivery of the Army telegram and the nature of the message would have surely caused tremendous worry to his family.

Western Union to Elizabeth Leinhauser, Dated November 29, 1918: DEEPLY REGRET TO INFORM YOU THAT IT IS OFFICALLY REPORTED THAT FIRST LIEUT OTTO P. LEINHAUSER MACHINE GUN BATTALION WAS SEVERLY WOUNDED IN ACTION OCTOBER THIRTIETH, FURTHER INFORMATION WHEN RECEIVED.

◅ৡ

October 28-29, 1918 – THOMAS

My Company is reorganized and I have the guns you wrote of. They are really worth waiting for. They are marvelous guns. It was very easy for us to master them as this is the third gun we have had and this one is comparatively simple.

Things are about the same with me. We are very comfortable and have been blessed with three days clear weather. October 29, just got news of Austria's vote. It rather looks like peace for the minute, but I suppose there will be quite a bit more of it yet. Nobody wants the war to go on, but unless Germany really admits that she has had enough, it will go on without a breathing spell.

I wrote this letter to you more especially to enclose you this paper which is one of many dropped by Boche planes over our lines. It is rather a unique souvenir. One of my men found it about 200 yards from where I am now.

I was up at the front the day before yesterday. It was still the same. I went up to the lines to make a little reconnaissance and had a Hun sniping at me on several occasions. But the little bullets are not bad. It is the big ones crashing that I don't like.

Fritz wasn't doing much shelling however, so I really had a nice trip. The Old Division has its tail way up in the air now, and would put up one hell of a scrap if called on. Give us a start and we could go strong now.

❧

On October 29, Major Huidekoper wrote to Major General Cronkhite that Captain John Kean was dropped from the rolls of the Battalion and that Robert Ballantine Bradley (1886-1953) was promoted to Captain to fill this vacancy (Headquarters Correspondence).

On that same day, Field Order No. 27 was issued to the Battalion and read in part, "The First American Army, while continuing its operations east of the MEUSE, will attack on its front west of the MEUSE in the near future. The 80th Division will cover the left of the 5th Corps. It will seize the high ground to the north of SIVRY lez BUZANCY on the first day. The first objective IMMECOURT (exclusive) – ALLIEPONT (inclusive). Second objective MALMY – SIVRY lez BUZANCY (inclusive). The 313th and 314th Machine Gun Battalions will, under direction of the Division Machine Gun Officer, execute long range overhead and indirect fire from H minus 1 hour to the time of safety of the infantry advance. After the execution of this fire, these battalions will not move forward but will revert to the Division Reserve. Combat troops will be in position at D day at H minus 4 hours. The attack will be pushed with the utmost vigor" (Stultz 508).

The next day the Division received orders to move forward. At 11:00 AM the 313th Machine Gun Battalion marched forward from Le Neufour, through Le Four de Paris, Hameau Détruit, where they rested for the night in Bois d'Apremont.

D Day was set for November 1 with artillery preparations set at 3:30 AM. The infantry began advancing behind a moving barrage at 5:30 AM. Sergeant Major Affantranger wrote of the Battalion's location, "On October 31st we left the above location at 4:00 PM and marched to location north of Saint Juvin for firing the opening barrage. Companies took up positions on an approximate line from K-8161 to K-9159 on Buzancy Map 1/20,000. Just before taking up this position all packs were taken off and put in a former stable and we had no more than vacated the place than a big shell came over and hit the building, setting it on fire. It sure was a close shave" (Affantranger 9).

CHAPTER 11
THE FINAL PUSH

At the start the new offensive, the First Corps faced a German defensive line that stretched the 80th Division from the southern part of Bois de Bourgogne, down to Saint Juvin and over to Landres-et-Saint-Georges (Craighill 70). The Division was called upon to attack and secure the high ground north of Sivry les Buzancy, located about 10 kilometers north of Saint Juvin. The jump off line was the Saint Juvin-Saint Georges Road. The difficulty in taking enemy machine gun positions in this area was earlier identified by officers that scouted the area only days before the big push. Because the offensive was originally planned to start on October 28th, some of the infantry officers made reconnaissance of the area. Senior officers up the chain of command were warned that a barrage could potentially over reach many of the significant defensive positions held by the Germans due to the lay of the terrain (Lukens 120).

The 160th Infantry Brigade was made up of the 319th and 320th Infantry Regiments and the 159th Infantry Brigade consisted of the 317th and 318th Infantry Regiments. The Division strength stood at 12,897 men. General Cronkhite used the 160th Brigade to lead the advance on the first day of battle. The plans called for them to move up to the front lines that were being held by the 82nd Division. The Brigade moved through the positions held by the 82nd without the enemy expecting an attack. The 159th Brigade came in behind 160th and held the Division's reserve. On October 30-31 the troops waited in their foxholes keeping out of the view of the enemy scouting planes.

The 80th Division sent two Infantry Regiments, side by side, over the top at H-Hour. The 319th Infantry took the right side of the front line and the 320th Infantry was positioned on the left. The 313th and 314th

Machine Gun Battalions supported the attack with a machine gun barrage. The two machine gun battalions were initially attached the 160th Infantry Brigade for the start of the attack, but were ordered not to advance with the infantry.

Historian of the 319th Infantry recalled the start of the attack: "During the night machine guns had been brought up and put in position from which they could rake the German front line. There were seventy-five machine guns to the regimental front. At 5:00 AM they opened fire. It was terrific. The air was filled with smoke, gas, and powder fumes. The machine gun fire was so effective that large quantities of trench mortar shells were later captured in the German front lines as they were unable to work their guns" (Ryman 53).

Major Huidekoper recorded the 313th Machine Gun Battalion putting down their machine gun barrage at 4:30 AM and fired until about 6:10 AM. The first wave of the infantry assault was spread over an area of about two kilometers wide. The 320th Infantry occupied the left side and included Companies K and M, each company having about 50 men. At 5:30 AM these 100 men went forward with about ten yards of space between each man. They followed the rolling barrage while incoming enemy shelling fell upon them. Companies I and L of the 320th Infantry followed behind the first wave. Lieutenant Englar McClure Rouzer (1887-1980) of the 320th Infantry recalled the scene: "This unorganized crowd of about 75 men, recruited after darkness and mostly unknown, was placed under my command. In addition to the telephone, we had all kinds of signal apparatus, a bunch of pyrotechnics that would have delighted the heart of any boy, panels for airplane signaling and finally, late in the evening, we received a basket of pigeons. It all sounded very well, but the German shells soon put our telephone out of commission, red rockets prove to be white, our aviators were taking a vacation that day and my next site of the basket of pigeons was three days after the Armistice when, with Colonel Gordon, I went over the battlefield and ran across the basket and the dead pigeons beside a fresh grave that told its own story" (Lukens 146).

As Companies K and M of the 320th Infantry moved forward, they were met with opposing machine gun fire. As warned what may occur, the American Army barrage did not destroy significant machine gun nests located on the northern slope of Ravin aux Pierres. The assaulting infantry were targeted by the well positioned enemy guns and the advance came at a high price. After about three hours of fighting and multiple casualties, the 320th Infantry was finally able to pass through this initial ravine. Lieutenant Lukens wrote of the first day, "Our whole line had suffered heavily and had fought for every yard of ground on that first day, but our battalion, which formed the assaulting waves of our regiment, had been caught in an especially bad hole. The American barrage, tremendous as it was, had at that point been too 'long,' and had left untouched a row of Boche nests between our men and the bombarded ground, so that when 'H' hour came the battalion was met with as murderous a fire as though the barrage had never fallen. The Major and the Colonel had known of this defect in the artillery plans the previous night and had appealed frantically to have them changed, but it was a Corps plan and someone on the Staff, way back in safety, had 'known it all,' and had refused to amend the orders to the batteries. It was no more the fault of the artillery line officers than of the infantry; like most blunders, it was made higher up, or, at least, farther back. All day men had fallen and little advance had been made, but meanwhile the 319th on our right was making better progress, and when early the next morning a new start was made, it was found that most of the Boche had pulled out on account of this menace to their flank, and our advance gained speed at a surprising rate. Then later in the day the fresh 159th Brigade relieved the 160th, and went on at a merry clip for the momentum was so great that the Boche guns could not stop long enough to fire, and the machine guns that our men overran and cleaned out were in improvised rear-guard positions rather than in organized system of protected nests" (Lukens 120).

The advance of the 319th Infantry on the right side indeed pushed farther, and at a faster pace than what the 320th Infantry encountered on the first day. Companies E and H of the 319th Infantry passed through the 82nd Division at 5:30 AM, followed by Companies G and F some 500 yards behind the first wave. The 319th Infantry attacked in liaison with the 2nd Division Marines on their right. They were hoping to take Imécourt as their first objective.

As the 319th Infantry advanced, their initial casualties were heavy, but their counter attack was just as fierce. As they pushed through the day they were successful in forcing over 200 Germans to surrender from their trenches along with forcing the enemy to give up multiple machine guns and field artillery pieces. By evening, notwithstanding their heavy casualties, the 319th Infantry advanced the Division over 8 kilometers on the first day to reach Imécourt. However, the rapid advance exposed their left flank giving the enemy an opportunity to attack Companies E and G (Ryman 54).

Upon completion of this first day's barrage, the control of the 313th Machine Gun Battalion was returned to the 159th Brigade Commander, Lieutenant Colonel Buchanan. This field message was sent from Major Huidekoper to Buchanan via a motorcycle messenger, "Barrage successfully completed 6:10 AM. Only two casualties. P.C. at K8851. Transport on Road Chehery to Exermont between Harold P.C. and Exermont. Two companies at K-8160. Two companies at K-8958. Will remain here and await further orders" (Headquarters Correspondence).

The infantry advanced without the support of the machine gun battalion and Major Huidekoper later recorded, "With the rapid advance, the difficulty experienced by infantry commanders in accurately locating any machine guns and the uncertainty as to exact location of friendly troops, the opportunities to machine gun fire in support of infantry attacks were very few" (Headquarters Correspondence).

Despite not advancing further with the infantry regiments, the officers were pleased with the results of their new gun. It was the first time the Battalion went into combat with their Browning Heavy Machine Gun. Each gun fired about 4,000 rounds when they attacked at Saint Juvin and the gun performed well as Major Huidekoper wrote, "Stoppages were very few, and in most cases were due to faulty ammunition, faulty bolt loading or incorrect headspace adjustment and not due to mechanical deficiencies in the gun. The simplicity of the gun, freedom from stoppages, its rapidity of fire and close grouping all tend to imbue the men with confidence in it. The range of the gun should in my estimate be increased. The tripod could be made both simpler and lighter. It is, however, the best machine gun ever used by the United States Army" (Headquarters Correspondence).

Following the end of their barrage, the Battalion assembled in a ravine about 1 kilometer west of Sommerance on the evening of November 1 and waited for their next orders.

November 1, 1918 - HAMILTON

Well, I've been in another big attack. The First American Army went over the top on September 26, 1918 and again this morning. Among those present on both occasions was myself. Someday I'm going to write about the psychology of going into an attack, just now I've too much else on my mind, but it is a darn interesting subject and the most interesting thing about it is that nine out of ten people feel exactly the same way. The tenth man is a fire eater and is out for blood. When he smells powder he wants to kill something. The other nine men don't like it for a bang, and go over the top with a strange mixture of emotions. I think almost everyone is scared, and your mind works around in a circle, and the circle contains the following possibilities: 1. A nice blight and visions of a soft white bed and a soft eyed nurse. 2. Being blown to absolute atoms by a large shell, most unpleasant picture, immediately banished from thought only to recur. 3. Doing something heroic, and getting a medal, and being given the freedom of Tenafly, New Jersey. Kissed by beautiful girls fêted by Dukes, etc., and all the while, most modest about it all. 4. Just being shelled, and gassed, and cold, and miserable, and unfed. This is so probable that it does not awake the imagination much. 5. Peace, oh! oh! oh! Blessed peace!

And so it goes, and so you go, over the top with the best of luck, and your mind a whirl. After all, it is a great adventure, the greatest almost in the world. You never know five minutes ahead what is going to happen and I've given up guessing. My word, what an adventure. I don't think anybody has ever properly written it up. The dark narrow roads jammed with every known vehicle of war from a bicycle to a tank. Traffic blocked for 5 miles in both directions, everybody cursing, and swearing, and trying to get his particular thing through. Dead horses, tired men, the smell of high explosive and blood. Rolling kitchens, walking wounded, Army mules, motor trucks, and shells, shells, shells. The general's cars with red stars on them and the right of way. Immaculate U.S.M.P.s Military Police standing at shell torn crossroads, in shell torn villages. Traffic like 5th Avenue's best. YMCA girls way up front, causing a furor wherever they go. Everything is as dark as the 'can and must' hole at Cedar Ridge because the attack is to be a surprise and Jerry has been known to bomb the flicker of a match.

Hallelujah, Amen, but I don't reckon I'll ever forget these marches up to the front lines the night before a big push. When there are the long pulls across country after you have left the road, when you probably lose your way, or your guide does it for you, and you go stumbling into shell holes and barbed wire with the company cursing and sweating with their machine gun kit behind you. And the word is passed up from the tail of the column to go a little slower as they are double timing and can't keep up and you are going as slow as you can walk. And then the getting into position with old Jerry sending up flares and you wondering whether or not he knows that you are going to be up and at him in the morning. And so I could go on indefinitely, and maybe someday I will write it all up, but not today. Sitting in a 6 x 3 bivvy under shell fire, waiting for orders to move up again.

November 1, 1918 – AFFANTRANGER

On November 1st the barrage was fired from 4:30 AM to 6:10 AM. It was another peach of a barrage. Of course lots of funny incidents happened, but one particular thing happened that I will never forget. This first night Headquarters Company were bivouacked on the side of an embankment which looked pretty good as a shelter from the big ones that Jerry was sending over. In the particular dugout or hole in the ground that I had were also Kyle Huff [1901-1963] from New Mexico, John Wilson [1895-1919], a fellow by the name of Anderson [Henry Brown Anderson 1894-1980], who had been studying for the ministry, and I think Welk [Leroy Edmond Welk 1891-1983]. Huff was a fellow that had joined the Army to see some action and funny as the devil. Anderson was a quiet easy-going sort of fellow, and the two of them together were a laugh at any time. Every time we would get to sleep a big one would come over and someone would holler 'Gas!' and on would go the darned old gas mask. Anderson told Huff that he would sleep with his gas mask right on his chest as per instructions so that he could find it if the gas alarm were given in the middle of the night. Huff just sort of laughed and in his funny way said, 'Yeah, I guess you are right about it Andy' and then deliberately took it off and placed it under his head for a pillow. Well, we finally got to sleep and we were knocking them off in great shape, considering the noise, when all of a sudden a big shell landed very close or in the hollow where we were. The Sentinel yelled 'Gas!' in my mask was on in the prescribed six seconds all right, and then I began to feel around to see if the rest were okay. Huff was sure in a pickle. It was pitch dark and he was yelling 'You have got my mask, where the hell is the damn thing. Dammit to hell who moved that mask etc. etc."

I sure thought he was a goner, and he probably would have been had there been any gas. In spite of the seriousness of the incident it was the funniest experience I can remember. He was the most scared boy in the Army right then. After the signal to remove masks had been given Mr. Huff immediately lit a candle against orders, but covered with a blanket, and proceeded to tie the mask on his chest and keep it there. I never laughed so hard in my life and he said 'Shore nuff, I believe Andy was right' and he never took the mask off again while we were in the lines.

This is the only one of the funny things that happened, but I could never relate them all and I will have to save them until I get back. I always managed to keep Huff close because he sure was a dose for the blues at any time.

That same night, I believe it was the closest a lot of us ever came to bidding goodbye to this old war. We heard the old shell singing through the air and could tell for some reason or other by the sound that it was coming directly toward our bivvy. It all happened in a few seconds, but it seemed a week and it seems as though everything I had ever done ran through my mind at that time at that time. The shell seemed to come over the top of our bivvy so close that if I had put my hand over the top it would have taken it off. It hit directly in front of the bivvy and tore a hole that you could bury a couple of horses in and scattered all over the place. The next morning they found pieces of shrapnel in every bivvy of the Headquarters Company but ours. I wrote a letter home immediately after that because I was for once satisfied that I could not be coming back. It was very little sleep we got the rest of that night.

I must remark right here about Major Huidekoper. During the night of the barrage, near daybreak, he sent for a runner and I sent Huff out and they went to visit all of the Companies. Huff said he was scared stiff all of the time, but the Major seemed never to worry a bit and would walk along with the shells bursting right and left of him and he never paid a bit of attention to them. Around the Companies he went, telling each Platoon they were firing slow, fast, or whatever the case might be. It sure is a wonder he was not knocked off, but he wasn't even touched.

Several other instances happened that led me to believe he wasn't afraid of anything" (Affantranger 10).

❧

Despite the difficulty encountered by the 320th Infantry on November 1, the Division was pleased with the progress on the first day of battle. Plans later that day called for the 159th Brigade to pass through the 160th Brigade to take up the attack. It was 12:30 AM, November 2, when a field message arrived with orders to give the 317th Infantry two companies of machine guns. Companies A and D of the 313th Machine Gun Battalion, along with Battery E of the 321st Field Artillery, were sent to support the 317th Infantry in their move to outflank the woods north of Alliépont, just west of Imécourt. Their objective was to move the Division farther forward and obtain the ridge west of Buzancy. The 317th Infantry staged their line along the Bayonville-Verpel road. Orders called for an 8:00 AM artillery preparation, followed by a 10 minute standing barrage.

The 317th Infantry advanced forward on the right sector of the Division the morning of November 2. The 3rd Battalion, along with D Company of the Machine Gun Battalion, took the right position. The 2nd Marine Division was on their right. The 1st Battalion, along with A Company of the Battalion, moved forward on the left. A machine gun barrage was put down to support the infantry's advance. The 317th moved forward at 10:00 AM and by 1:00 PM they advanced into Sivry les Buzancy. Further progress beyond this point was held up by enemy fire that came from the ridges north and northeast of Buzancy as the enemy concentrated a defensive front line to protect their subsequent retreat.

"Part of A Company, Second Platoon under Lieutenant Whitten [Harold Edwin Whitten 1893-1967] in Buzancy are under heavy shelling. That night a shell kills Private John Manion [John Francis Manion 1894-1918] and wounds several others in Buzancy" (Devir 29).

The Germans were falling back to the area around Harricourt and Bar-lès-Buzancy. Major Huidekoper wrote, "On November 2, it was reported that the enemy was in full retreat. Early reports from the advance units of the Brigade showed the enemy was retiring, covering his retirement with a skillfully arranged defense consisting of machine guns and artillery, which by heavy firing during the day and early hours of the night endeavored to delay our advance. After midnight this fire was decreased and the defense was withdrawn to a new and previously organized position" (Headquarters Correspondence).

November 2, 1918 - HAMILTON

I said you never can tell what is going to happen, and you can't. The afternoon of the first day, we were recalled from our advanced positions and moved back about 2 kilometers and bivouacked for the night. Bobby Stoddart and I, and two orderlies, slept in a 'bivvy' about as big as a Pullman lower, and it was a squeeze. At 2:00 AM I heard them calling for A and D companies and I shivered for fear they would want C Company to go too, but my luck was good, and they didn't take us out. Although Companies A and D had to march at about 3 AM, and it was darn bad.

Today we set out about three in the afternoon and marched to [Sivry les Buzancy]. We got there after dark and found the town just evacuated by the Germans and in pretty fair condition. I put almost the whole company in an old barn full of straw and we lay down to get a little sleep. He shelled the town during the night and hit the house next door wounding 20 men [318th Infantry].

While A and D Companies were settled in with the 317th Infantry, B and C Companies of the Battalion were ordered to report to the 318th Infantry. They marched forward from their reserve positions in the evening and joined the rest of the Battalion at Sivry les Buzancy to billet for the night. The march took place during a pouring rain and the men traversed muddy, congested, and shell torn roads. The regimental headquarters was established in the village and any available building or barn was used to house the weary men. In one of these barns a group of officers from the 318th Infantry gathered for a conference that evening. The building was about thirty yards from the regimental headquarters. While planning took place in the barn to prepare for the next day's attack, a German artillery shell came through the roof and exploded, killing or wounding many of the officers. This was a tremendous setback for the Regiment as many of these officers were slated to lead the early morning attack.

237

For the next few days the 159th Brigade continued to keep pressure on the retreating enemy forces and pushed the line forward. Plans called for the attack to continue on November 3 with a change in the Division's direction, advancing northeast instead of due north. The 318th Infantry was in line on the left, with the 77th Division on their left. The 317th Infantry was still positioned on the right with the 2nd Marines on their right. By morning a gap of almost 1 kilometer occurred between the Marines and the right-side of the 317th. The 3rd Battalion of the 317th was ordered to close up this gap and extend their line into the sector being held by the Marines. This move required the 1st Battalion of the 317th to cover a greater portion of the front line. Despite this larger sector, the 317th advanced quickly and by noon they advanced over two kilometers.

On morning of November 3, Major Burdick's 3rd Battalion, 318th Infantry, left Sivry les Buzancy ready to lead the day's advance. Company B of the Machine Gun Battalion was assigned to support Major Burdick's unit. The infantry occupied the left side of the Division's zone and moved into position about 7:15 AM that morning. The attacked called for advancing at 8:00 AM through an area that was previously in the zone of the 77th Division. Major Burdick did not have an exact location of the 77th Division's front line in that sector, but expected the enemy to still be holding a defensive position near Harricourt as they moved forward in a northwesterly direction. Major Sweeny's 1st Battalion followed behind Burdick with Company C machine guns as their support.

The advance was slow as the men traversed through a swamp located just south of the Buzancy and Bar-lès-Buzancy Road. The area though which they passed was under heavy artillery shelling. It was during this advance on November 3, 1918 that Private First Class Wallace Ben Holland was killed. His machine gun squad was hit by an artillery shell killing Holland and wounding two others. Captain Robert Stoddart provided an eyewitness account of Holland's death in a report to the Division Adjudant, Major Carl H. Tobey (1888-1954) stating, "The soldier was killed by shell fire in a field 1 km south of Buzancy while his company was following an assault Battalion of the infantry" (Burial File).

For two days, Holland's body remained on the battlefield as the fighting continued. He was buried in a shallow grave in Buzancy on November 5, and a wooden cross was erected to mark his burial with one of his metal identification tags attached to the cross and the other tag remained on his body. Chaplain Luther W. Clark (1886-1957) of the 305th Engineers completed the Grave Location Form specifying the location of Holland's burial with grid coordinates that later identified the position of his temporary grave.

Back home in Pennsylvania, Holland's family received an erroneous report in mid-December stating that Holland "had been seriously wounded in action in France on November 5" and that the "extent of his injuries are not known" ("Union City Boy"). It is unclear when the family unofficially learned of his death.

Private John W. Charles Jr. (1896-1918) was wounded by the shelling and had to be transported to a rear hospital, but he only survived ten days and died from his wounds on November 13, 1918.

November 3, 1918 - AFFANTRANGER

The Battalion P.C. moved from Sivry to Buzancy, arriving there about 4:00 PM while the Germans were going out the other end. The town was still burning and the Germans were shelling it to beat the band. The Battalion P.C. located in a building on the Main Street in a place used by the Red Cross of the Germans, on the eastern side of the road to Bouziers 100 feet south of the road to Thénorgues. Casualties to date, one man killed and nine wounded, four horses killed (Affantranger 10).

November 3, 1918 - HAMILTON

We got up at 4:30 AM and had a hot breakfast and marched out. We were with and assault battalion and had no idea what we were in for. We marched into heavy shell fire going up to position and I had one man killed and two wounded.

We then attacked the advance practically without resistance for 10 kilometers. This was the first time I've gone along with the first infantry wave and it was great sport. We were held up just as it got dark by heavy machine gun fire, but it was too dark to attack; we dug in for the night. We had a wet rainy night. I slept out with my orderly under a tree.

∽

After the 318th Infantry made it across the swamp, Major Burdick's Battalion advanced rapidly and made liaison with the 77th Division near Bar-lès-Buzancy. At 3:00 PM the infantry reached as far north as the Saint Pierremont-Sommauthe road, but they were pushed back by harassing machine gun nests that continued to defend the enemy's slow retreat. It took the evening of November 3 and into the early morning hours of November 4 to destroy most of these machine gun nests. At 8:00 AM that morning, Major Sweeny's 1st Battalion passed through the 3rd Battalion to take up the fight.

Major Sweeny was given Company C of the Machine Gun Battalion, along with two Stokes mortars and two 37mm guns. His advance that morning was rapid, but this progress also led to having both his right and left flanks dangerously exposed to the enemy.

"In order to make further progress, it became necessary to take the town of Sommauthe and the dominating heights of Hill 314 just south thereof, within the sector of the unit on our right. This was done, the town was handed over to D Company of the 317th Infantry, and the advance proceeded" (History of the 318th).

The 317th Infantry, on the right-side of the Division, had their 2nd Battalion pass through the 3rd Battalion at 6:30 AM and continue the attack. The 2nd Battalion moved forward and occupied Vaux-en-Dieulet, but by 7:00 AM it was stopped by the enemy who had taken Hill 314 just south Sommauthe. The 1st Battalion fought hard to reach Sommauthe by 10:00 AM and with the 318th Infantry flanking from the west, Hill 314 and Sommauthe were eventually taken by the Americans. The 318th handed the hill over to the 317th and the entire Brigade was ordered to advance to Beaumont-Stonne road.

On the left, the 1st Battalion also received fire from three key German positions, namely Hill 278, La Polka Ferme and Ferme d'Isly. Hill 278 was within the zone of the 77th Division, but the harassing fire stretched far enough to reach into the sector occupied by the 80th Division. It took the entire day of November 4 and into the early morning hours to ultimately take these three strongholds. During the morning of November 5, patrols with the 1st Battalion made their way past La Polka Ferme and Ferme d'Isly and stopped at a steam east of Mont du Cygne.

November 3, 1918 - AFFANTRANGER

The Battalion P.C. moved at 4:00 AM about 4 kilometers north of Buzancy where we bivouacked for the night in a ravine. Jerry bombed Buzancy that night and it was the worst bombing that I ever heard or saw. There must have been 10 or 15 planes that flew over our heads towards Buzancy, and when they arrived they all dropped their loads. I wish you could have heard it. We sure had moved out of that place in time alright.

At 9:07 AM the Battalion P.C. moved to Sommauthe, locating there in the northwest corner of Central Square. At 2:15 PM Company D was transferred from the 3rd Battalion 317th infantry to the 2nd Battalion per verbal orders of Colonel Keller (Affantranger 10).

November 3, 1918 - DEVIR

The whole company passes through Buzancy. Private Hoburn [William Roy Hoburn 1892-1918] is killed and several other transport service are wounded when a shell lands in their midst at Sirvy. Gun teams in platoons under command of Lieutenant Lunden and Whitten continue on chase of the enemy. The first platoon under Lieutenant Lunden are forced to seek shelter on the side of a hill when a German sniper opens fire when the platoon is between a strip of wood. Men are up and at 'em again and the platoon stops on the hill of the valley near Vaux awaiting orders.

In the meanwhile, a fleet of more than 200 Allied planes flew toward the Jerry lines. Shortly afterwards these machines returned. Thirty minutes later several air machines came toward Lunden's crowd whose machine-gun fire attracted attention. Here it was seven Jerrys and three French aeroplanes. Six of the Hun chased two of the Allied planes well in the vanguard, a Frenchie and Hun entertained with a spectacular battle. At times the pair weren't off the ground more than five feet. In an effort to down the Hun Aviator the Frenchie dipped his plane under the Fritz to attack. The German let him come up and then barked his machine gun. The Frenchman's machine was hit in flames were coming from it. Seeing this the Allied airmen made a dash across the valley some 200 yards wide with the Hun in pursuit. Three fourths of the way over the French machine was seen to dip and lucky enough it hit the opposite bank with a thud nose down and turned a complete somersault, the impact throwing the aviator to the ground. The Hun was just overhead and seeing the Frenchie let go his machine gun fire and this caused the Allied airmen to run down the hill 10 feet where he flopped over. His clothes were ablaze. Two men of Lieutenant Lunden's platoon rushed over to where the Frenchie lay and ripped off his burning suit and gave first aid. While administering first aid a Jerry machine gunner, apparently having of observation on the scene cut loose his fire which caused the first-aid man to get down and avoid being hit. Later the Frenchie was taken to a station back a ways. In that air battle the Frenchie received two nasty wounds on the thigh (Devir 31).

November 4-5, 1918 - HAMILTON

Today we stopped where we were and the support battalions took up the attack. They had plenty of resistance and didn't get ahead very fast. We did nothing but lay in the sun and dried out our blankets and praised God that somebody else was doing the attacking. We had hot meals sent up from the kitchen and everything was good. The next day we took up the push again and went about 6 more kilometers. We spent a bad night in the rain, under more or less shell fire, trench mortar, and machine gun fire. The rain being by far the most disagreeable of the three.

∽

At about 6:30 AM the 1st Battalion was waiting at the steam for the 2nd Battalion to pass through their position. The continued advance of the 318th Infantry took the men through the forests of Bois de Saint-Pierremont and Bois de la Berlière reaching Warniforêt, located on the Stonne-Beaumont road.

The advance to Beaumont-Stonne road was key for the Brigade as the Germans were steadily moving north across the Meuse River on route to their main resistance in Sedan. Efforts were being made by German patrols to slow the advance of the American Army as the enemy pulled back. The Division was on a course to position its 159th Brigade from Beaumont to Yonq, a front line over 2 kilometers facing northeast.

The Division needed to relieve the battle weary men and anticipated being relieved by the 1st Division. Orders called for the 317th to stop at

Hill 275 and wait for the 1st Division to pass through the line. This occurred at 6:30 AM on November 6. The advanced units in the 80th were relieved and ordered to rejoin the rest of the Division near Sommauthe. The 2nd Battalion, 318th Infantry was the one unit in the Division that advanced closest to Sedan.

All companies of the Machine Gun Battalion were relieved from assignment with the 317th and 318th Infantry Regiments between the hours of 2:00 AM and 6:00 AM on November 6 and the Battalion assembled in the woods about 1 km north of Sommauthe on the morning of November 6, 1918.

November 6, 1918 - AFFANTRANGER

Of the four Companies of this Battalion attached to the Infantry Regiment of the 159th Brigade, one was for four days continually with a front-line Battalion, and during that time marched about 30 km, without limbers, and the men carrying their complete kit. The minimum march of any Company of the Battalion without limbers was about 20 km. The going for the most part was very heavy and in many places difficult, considering that the average load of each member of the gun squad, in addition to his pack and personal equipment, was over 40 pounds. The mobility so highly desired to a certain degree impaired (Affantranger 11).

November 6, 1918 - HAMILTON

Today we were relieved by the 1st Division and we moved back about 2 kilometers and bivouacked in a wood. We stayed there two nights and then marched south 10 kilometers and bivouacked again and then 10 kilometers more the following day. It is all wet and disagreeable. I think in the long run that rain is worse than shell fire, but I don't like either. Although, this push has been lots better than the first. We advanced all together about 25 kilometers and took the fortified town of Buzancy, several thousand prisoners and several hundred guns. Our outfit had very few casualties, although some of the others had plenty.

Major Emory [German Horton Hunt Emory 1882-1918] was killed, and Reese Niven [Maurice Philip Niven 1887-1918] and Colonel Welch [Harold Echalez Welch 1879 -1918] and a lot more who I knew. I think the old Boche began his retreat before our attack came off, but I think we would have driven him anyhow, but not so far or so fast. The Yanks are still going strong and I feel perfectly sure that he will go back to his own frontier peace or no peace. Peace is coming. We may have to push again, and I may have a lot more unpleasantness, but peace is near and I really don't believe we will have much more. Altogether, I haven't seen much action, but I've been in two big attacks and have been in an active campaign for about three months. It has been impossible to keep up this book during the fight. One has too much else to think about, and after it is all over, you hardly feel like going over the whole thing again. It should be written down from day to day as it occurs, but I couldn't do it.

The Boche retreat has been a work of art. He moves back his infantry, leaving plenty of artillery protected by machine guns. He uses his artillery wonderfully, hits what aims at, aims at everything in range and makes one gun do the work of ten. He places his machine guns cleverly in hedges, in woods, in cabbage fields, almost anywhere. These machine guns are almost impossible to dislodge without artillery and the old Boche would just stay long enough for us to get our artillery up and away he goes over the hill. Our artillery, when I saw them last, were getting pretty fed up with digging in and getting all set to fire only to find that their targets had moved out of range. Others may have had different impressions, but where I was, the German retreat left nothing behind. No equipment, no clothing, no stoves, and not much ammunition. It was hard to believe that he had been there in force at all. The Yanks left nine times the amount of stuff in their advanced than the Germans left in their retreat. If the German morale is bad, they certainly don't show it in their retreat.

The last few days that I was there, it was a rear guard action, pure and simple, with the old Boche still showing us something new about tactics. There is no use talking. The Boche is licked, but we haven't licked his tactics. In the attack, in the defense, in the retreat, he has always been about 2 jumps ahead of everyone else. He has thought of everything first, with the one exception, tanks. He has led the way, all the way, and has proven again and again that he knows more about the war game than we do. The Boche is licked, thanks to the indomitable Poilu, the stubborn Tommie, the impetuous Yank, and perhaps to God himself. We had more men, more money, more material, and in the long run, he didn't have a chance. But my hat off to you Mr. Fritz, you are a better soldier than I am, or ever will be.

Yes, the war is won. The great German dream of Empire will never be realized. The whole great fabric of the German force, and intrigue, and treachery, has come crashing down. Bulgaria, Turkey, Austria, Germany, just as Dad said they would, and it was just by a hair that we didn't have the other thing happen. Just a hair between Germany, down and out, and Germany controlling half the world. By George, I'm glad I was in it. I'm glad my mite was in the last smite.

CHAPTER 12
PEACE AT LAST

The order to move further to the rear was issued on November 7. The 159th Brigade was instructed to move at 7:00 AM on November 8 from Sommauthe and travel via the route of Buzancy, Thénorgues, and Briquenay where "foot troops were not to march on roads used by horse and motor transport, except where no other road is practicable, such as bridge crossings and through villages" (Headquarters Correspondence). The Battalion spent the evening of November 8th in Thénorgues. The Battalion commanders located themselves in a building directly opposite the village church. The next day the Battalion left Thénorgues and moved south to billet in Champigneulle.

November 9, 1918 - HAMILTON

We are now back in billets. We don't hear the guns anymore, nor do we have to wear a tin hat. It is a rather indifferent billet, having been shelled by both sides without regard for private property. This house is in shreds to say the least, but the roof extends over the part of it occupied by the officers of C Company and it has a floor and a fireplace. Altogether, it is tres bon billet and I hope we will stay all winter. We will not stay, however, but will probably move on tomorrow. Nobody minds much. We are going south, away from the war and everything is going to be all right. Mail came in, and some hot chocolate and some soup. I don't know what more a fellow could want.

November 9, 1918 - THOMAS

We are temporarily through this show but suppose we go up again immediately if this war keeps up. We got through pretty well this trip as we chased the Boche about 15 miles in four days after we started.

We are in hopes of course that this is the end of it and it looks very much that way. Of course it may go on indefinitely, but the tide has turned. I think the Boche wants peace as much as anything from what the prisoners say and if it could be given with a surety of no more war it should be.

November 10, 1918 - HAMILTON

Moved back 10 kilometers more. This time we are in an old German artillery P.C. It is pretty comfortable. It is a jolly location snuggled up against the side of a hill and it's a lovely fall day, almost like Indian summer. The first good day in sometime. We need all the good weather they can give us as the roads are well-nigh impassable.

I saw the best air battle I've seen the other day. A Jerry and a Yank, and it was right over my head. They ducked and swerved like two swallows firing at each other all the time and each one striving for the advantage. Then suddenly they came up abreast on the same level not over 50 yards apart, each one trying to get his machine gun on. They both opened fire at once, the tracer ammunition plainly visible, and the Yank got one in his gas tank and came down like a plummet in flames. I could have cried with chagrin, but by gorry it was a good scrap. I wish I was in the air service.

The move south, away from the front lines, put the Battalion in the village of Cornay on November 10, the day before the Armistice was declared. The entire Division was scattered around the Neuvilly-en-Argonne area as the news of the signing was passed through the ranks.

November 11, 1918 - AFFANTRANGER

The Battalion marched to a ravine 1 km north east of the Lachalade. It was while on this march that a Major came along on horseback and hollered that the Armistice had been signed. Maybe we didn't do some yelling then. It was sure great. On arriving at Lachalade we found out that it was true by the following memorandum received from Brigade Headquarters: 'At 11 o'clock in the morning conclusion of the Armistice has been announced at Paris by volleys of guns fired from the field of Mars. The population has not been surprised by the event, for it was expecting it from hour to hour, and foreseeing the signing of it had, in the course of the last few days, literally empty the stores of all their flags. The government communicates this afternoon to the Chamber the conclusion and the conditions of the Armistice.'

It sure looked like home for us and we were happy bunch I want to tell you. I guess even Huff had finally seen enough dead Germans and had had his fill of war (Affantranger 12).

November 11, 1918 - HAMILTON

Did 25 kilometers through the most awful roads and landed here where we got the whole company into French billets, dugouts in the side of a hill, dry and quite comfortable. Heard officially that the armistice has been signed and that Bill Hohenzollern [German Emperor Wilhelm II, House of Hohenzollern] has abdicated. My gorry what news, the war is won, it's all over, it's over and I'm alive, we will go home. I'm going to wear low shoes and silk socks again. Oh Allah is great, praise be the Lord. The best that could happen has happened. The complete overthrow of the German military autocracy. We have not fought in vain, we've done the impossible, we've licked the unlickable Boche. Good old Frog – Good old Tommie! GOOD OLD YANK!

The French soldiers are kissing each other and beating the Yanks on the back. Everybody you see wears a broad grin. What we will do nobody has an idea as usual. I suppose we will go to a back area and drill and shine up for a parade in New York and sit tight to see whether or not the old Boche wants anymore war and eventually we will take a transport a transport with lights on it and go home. Six months should do it at least, six months, six months.

❧

The Battalion was resting in the commune of Lachalade, and spent one week resting and repairing equipment. "Our stay at Lachalade was very short but sweet. It was great sitting around the fireplace at night thinking of getting home, but then the thought came to us that perhaps we would be kept here for the Army of Occupation" (Affantranger 13).

A week of rest also provided the Division an opportunity to muster the men to determine if any troops were missing from the ranks and account for the dead and wounded. Toward the end of the week an accounting of the men took place and all men formed for inspection. These inspections also turned to memorializing the dead as the commanders read the names of those men in the unit who were killed. The Chaplains offered prayers in memory of the fallen.

During the Third Phase the 80th Division suffered a total of 278 dead and 1,027 wounded. The Division's Summary of Operations for the time period of November 1-6, 1918 recorded:

313th Machine Gun Bn: 2 killed, 3 died of wounds, 16 wounded.

317th Infantry: 24 killed, 13 died of wounds, 153 wounded.

318th Infantry: 20 killed, 3 died of wounds, 83 wounded.

320th Infantry: 57 killed, 24 died of wounds, 326 wounded (80th Division).

&

November 12, 1918 - HAMILTON

I am sending you the last installment of my diary. I don't believe I'll continue it because the war is over and the thing was supposed to be a war diary. I have very little news except that we got back safe to billets and arrived after a 20 mile hike to get the good news that the Armistice is signed. I don't know yet what that means, but I guess we won't have any more fighting to do, and we should be home inside of six months. I will send a wire to the family as soon as I get to a place where messages can be sent.

The news seems too good to be true. It's hard to realize that we've won the war, but we have won it, beyond the slightest doubt, and I can't help feeling that the work of the First Army on the critical Verdun Front had quite a bit to do with it – but then I guess everyone is proud of his own outfit.

November 12, 1918 – THOMAS

Well, the war is finished and I am glad it is for one. It is one thing to keep up while you have to, but there is no glamour or romance in this war. It is hard, mere soul-trying work. Our Division came out with flying colors, I am glad to say, but our Battalion was handicapped by the style of warfare. It did well, considering everything, and would have done better if the occasion had arrived. I'll try to write you all about it when I get a breathing spell. But at present we don't know what we are going to do. We are just north of Sainte-Menehould in the Argonne, and are just out of the line. All time is spent in cleaning up. I suppose it will be six months before we start back, and we will all get rather impatient before it is over, but I want to get the bunch back now I have got them here.

༺

After a week of rest, the Battalion took on the difficult task of marching 150 miles south to the 15th Training Area in the French Department of Yonne. The average daily trek was about 20 kilometers, or 12.5 miles, but the daily distances were extended in the latter days of the movement. Field orders were also issued with the names of villages where the men would billet for the night, but not all locations could accommodate the men under-roof and so it was often necessary to bivouac the men in any available open field. For most of the trip, the weather conditions were favorable, but during the last three days of the journey the weather turned to a combination of rain, snow and sleet.

It was during this time period that many of the wounded soldiers who were able to rejoin their units were being released from the hospitals and ordered

MILLER

to catch up with their command as they units headed to the training area. Sergeant Joseph Miller (1894-1926) of Meadville, Pennsylvania, sailed to France with the Battalion as part of A Company. Less than a month after arriving, Miller was kicked in the head by horse and on July 4th was transported to the King George Hospital in London, England for medical treatment. The extent of Miller's injury caused him to miss the majority of the war while he recovered in England and he was released from Base Hospital No. 29 on October 22, 1918. Travelling across France with about 21 other soldiers, he met up with the Division, then located in Clermont, and found his Battalion First Sergeant. Miller wrote, "We found a kitchen here for the 80th Division men only. Stayed at some old shack in the hills with plenty of straw, waiting to be transferred to the Company. On November 9, we laid around waiting for orders. At 9:30 PM heard a lot of shooting in the valley. Someone thought peace was declared. November 10, we done our own cooking on a little stove. Had bacon and coffee for breakfast, and coffee and bacon for dinner, and bacon and coffee for supper, still waiting for orders" (Miller).

November 15, 1918 – THOMAS

I am temporarily in charge of the Battalion and will be for a few days or weeks, and for the first time since my Army life began, can hear reveille blow and go back to sleep with a clear conscience. However, it gets dark over here at 4:30 PM and our regular bed time is 7:00 PM, so 6:30 AM is not bad.

Well, it's all over and all that is left is rumor. We have gone from Nice to Russia, according to the Brigade quartermaster or the veterinary or somebody who springs a hot one. I don't know nor care much where we go. Very probably back to a rest camp or maybe south. Rumor is pretty strong that we are not the honor division to occupy Germany. So everybody is putting on as much dog as possible and trying to get snap into the men. It's not so easy now so they can't help the letdown feeling, but it is coming back by degrees.

We got out of the line five days before it was over. It took us three days to hike back over our advance in the same number of days, so you know we were going some. We tore about 16 miles in three days.

You asked me for a description of a show. I can't give one I'm afraid, but I can give a general idea of what it is. The honor of war is not the actual fighting, because you are held up by excitement at that time; it is the ceaseless grind of inconvenience and filth and hunger and uncertainty. It is not human and although if another war came I suppose everybody would be damned fool enough, myself included, to come again. I hope there will never be another.

To begin with, we got out of one show, our first, in which I lost about 70 men, chiefly gas. We got back and it was drive, drive, and drive trying my best to make a company in two weeks like my old company that had taken a year. Replacements coming in, men sick, and rain and mud, then the order to move. This order always comes at 11 PM. You go and get in and move at 6 AM to a pretty good place close up. Then the next day you personally go up to reconnoiter. You find the shells breaking and are sniped at just as before, but your nerves are all back and it doesn't seem a bit bad. Then back again.

The next day you hike with your company up to the place close behind the lines, then the night following you move up. Of all the bad parts of war the worst is getting men over a road, and also your transport when the road is blocked and shelled. You curse and swear and move a little bit at a time. We got almost up to our position last time and were dropping packs in an old barn and Fritz dropped three shells square in the barn. It destroyed quite a number of packs and didn't hit a man but it had all of us clawing into the dirt. We got up and dug in and then the barrage came down. That is fine to hear, when they come from behind. Then the infantry comes filtering by, seemingly indifferent, and disappear out front. All this time Fritz is dropping them back and they seem awfully close when you are in a little bivvy below ground. Then the men will crawl out and look and you have to go all around and keep them down, and the man right next to you gets shot by a rifle bullet and a shell breaks near and knocks out four men and it is nothing out of the ordinary.

No orders coming to advance, we have finished our part, the combing machine-gun barrage, we stay there all day. Can't get any reports except wild tales about success or repulse and so you dig in a little more at night and prepare to stay. Just as everything is finished for the night the order comes to move transport and all back about 2 miles. Back you go dog tired. Dig in for the night as shells are breaking all around. Pass out there in a blanket and overcoat, both wet and in mud several inches deep, but the sleep is blissful. Then 10 minutes after, it seems, really at 2 AM, a call from the Major. Your company is to move out with a battalion of infantry at 4 AM. They are going through the battalion in the front and you go with them. You kick your company out, literally and pack up and report. Then hike through the battlefield of the day before. Everybody full for guts, but a bad time of the day. Dead men, dead horses, stragglers, wounded, mud, rain, filth of all descriptions. Nobody knows where we start from or who is on our right or left, but will go anyway. Let a real Brigade try it. A halfhearted barrage and we are gone. My men are carrying their guns, tripods and 4000 rounds of ammunition per gun and keeping up with the infantry. Then we hike and stop and get a target and bring up the company and the infantry has got by. Then in the afternoon they strike machine gun nests and reach their objective and we come up to protect the flanks. We get out and find about 10 o'clock that the infantry are on a road back of us and my headquarters is in front of their line, but all I can do is to go out and tell my men and try to cheer them up. Shells and whiz bangs all night and goes again at day light. Men so tired they can't move but go all day and take positions at night. Have to force men to dig in. Rain and cold all night. You get up and wander around as there is no place to sleep. At 2 o'clock we are notified that we are in support and move a little slower. A few shells then dig in for the night and the order comes move up immediately 6 kilos. Transport has caught up there so out you start. Horses and men pulling limbers through mud. Nobody knows whether the road is the right one. Down in the mud with their overcoats shielding sickly match and study the map. Our man says front lines haven't advanced that far, but out you go and get there. Told to stay there and find old Boche camp. Much rejoicing, get all settled. Rain, rain, men sick, two horses dead, then the order to move up 8 kilos comes just at dark. Start out at one and go up to an area where shells are dropping like hail. Get to town and try to locate infantry. Darkness and raining and shelling and finally get them located. Halt company in mud a kilo back, send a lot of runners and go out in the dark to select positions to place guns the next day. 2:00 AM orders come. Division relieved and get out night then. Pass relieving divisions coming in. They are swearing as you did the night before. Move back to your kitchen and have a hot breakfast and hike back to your Battalion. Show over temporarily. Then we did so well we get a rest. But we don't, but peace caught us.

I can fill in details to you one of these days. We have been lucky and haven't caught much. My own part in this war has been exceedingly negligible, but the experience is there. The French and English who fought it four years are the men. All of us could do it, and would do it, but I'm glad we did not have to. This is a poor effort. Will try to write a funny one next time.

November 21, 1918 – THOMAS

We are in the process of hiking about 100 miles and expect to land about the 2nd or 3rd of December. We are going back to comfortable quarters and rumor has it to go into Germany a little later. Another rumor is that we go home to parade. One about as likely as another. I don't care very much, I am going on leave about December 1st. I don't feel much like spending the money but think it would be very foolish to be over here and not run around a little. I'm going to Nice, I think, as I hear wonderful reports of that vicinity, so you can picture me about the time you get this as bathing in the Mediterranean or braving the banks at Monte Carlo or most anything like that. At present, I'm strolling across France and although it is pretty cold, it is not so bad.

I guess you are glad as is everybody that it is all over now. It seems a little hard to realize and I was afraid to believe it until I knew it absolutely. I suppose we will come wondering home sometime about April or May, but I'm afraid we'll have a hard time getting back as fast as we came over. Nevertheless, we can hope for the best and I wouldn't mind the German experience, should such a thing become necessary.

Just at present I'm trying to get the Battalion over a rather strenuous hike as the Major is on leave and will only return at about the end of our trip. It is a wonderful country we are seeing now, though by the time it is all over I will have just about covered France.

There was nothing pretty about this war. I'm even glad to get away from the lines. Today, for the first time we are in a town that has never been shelled and we have been coming almost directly south for eight days. Of course we crossed from the new front lines through the old. They have German prisoners all through here rebuilding the destroyed places, which of course is as it should be. But to get a bed to sleep in at night is fine, and to be able to have lights and burn fires is unbelievable. I hope my watch has arrived.

It was a funny year for that epidemic to come, wasn't it? We haven't had a great deal of sickness, except the usual things. No cold to speak of. I lost one man with pneumonia the other day. I lost quite a few good friends since we started. The Division lost a bunch of good officers. Two of our officers came back yesterday from the hospital.

Edward J. Quinn (1895-1918) of D Company, died of pneumonia on November 2, 1918. A month earlier, Private Eli Hornick (1894-1918) of B Company, also died of pneumonia on October 19, 1918.

November 28, 1918 – AFFANTRANGER

On Thanksgiving day our mess Sergeant cooked us beans and the whole of Headquarters company got the dysentery from them, some quite bad and others not too bad. I was in such bad shape I could hardly walk, but made up my mind that I was going to walk every step of the way. There were two or three ambulances which ran from where we were marching to Sennevoy le Bas, picking up stragglers and sick and carrying them on to our destination. Major Huidekoper was not with the Battalion during the march and Captain William G. Thomas of Company D was placed in command. He insisted that I take an ambulance, but I stated that if it was alright with him I wanted to make the entire trip on foot. He laughed and said it was alright with him (Affantranger 13).

November 28-29, 1918 – DEVIR

Thanksgiving Day. March 32 kilometers to Mussy. Note of interest, the men get Bully Beef sandwiches for dinner. November 29, the worst ever. The Company staggers into Sennevoy le Bas after a 40 kilometer hike (Devir 33).

November 30, 1918 – HUIDEKOPER

The Battalion left Lachalade on the morning of November 18, 1918 and with the exception of the first four days of the trip had absolutely no delay of any kind. During the first four days, the Battalion marched in the rear of the Brigade and was unnecessarily subjected to halts and irregular marching periods, which resulted in arrival after dark. During the rest of the trip, however, owing to the excellent marching schedule, there were no interruptions in the march and the Battalion arrived at its destination, no matter how long the march was, before dark.

For the first few days billets were unavailable for most of the men. During the last week of the March, however, all men of the Battalion were undercover every night. At no time during the march was there any trouble or delay in securing rations for the men. The dump was always known in sufficient time in advance and was situated near enough to make it easy to procure rations. Forage for the horses, however, was scanty. During most of the trip only enough forage was received to give the horses about four or five pounds of oats and eight or nine pounds of hay per day.

The marching of the men as a whole was excellent and their health was good. Eight men were evacuated during the march on account of sickness, but no men fell out or were lost during the trip.

On their arrival at Sennevoy les Bas, November 29, the spirit and condition of the men was excellent. The only real and pressing lack was shoes. Many men suffered on the march from worn-out shoes (Headquarters Correspondence).

∽

Arrival to the Training Area brought with it a number of changes in the Army leadership positions. General Cronkite was assigned as the first commander of the Ninth Army Corps in Ligny-en-Barrois and Major General Samuel D. Sturgess took command of the 80th Division. Lieutenant Colonel Oscar Foley became Assistant Provost Marshal in Paris and the position of Division Machine Gun Officer was transferred to Lieutenant Colonel John Cocke.

While peace talks began in Paris, the Battalion rested for only a few days before returning to the arduous regiment of training and drill. Their day began with 6:15 AM Reveille, six hours of school for the officers, and machine gun training for the enlisted. The Division Machine Gun School was started in Gigny-Bussy training the men in a two-week course. Close order drill occurred every night with Taps set at 9:30 PM. The men started to receive replacement equipment with shoes high on the list of necessary replacements.

In late November, the service chevron was approved to be issued to all men who served at least six months in the theatre of operations. The chevron was worn on the left sleeve cuff. The wound chevron, equivalent to the Purple Heart medal, was also being issued and was worn on the right sleeve cuff.

The Battalion provided the Division with a list of the men authorized to wear the wound chevron. The majority of the men on the list were identified as being wounded from gas. The official shoulder insignia of the Blue Ridge Division was also issued in the Training Area.

December 1, 1918 – HAMILTON

Well it's all over. I've been to the war, and what is almost as important, I have come back again. I had the great satisfaction on November 3rd of telling my men that the Boche was in full retreat, and the next few days we spent in a rather unsuccessful effort to get close enough to hit him again. We were hot on his trail all right and I think the armistice just about came in time to prevent one of the greatest defeats the world has ever seen. We were just fairly swooping on his trail when we were relieved by the 1st Division and so did not have the pleasure of taking Sedan or of actually being in at the death. The armistice came five days later while we were marching back. I did not believe it, nobody did. The bombardment during the 6 hours between the signing of the armistice and the cessation of hostilities was something fierce. So we shrugged our shoulders, we had peace talks before, followed by big bombardments and we were from [-] but that night it was confirmed and we knew it was over. There was remarkably little enthusiasm. We certainly did not cheer. I think we were still pretty skeptical and it was only as we gradually received word of the terms of the armistice that we began to realize that the great job that we had come to do was over and that we were still alive.

It was a great thought, it comes back to me with a rush every little while and makes me want to get up and holler, and roll on the grass, and make an ass of myself generally. Our Division, unfortunately, was not chosen to go into Germany. They took five regular army divisions, four National Guard and just two National Army. I was sorry to have missed it, but it couldn't be helped. I consoled myself with the thought that at least we would not have a 200 mile hike, and then what do they do but make us hike all the way from the Argonne to here, about 160 miles. I dodged that by going on leave.

I didn't know when I went on leave that the hike was coming. I thought they would go on the train, but no trains were available and 2 days after I left for Paris they left for here walking on their flat feet. I went to Paris which I had never seen before. Paris was wonderful. They had gone wild a week before when the good news had come but they were still wild enough. The whole city was hung with flags; everywhere were captured Boche guns, and everywhere people, funny little French girls in all kinds of costumes, went careering around the streets singing and laughing and throwing confetti. Great flocks of them would surround a poor unsuspecting Yank and not let him go until he had kissed the whole gang. It was great stuff.

Mary Polhemus [Mary Bartow Polhemus 1890-1981] is at the base hospital in Bordeaux. I had a note from her there. She had been nursing my old Captain John Kean, whose wound was a lot more serious than at first appeared. The shrapnel had gone in the point of the shoulder and broke his collar bone. I don't expect he will be back now and rather hope not, because it might mean that I will lose the company, although that's rather unlikely.

This place is a terrible mud hole. My billet is fair but the men are pretty badly off. They are all quartered in an old farm, but like most French farms it is on low ground and the other day we struck water after digging down 4 feet. I hope the men don't get sick, but conditions are very bad and as lots of the men walked right through their shoes on the last hike, that doesn't help any. Everyone has cooties except the officers. I have installed a 'decoutyizer' and although it gives them 'an awful freicht' they are a hard thing to cure. They are as big as this [drawing of an insect] and bite like billyo. They drive the men almost frantic, some of the men actually go without underwear, and it is cold here too, because the cooties don't live on a man without underwear, it's too cold for them.

December 1, 1918 - THOMAS

We finished our hike yesterday and covered 68 km or about 41 miles in the last two days. I had the Battalion for the hike and didn't lose a man in the 12 days of about 160 miles. Am a little cocky about that. We are in a little village called Sennevoy-le-Bas about 12 miles from Châtillon-sur-Seine, and will in all probability be here for a month or two. I have a wonderful billet and as soon as I can get the men comfortable will be okay.

The Major is back, so I'm back to my Company. All the men got drunk the first night, as was to be expected, but have settled down now and will only have occasional outbreaks. We are preparing big things for

Christmas, within our limitations, and are doing everything we can to make ourselves comfortable and keep the men amused until we start back.

I walked into young Ed Cansler [Edwin Thomas Cansler Jr. 1890-1950] the other night. He's a fine looking soldier he gave me news of Tom Gathier and a few more. You remember my writing you of a boy named Duff [Joseph Miller Duff Jr. 1889-1918] that I said sent to Training School. He used to coach N.C. One of the finest men I've seen in the Army. He got his commission and then got killed. It was a real blow to me. That Argonne finished a bunch of my friends. My wounded are drifting back one and two at a time. I hear with quickened pulse that Jimmy is on the way back. It means my life is one sweet dream from now on. I expect him in any day now.

December 7, 1918 – THOMAS

The next few months are going to be pretty hard. We have a heavy drill schedule and no incentive. I'll be very glad when it is over so we can come on home. The only thing is to try to keep the men's spirits up. They have it harder of course. No form of amusement whatsoever and not very good billets. We hope to move on anyway as you very soon get tired of one place. I have a peach of a billet, and am altogether very comfortable.

I'm torn between conflicting desires, but now that it is over I am ready to get home. They send around blanks to be filled out giving you three choices. Regular Army, Reserve Corps with immediate separation from the service or just plain immediate separation from the service. I took the latter because I didn't know what I would find in the way of a job when I got home, and whether I could get a job that would allow me a month to six weeks every year for the work. It will be comparatively easy to get my reserve commission back if I want it.

We have inspections every day now, and squads right and squads left, which is intensely boring, with no incentive, but really after all makes time fly.

December 9, 1918 - HAMILTON

When the war stopped bang, I also stopped this book! I began the thing as a war diary way back in May 1917 and the war being over, there seemed no excuse for its existence. However, after a month of writing nothing I am starting it up again from sheer force of habit. After all, the story isn't finished yet and I might as well fight it out to the bitter end.

We arrived back at our billets on November 11, the day of the Armistice, and three days later I went on leave. I went to Paris and then to Nice and after seven days there returned to Paris and there found that the Division was marching down from Lachalade in the Argonne to Sennevoy-le-Bas near Châtillon. It was a rotten long hike and I was glad enough to miss it. As it was impossible to pick them up on the march, I went to Diou and waited there until they arrived here. Then I came out and joined them. They had a bad time, but in spite of being through their shoes, the company had completed the 160 mile march without the loss of a man.

This village is like a million other French villages, just a cluster of stone houses grouped together around a church with a tall spire. As usual the town is built in a hollow and I don't believe the ground ever dries out. It is a swamp now. The company is billeted in an old farm, a rotten low lying place with a moat around it. It is neither dry, sanitary nor comfortable and what's more the men are terribly crowded. I suppose it will be better to spend the winter here than in the line; but at least there is excitement in the line and one's chance of living in a hole like this or in the trenches would be about 50–50.

The horrors of peace are almost as horrible as those of war and we have now left the easy 'Let her rip' attitude of the frontline for the inspections and drills and red tape of a training area. We are all frankly bored. There isn't a man in the company who is thinking of a single darned thing but home, and yet we are supposed to take these men and whip them into tip top fighting trim again in case the Boche should resume hostilities. So we have to go back to the old stuff and try to teach a lot of men what there is no longer any stimulus to learn. I suppose it has to be done, but it doesn't make it any easier. Also the men have no shoes and it rains a perpetual drizzle; it gets dark at 4:00 PM and we have no candles. Bah!

December 10, 1918 - HAMILTON

The days stretch out into the future as far as the mind I can reach, utterly cold and miserable and devoid of interest. We have a new

Divisional Machine Gun Officer [Lieutenant Colonel John Cocke] and he is in an effort to justify his existence and is being most unpleasant. Teaching tactics is bad enough when you are preparing for actual combat, but when you try to make it interesting to a game like this, who will probably be out of this Army for good in three months, well, it is not easy.

I have a fierce letter from brother Ken, which advocates my beating the old Boche to a bloody pulp and that he should enjoy going into the trade war with Germany after the peace is signed. Good old fighting Ken, he missed the biggest scrap of all time by going into the wrong thing, and is howling for blood now. I really don't quite get his point of view. I can't see there's any difference between the man who leads an assault platoon or the man who makes the rifles for the platoon to charge with. The war is either right or wrong: you can either fight with us or against us; there is no middle ground. You can't fight without hate because hate is the essence of war. We fight to kill the other fellow; if you don't do that, you aren't doing your job. Kill the other fellow, that's all you have to do, that's the way to win, there's no love in that. The people that try to mix war and Christianity are pure hypocrites. You might just as well try to mix Christianity with a war on mosquitoes or on tuberculosis or on the potato bugs. I don't love rattlesnakes or measles. I hate to them and I try to destroy them. You don't do it by praying; you need a big stick. All the prayers in the world wouldn't have stopped the Germans at Château Thierry if one Yank regiment hadn't been able to shoot straight; all the powers in the world wouldn't have taken Montfaucon if they hadn't outflanked it. Prayers may save souls, I have no doubt about it, but they don't win battles; and the people who support the war but don't believe in fighting, who pray for victory, but don't use a bayonet; or like a women who prays to remove dirt instead of using a broom. I'm not shooting at Ken particularly but just at the creed in general which has been as far as the war is concerned utterly untenable. If you want to fix a broken bone you can either pray or use a splint – if you use both you have no faith. If you want to win the war, you can either pray or use a bayonet. If you do both you lack confidence –and take it from me it's the most bayonets that do the trick. The conflicting prayers of the opposing forces neutralize each other – the battalions with the most guns and most bayonets, kill the most of the other fellow. No - Ken went in the wrong thing – he should have had a battery or an infantry company and worked out his feelings in the straightforward way. And I can't help feeling he will always regret the choice he made – especially in the bloodthirsty mood he's in now. As for me, I've seen enough blood – I'd like to see the Kaiser swing from a tall tree with a few of his gang of cut throats – but as for a trade war – well I'd like to see things supplied by the people who make them cheapest and best. To Hell with boycotts and trade wars and tariffs – let's go for something bigger than that – let's buy wool from Australia – if we can get it cheaper – and knives from England if they are better, and toys from Germany – if they make the baby smile more. Let's hate like the Devil as long as we are at war, and then let's put our backs to the dark days behind and look for something better.

December 11, 1918 - HAMILTON

Wet weather. We were supposed to go to the range this morning, but I took the company to the wrong place and then the rain came down so I marched them back again. I have 40 men confined to the barracks on account of being entirely through their shoes. It's pretty unsatisfactory all-around. I wonder if we will go to Germany. I'd a heap sight rather do that than lie around a place like this, but I'm afraid there isn't much chance of it. I think we will probably be here all winter and then will go back to our wives and mothers and collie dogs and the things we love. I've talked to lots of men and the main reason for going home is food.

Practically everyone looks forward above all else to bacon and eggs, or soft shelled crabs, or oatmeal and cream, the way I do, or some other article of food which Uncle Sam does not supply. Of course there are lots of smaller things that calls a man home, a clean bed, and personal liberty, and a porcelain tub, and perhaps some little bright eyes somewhere. But what really calls the boys home, is the home grub and I haven't a doubt that it's been that way since the beginning of things.

December 11, 1918 – THOMAS

Where we were in the line nothing possible could have been worse it seemed, but drilling all the time seems just about as bad. You adapt yourself so very much to circumstances. When you are in the war itself you felt very much like talking about it, but nobody talks about it much now. Everybody knows everybody else's experiences so they can't put anything over. I imagine this war will have a lot of stories told about it by the time the Army gets home.

My old men keep drifting back. Jimmy is back with a wound stripe, and as wonderful as ever. I am trying to learn French and doing fairly well, but I would rather be back home. I hope I come soon.

Have got all my stuff back from Boulogne where it was stored. I don't need a thing now so don't bother about sending any more socks or things. I am awfully glad about the gloves. I do need a warm pair of gloves more than anything. Two weeks from today is Christmas. It is hard to realize. Love to all. I hope you have a wonderful New Year. I think it is rather wonderful to be living at all in the last year or two.

December 16, 1918 - HAMILTON

I don't know why I'm keeping this magnum opus up; there is no point to it anymore. I have 60 men marked 'quarters' today on account of sickness or shoes. We had to hold classes for them indoors. This is a great bore for everyone. I ruled that the man marked 'quarters' could either go to his bunk and stay there or was well enough to learn the anatomy of a machine gun.

We are being terribly harried by inspectors of all kinds. They come around, ask pointed questions and raise Cain about everything. An inspector from 'Army' came around inspected the whole 159th Brigade. He didn't see a thing he that he liked except two men in C Company that gave him a snappy salute. He finally arrived at General Jamerson's headquarters who is in command of the Brigade. He began to criticize the headquarters. General Jamerson is a pleasant man with nice grey eyes. He looked at the inspector and his eyes twinkle. They were both brigadiers. 'Look here General,' said he, 'have you ever been near the front?'

'No,' said the inspector.

'Well,' said General Jamerson. 'My men have. They have been through some of the stiffest fighting of this war. They know how to take care of themselves and are alright. I'm fed up with you. Get out.'

But the relief was just temporarily. A whole flock of inspectors and professional agitators are constantly dogging our steps and making life miserable. Not one of them ever heard a bullet, or saw a trench, but here they come and tell you 'your billets are not homelike' or 'that the men shall drill five hours a day without regard to the weather' or 'that there should be partitions between bunks,' when you have no bunks, or 'that there should be ten minutes snappy close order drill after retreat at night.'

Retreat is at 4:45PM every day. I stand in front of the company and am supposed to give them ten minutes 'snappy close order' drill. My word! This certainly is developing into the worst war I've been in. They are standing in mud to their ankles.

'Company!' Terrific splash.

'Attennnnnnn-shun!' Mud flies everywhere.

'Present arms!'

'Order arms!' Small splash.

'First Sergeant!' You can hear the First Sergeant come splashing around the end of the company, but it is too dark to see him. He comes to a halt, and you can tell from the splashing that he almost lost his balance trying to do a snappy right face.

'Dismiss the company.' The First Sergeant says, 'Inspection, arms. Port, arms. Dismiss.' A terrific splash and C Company goes tearing off to supper.

December 17, 1918 - HAMILTON

It has rained a cool drizzle for a week. John Kean came back to the company after being two months in the hospital. I don't know what his status is but I seem to be still in command of C Company. I have been trying to get a pig for the men for Christmas dinner, but without luck. It is impossible to buy anything.

Colonel Cocke, the new D.M.G.O. is sick in bed and there isn't a machine gun officer in the Division who doesn't fervently hope he doesn't recover. He certainly is about as popular around here as the flu. I have enough wool socks now to last until 1924. I will never wear any other kind again. One of the boys in our medical detachment took a long drink of carbolic acid, thinking it was cognac, and died tout d' suite as was rather than expected. It was hard luck, but he should have known better. This narrative is getting gloomier and gloomier.

The soldier that Captain Hamilton was referring to was Private Leon W. Spiro (1898-1918) of Philadelphia, Pennsylvania, who died accidentally. The death of Private Spiro was reviewed by a board of officers and sent to the Central Records Office, Adjutant General. The findings reported, "Private Spiro of the Medical Corps, 313th Machine Gun Battalion died at about 8:40 AM, December 15, on the ambulance between Sennevoy le Bas and Laignes, death caused by carbolic acid poisoning. His death was due to the carelessness of the deceased and the noncriminal carelessness of two other members of the Medical Department, Sergeant William G. Jahraus and Private Oscar A. Bosch [1887-1963]. His death was in the line of duty and not due to the soldier's own misconduct" (Company Records).

Sergeant Jahraus stated, "We got up this morning and wanted to get some milk for breakfast in a canteen and it had a bad odor in it, so went in and got a bottle supposed to contain cognac which had been purchased by about five members of the Medical Corps, and had been there for several days. I asked, "Who wants to drink this?" Spiro said, "I'll drink it." And he drank it. As soon as I got the bottle I got a smell of carbolic and put it up on my nose and hollered at him right away. "Don't drink it Spiro." I gave him alcohol right away and he drank about two or three swallows" (Company Records).

Private Bosch stated in the report, "Sergeant Skonieczka [Francis Bronislaus K Skonieczka 1895-1960] from Company D came around last night to get some carbolic acid and he gave me a wine bottle to put it in as he wanted to use it as an antiseptic wash for a rash that he had on his body. I put in about two teaspoonful of carbolic acid in the bottle and told the rest of the medical corps that I was placing it on the top shelf and to give it to Sergeant Skonieczka when he called for it the next morning" (Company Records).

The Battalion Surgeon, First Lieutenant Jarman, was called to the infirmary and attempted to flush Private Spiro's stomach out, but after recognizing that he could do nothing further for the soldier, he ordered Private First Class Peter G. Mainzer (1892-1972) to take Private Spiro in an ambulance to the Camp Hospital located in Laignes. Private Spiro was pronounced dead at the hospital.

∾ક

December 18, 1918 - HAMILTON

The men on the base depot say that the Division will go home very soon. Most rumors seem to start at the dumps. There they are pretty close in touch with Corps, and if you really want to know what the Division is going to do, you want to talk to the men at the ration dump. He will either have the dope or he won't, but in any case he will tell you a darn good official, straight from the Corps commander, lie. I can't see how we can be.

February they could begin to send the original 30 Divisions, which they intended to keep here. I don't see how we have a chance before that. I think that there are just about 30 organized Divisions in the A.E.F. at the present time.

December 20, 1918 – LEINHAUSER

Left the hospital at 7:00 AM and arrived back to the Battalion at 4:00 PM. Some mud hole, wet and disagreeable. I got soaked to the skin. Still raining and not feeling too good.

December 21, 1918 - HAMILTON

Nothing special has happened. Today is the shortest day of the year and I'll be glad to see them lengthen out. A day that doesn't get light until seven and gets dark at four is not worth having.

Lieutenant Otto P. Leinhauser of this Company returned to duty from the hospital today. He blew himself up with the detonator of an aerial torpedo the day before the November 1st attack. It certainly made me mad to have him do it. He is 6 feet and weighs 220 pounds, built like a God and one of the finest looking men I've ever seen, and the best platoon leader in the Battalion. And here he goes and gives himself a blighty the very day before we were supposed to go 'over the top.' He should have had a General Court Martial, but was let off on account of his exceptional ability. Anyhow, he came back to us yesterday and the administration of the company is greatly improved.

He has command of the 3rd Platoon of C Company ever since the beginning, and his men worship him. The 1st Platoon is commanded by Bobbie Stoddart, who is one of the best officers I've seen in the Army, and would certainly have had a Company if he had been in the Infantry instead of in the machine gun company.

The machine gun company, being far smaller and incidentally better, has had fewer promotions than either the infantry or artillery. I was born lucky to get mine and that was simply a combination of lucky things. Captain Kean has gone back to Bordeaux, but I believe will return to the Battalion soon again. I believe I am to keep my Company, but don't care much about that now. There isn't much fun in it at present, what with inspections and reviews and gosh knows what not. Leading a Company in the war is alright, but as for leading them in a parade, well I don't care for it much.

December 22, 1918 - HAMILTON

Today was Sunday. I finally bought a pig for Christmas for the Company after a lot of trouble. He was très beau cochon [very beautiful pig] and weighing 115 kilos vivant [living] and we slung him by the ears into the rear of the Ford and brought him home in triumph. He is really a crackerjack and I hate to have him killed, but tomorrow the deed must be done and a very 'vivant couchon' will become very 'mort couchon' [dead pig].

December 22, 1918 – THOMAS

We are still in this mud hole and the future is still very uncertain. All of the rumors are working and carrying us daily from Russia to Austria or Germany or Bordeaux. The drill is of course monotonous, but even that helps to kill time. I haven't been away from here in the time since arriving, and don't expect to take a leave unless we are here after February 1. Then I will have enough saved to take a good trip and still have money. I am very close with money these days, strange to say. There is absolutely nothing to do here, either for the men or the officers, and of course it is very tiresome.

Jimmy is back though, with his wound stripe, and as fine as ever. We have a fine mess, but it costs about $45 a month, a piece. However, that is all I spend money for, so don't begrudge it. I hope, however, that we can get on home before very long, as I would like to get out and go on to work again. With all the kings and presidents paying a visit to Paris and 'Mrs. Wilson kisses little girl stuff,' I suppose peace will wait a while longer.

Our men are very good, considering what they used to be, and are a very well disciplined crew. We don't have any trouble from them, but the spring is going to be a long drag if we are here that long. I've got some nice plans if I ever get home and I am saving money for them, but just at the present sitting, it is not very helpful.

The day after tomorrow is Christmas. I don't feel at all Christmassy, but didn't expect too much. I hope it will be the last Christmas I ever spend away from home.

December 24, 1918 - HAMILTON

Tomorrow is Christmas day and the Government has kindly issued us canned salmon and beans for our Christmas Dinner instead of the annual fresh beef. I am jolly glad I have that 'tres bon couchon' now deceased. Our rations have been usually pretty good and we get excellent fresh beef almost every day. Why they should give us a worse ration for Christmas than usual, I can't imagine, although they probably couldn't help it.

Christmas Eve most everybody got drunk, or tried to, or both. I don't see any reason why they shouldn't. We don't have very much trouble with booze as a rule. The French restaurants are open for several hours every day and are allowed to sell anything but alcohol to the men. The men do get more or less alcohol just the same, but it is very expensive and there is much less drunkenness than you would suppose.

I have a dozen men in the Company who give me pretty constant trouble, but for the rest, a few go on occasional sprees, and a lot are total abstainers, and C Company is a practically rough company. They were recruited from the slums of Erie, Pa. and a lot of them are the very roughest kind of roughnecks. I can't understand why they are so easy to handle. We have been in France six months now and I've only had one venereal case in my company. Tell it in Gath, and publish it in the streets of Ascalon, so that the people will stop writing letters to the press about the corrupting influence of the Army. One man out of 250, in six months, and I believe he was the only case we have had in the Battalion, over a thousand men, including replacements.

December 25, 1918 - HAMILTON

Christmas Day. The General commanding the 159th Infantry Brigade has issued an order to his officers saying that they will attend a party at the Brigade at 3 o'clock this afternoon and that the 'Egg nog barrage would go down at 3:00 PM and would continue until dead.' I don't think I shall go. Egg nog makes me extremely sick. I don't like booze very much anyhow. Beer is fair, although I like tea better. As far as whiskey, rum, champagne, cognac, liquors of all kinds, I don't like them for a hang. I drink them when I have to, but get along far better without. Let prohibition come, bring on your tea and buttered toast.

December 26, 1918 - HAMILTON

Every day I take a shot at something different. I must be getting terribly sour. Today it is the Marines. The 2nd Division is generally known as the Marine Division, but it is composed of one regular Army brigade and one brigade of Marines. The Division is a good one, but whether the regular Army brigade or the brigade of Marines is the better, would be hard to say.

They were next to us in line in front of Buzancy and I have a fair chance to judge them. The Marines are good, of course, and have a fine esprit de corps, but except for their button on their cap, look just like anybody else and straggle as badly on a long march as the National Guard. They did good work at Belleau Wood, but although they are credited as being at Cantigny, I don't think they fired a shot, and at Château Thierry, the best work was done by some regular Army regiments. Their infantry was no better in the last attack than any other. We advanced with them and although we were a head of them the entire time, you heard of the 'superb dash' of the 'Marine Division' but the fact that the 80th took a very strong town of Buzancy, is not even mentioned. The Marines had five times our casualties in the last attack, but just because they try to show up the 'Green' National Army Divisions on each side of them. Unnecessary casualties. The Marines will tell you proudly, 'Why damn it, we had 3000 casualties at [-]!' Yes, and damn it we had 300 and had more difficult ground. Tell it to the Marines that success in battle is killing the other fellow without being killed yourself.

What the deuce good are 3000 casualties unless you inflict 5000 in getting them? The Marines have done good work in the war, I don't deny it, and their brigade is one of the 60 or 70 infantry brigades that helped to lick the Hun, but after all, what is one brigade. 8000 men, in an army of a million. What the Marines have had is some damn good press agents who have made it as though the Marines won the war, while a Division like the 1st, which has a far better record, is hardly ever spoken of. If the Marines had broken the Hindenburg line instead of the 30th, if they had taken Montfaucon instead of the 79th, if they had taken Buzancy, even instead of us, why the world would be rung with it. Instead of that, most of the Divisions who did splendid work, such as the above, are unknown and never will be known. It was the unknown ones that broke down the Boche along the Meuse, and if you see the Marines, you can tell it to them. Y.M.C.A., Aviators, Marines, tomorrow I shall take a potshot at something else.

December 29, 1918 - HAMILTON

I am sending this book home today. I think less and less of it as a literary effort, but it certainly is lots easier than writing letters. Today was wild and wet. I didn't do anything but develop a bad temper, which of late has been chronic.

December 30, 1918 - THOMAS

I haven't written you in sometime. Due somewhat to the many Christmas celebrations. The men had a fair time. Jimmy got a lot of missile toe and fir and put it up in my room. I broke a vase in the operation and almost caused a billeting debacle. After going all over the country, I finally managed to buy two hogs at $150 apiece and was going to have them barbecued for Christmas. Everything went fine until about 6 o'clock Christmas morning, the hogs caught on fire and almost burned up. Enough was saved though and this with a keg of wine and a few grapes and nuts were the Christmas dinner. However it wasn't bad. After lugging the phonograph all over France, into the line and out, two or three times, it is working, and we had that playing, so it was very cheerful.

It is terribly boring here now. We live only in hopes of moving somewhere. Anywhere, it doesn't make much difference, but I'm afraid we are here for a couple of months anyway. There is not much sickness, thank the Lord, but we are living in dread of the flu. Of course everything is joked about. There is a very nice young fellow, a lieutenant, who is in a horrible fix. On one hike coming here, he was in a billet with a Frenchwoman who had lived in America. Thorne is very dark, and after talking to two or three of them for a while, the women pointed at Thorne and said 'oh, African.' They emphasized the last syllable. Since then, the whole Battalion has been on top of the poor boy. He is his Royal highness, the Duke of Africa, and the Ethiopian prince. His life is a perfect misery.

CHAPTER 13
HOMEWARD BOUND

The New Year brought hope for the men of the Battalion, but the monotony of the daily drill and training continued for them over the next several months. The Army understood the need to maintain discipline and preparedness if hostilities resumed, but it also served to keep the men engaged and physically fit.

As winter set in, the poor weather conditions added to the misery of the daily training regimen. The Division was concerned with the health of the troops, particularly respiratory illnesses and impressed upon the officers the need to maintain sanitary conditions and establish areas for drying the uniforms and shoes of the troops.

While trying to combat the influenza epidemic, the officers in the medical corps often clashed with the Division command about the constant training and the exposure the dismal weather. Division records in late January and early February reported that more than one fourth of the Division was unfit for duty as a result of various illnesses such as influenza and pneumonia. The Machine Gun Battalion had a large number of illnesses during one period and reported a 'non-effective strength' of 18.8 percent (Stultz 589).

The pressure from the medical officers resulted in relaxing the regimen of the outdoor maneuvers and allowed for an increase in indoor instruction. Schools were established during these winter months and allowed the men to take classes in various courses offered. Some of the subjects offered the men with basic skills needed in preparing for their return to civilian life, but the majority of the schools maintained a focus on military training.

Maintaining military discipline with the troops was a challenge for the officers when boredom and monotony set in. The men had their minds set on returning home and there was little to do during free time. When a violation of military code occurred, a Charge Sheet was completed with the soldier's name along with the offense, witnesses and outcome. The National Archives in College Park, Maryland has a collection of these charge sheets for the men of this Battalion that primarily reflect minor disciplinary charges that occurred while the men waited for their return home.

Charge Sheet: Private Glenn E. Murray [1890-1933], Company D, was found drunk while on guard duty at Sennevoy le Bas on or about 3:00 PM November 30, 1918.

Charge Sheet: Private Matthew Morris [1887-1950], Company B, did at Sennevoy le Bas, on or about the 3rd day of January 1919 violated standing orders of G.H.Q. A.E.F. by selling cognac to soldiers.

Charge Sheet: Private William F. Carroll [1895-1962], Company C, on 2 January 1919 behaved in an insubordinate and disrespectful manner towards Corporal Robert R. Edwards [1894-1988], Company C, who was then in the execution of his office, by saying 'go fuck yourself,' or words to that effect. (Headquarters Correspondence).

January 16, 1919 – THOMAS

I started out two weeks ago by myself and spent the first three days in Paris, which were wonderful. I then went to Lyons for a day, Marseilles for two days, then to Canes, Nice, and Monte Carlo for a week. I met a boy named Lowndes in Nice and have been with him ever since.

That is the most wonderful country I ever saw, and although I spend more money and I should, I don't regret it a bit. We met some wonderful people. One afternoon we went out to tea with some people. We were ushered into the most magnificent apartment you ever saw and met about four of the most ridiculous countesses and duchesses you ever saw. One of them was the sister of the Queen of Belgium. I talked in my most fluent French and looked out onto the most wonderful view in the world. I was invited to return, but became horribly confused when leaving because I forgot whether to put my extra hand on my back or my stomach when I kissed the ladies hands in parting. Did both however and got away strong, 'Mine own people.'

I am at present waiting a telegram with some money to get me back to my Battalion.

◆

The movement of officers into new command positions occurred regularly while in the Training Area. In early January, Major Robert H. Cox of the 314th Machine Gun Battalion served a short stint as the Acting Division Machine Gun Officer only to be replaced a few weeks later by Lieutenant Colonel Jesse M. Holmes. At the beginning of February, Holmes was then replaced by the Battalion's own Major Prescott Huidekoper to serve as the new Division Machine Gun Officer. Major Jennings C. Wise of the 318th Infantry was transferred to the Historical Section of General Headquarters.

January 20, 1919 – THOMAS

I'm glad my watch is safely home and hope you didn't have to pay duty on it. Today, I received a visit from one of my Sergeants who got his commission and is now in the Army of occupation. He brought me an Iron Cross which I was very glad to get. I'll try to pick up a few souvenirs before I come home, but when they were thickest, we didn't have time to bother with them, or have a place to carry them.

I remember one night we spent in a little town, where the Boche had left his dinner cooking on the stove, and there were about eight or ten of these officers' helmets in a back room. They sell for two or three hundred Francs each now, but we didn't have time to bother with them.

What I would like to bring you are some of the flowers from the Riviera. The roses there are the most gorgeous I have ever seen. I didn't tell you that I met Nell Lewis [Cornelia Battle Lewis 1893-1956] down there, did I? I took her out to dinner one night, and one morning we went down and looked at the flowers in the shops. I bought her an arm full of the most gorgeous pink roses you ever saw, with the most delicate blue red veins running through them and they cost six Francs, just a little over a dollar. Nell was fine. She is working for the YMCA at Nice and is having a fine time I think. We sat out on the promenade and thought and discussed what a wonderful effect it would have on the simple villagers if some of what we saw pass were turned loose on Charlotte and Raleigh.

I, naturally, spoke to several Countesses and Duchesses of my acquaintance, much to Nell's awe. There were no queens out that morning.

It's a different world from ours, mama, but with all its bright flowers and beautiful women, and picturesque scenery, ours is a cleaner, fresher world and I'll be glad to return to it.

The whole trip was fine though throughout, and although I spent some money that I had expected to save, I don't regret it. Paris was a disappointment. It rained both days I was there and the whole town has stopped work and is marking up prices for Americans. I saw quite a number of people I know, and enjoyed being there and that is all.

The whole trip was the first time that I had relaxed since I have been in the Army, and it was worth it to me. But, coming back wasn't so bad. My Company was all glad to see me and I had a lot of mail too. I had told this old man I was going to bring he and his wife a souvenir, which I forgot of course, but they came out and greeted me with open arms and were fine to me. But coming back to this mud and rain every day, it seems impossible that a place like Nice exists, with the sunshine always and blue skies and blue water. Chances for an early return seem pretty slim. We hear rumors of course, but have rather made up our minds to grin and bear it for some months to come. It may be that we will get home by spring, but I doubt it.

The 30th [Division] are coming right away I think, so Perrin Cothran [Perrin Chiles Cothran 1885-1959] writes me. They are pretty lucky. Tom Thornhill [Thomas Murrell Thornhill 1894-1972] is with me still and is fine young officer. I saw Bill Taliaferro [William Morrison Taliaferro 1893-1961], who has his orders home. He was hit on the night of November 2nd and was in the same barn with my Company transport. My Company was up farther. He is all right now though. Also saw Alex Worth [Alexander McAlister Worth 1891-1970] and several other people. You meet somebody everywhere you go, and somebody with new stories.

January 26, 1919 - THOMAS

The men are fairly comfortable and I am very comfortable, but never have anything to do, and not much to read. I am growing terribly fat and lazy. The men are very good though, and with a few exceptions, don't give any trouble. It is very hard on them though, and I'll be glad when it is over.

I'm just beginning to realize that I've been in the Army almost 2 years, and also how much two years practically separated from everybody I know means, and I'll admit, I'm very homesick. I suppose as soon as I get out I'll miss being forcibly pulled out of bed by Jimmy, now signed his name James, every morning and having a thousand little things to settle every day, but that's rather the nice part of it these days.

I had a pitiful letter from one of my boy's mother tonight. She just couldn't believe that her boy was dead. I had already written her all about it, but evidently she hadn't received the letter. It was awfully hard on some of them I think.

When we were up in the line and sleeping in rain and mud every night, we used to talk about the war being over, and having a nice place to sleep, and taking off our clothes at night, and not much drill, and it didn't seem like we would ever get tired of France, but of course now everybody is as sore as pups.

One of my lieutenants got his orders home while I was on leave, but even if I had a good reason, I think I would stick it out now and go home with my Company. They are just as homesick as I am, and a lot of them have wives and children. They keep wondering in one by one from the hospital, and I feel very proud of the fact that they fight to get back to the Company, rather than go home.

One of my buglers came in yesterday, and brought me a souvenir, a paper cutter made out of a shell fragment, one of the many that have already been brought in, and he immediately felt fully at home and borrowed 20 Francs. Then waxing extremely loquaciously he gave me a full history of 'Wild Adventures in Hospitals.' It reminded me very much of Penrod's 'Adventures among Carpenters.' It seems that in all of these adventures the said bugler, one Signor Dominic Restivo [1895-1972], had irreparably put to flight whole formations of doctors and nurses, daily arrayed against him, his object being to be put in Class A, and sent back to duty. He even passed words with a Colonel, the whole conversation being, "And he says, 'Well, how you are feeling,' and I say 'Alright,' just like that."

February 3, 1919 – THOMAS

We have had snow on the ground for three weeks now and drill is a little difficult. Nevertheless, between getting up a show, having a school and athletics, we managed to kill time some way or the other. I personally am living in dread of having to go to another school. I am well fed up with them, but it is not at all unlikely. They still go on and are just as boring, from all accounts, as they can possibly be. I have never in all my life been any more fed up than at present, but of course, it is part of the game and I'm going to play my string out after going this far, you know. We'll get out someday I guess.

All the dope is that we go to Camp Lee to be mustered out. It would certainly look like home to us now. The only thing we do have is good food. We have the finest Greek cook in the world. Have divorced him from many of the good old Busy Bee days, and he can cook wonderful kidney stew and pies, but he will put sliced pickles on both sides of the omelet.

February 9, 1919 – THOMAS

Nothing unusual going on now. I am temporarily in command of the Battalion. It only means I don't have to get up to reveille, which is quite a relief. Don't think it will last long. Nothing to do but eat and sleep here and try to keep the men as happy as possible. Winter breaks in about a month now, I think, so if we have to stay here it won't be so bad.

The Company had a show last night which was fine. It keeps their interest up and is awfully good for them, if you can get it started. It has been awfully cold here for several days, the coldest weather we have had. I am glad we don't have to be at the front these days.

February 21, 1919 – THOMAS

It is a good deal warmer here now and I think spring will break in about two weeks. We don't get any information on leaving. Will probably be here for some time yet. We may get home by May or June. It is awfully tiresome here. There is nothing to do, very little to read. All of our time is spent in getting things to keep the men busy and is a rather hard job. The men are mighty good about it and will be, but are awfully homesick. They are allowed to go on pass now, which helps. Jimmy is going to Paris Sunday. He's getting all ready for it now. We can let 20% of them go at one time, and they are really having an excellent time.

As far as my plans go, I haven't any. I want to come home and do nothing for a while, and have an invitation to Virginia Beach for a part or whole of the summer. I'll go there for a while, then I'm going to Louisville, probably for a while, then I'll have to get to work sometime I suppose. [Louisville was the home of Captain Thomas' future wife Katherine Beverly Leathers 1895-1995].

I am afraid Jimmy will be a little expensive for us. He's a nice boy though. He'll visit us for a while, I think. Those are his present plans I believe. He can stay as long as he wants to. He has been invaluable to me. He was bothered all day yesterday and I asked him what was the matter. He said he didn't want to leave me for five days to go on pass.

❧

A Division Bulletin dated February 22, 1919, provided the Battalion with the news they were all anxiously waiting to hear, an estimate date on when the men would be returning to the States. The Adjutant General of the American Expeditionary Forces wrote: "Divisions will return to United States in the following order: March: 27th, 30th, 85th, 37th, 91st Divisions. April: 26th, 77th, 82nd, 35th, 42nd Divisions. May: 32nd, 28th, 33rd, 80th, 78th Divisions. June: 89th, 90th, 29th, 79th Divisions" (Stultz 600).

February 25, 1919 – THOMAS

By the recent order, we are supposed to sail in May. We are hoping to beat that a little, but can't tell of course. Everybody is very anxious to get home, naturally. We are having very rotten weather. It is raining every day, but we hope to have spring in about three weeks. Most of our time is getting the men rid of cooties and keeping them well. Jimmy is on a trip to Paris for three days. He gets back tomorrow, I hope.

March 12, 1919 – THOMAS

We leave this area in about three weeks, I think, and should be on the way home by May 10th. When I was in Paris the other day I saw Colonel Foley. He is trying to get on the Liquidation Board and promised me he would get me on it also, if he could. It would be a fine experience, I think, and I hope I can land it. It would take me all over France and very probably keep me here for another year. Don't get worried because there is not much chance, I'm afraid, but thought I would tell you anyway in case it comes up later.

March 25, 1919 - THOMAS

It seems a long time since I wrote you, but we have been very busy packing up. Besides that we are to pass in review before the Commander in Chief tomorrow, which means a lot of preparation. We leave this area about a week from Thursday to go to Le Mans. We stay there three weeks, or a month, and then go to the port of embarkation.

We have turned in all of our guns, which is quite a job and expect to turn in all our rolling stock in a few days. This will mean a lot less work and travel and it means that we will only have to keep the men amused and happy until we get home. They are in fine shape now since they think they are on the way home, but they have always been wonderful. You haven't any idea that these men have been through cheerfully, not the front so much, that was bad enough, but made to go through everything else in the world, and have laughed through it all. The American soldier is a wonderful institution.

I've got to get up at 3:00 AM in the morning and march the Battalion 8 miles and be hiked around until 12 or 1 o'clock tomorrow, so I'll close.

◈

The entire 80th Division came together on March 26 for a review before their Commander-in-Chief, General John J. Pershing. The 313th Machine Gun Battalion marched about 12 kilometers from Sennevoy le Bas to a hillside just south of Pimelles where the review took place. General Pershing took over two hours passing through the platoons inspecting the troops and often stopping to talk to the men, particularly those wearing the wound chevrons.

After the General completed his inspection, a group of 12 men from the Division were formed together to allow the General to personally pin on the decorations awarded to these men. It was here that Alexander MacWilliam of the Battalion received his Distinguished Service Cross from

General Pershing. Just three days earlier, Special Order No. 82 from General Headquarters announced the appointment of MacWilliam as a Second Lieutenant in the Infantry. It is not known which rank MacWilliam was wearing at the time Pershing pinned on his decoration. Following the ceremony, General Pershing and his guests took their positions in a reviewing stand and the entire Division passed in review.

The next day, Division Field Order No. 2 was issued and instructed the Division to begin transferring from the 15th Training Area to the Le Mans Embarkation Area. Le Mans was the headquarters for the American Embarkation Center, but there we about 30 different villages surrounding the area that billeted the soldiers. The move started with troops boarding trains at Poincon beginning on March 30. The move required 20 trains to transfer the Division. The 313th Machine Gun Battalion departed from Pacy on March 31 and received following billeting assignments while on route to the Le Mans area: Headquarters Company, C Company and D Company were billeted at Saint-Vincent-du-Lorouër, while A Company and B Company billeted at Pruillé-l'Éguillé. In was in these two villages that each Company gathered to have their photograph taken to record the history of the unit. The photos were generally taken by independent American photographers. The C Company photo reveals the men standing outside the Hotel De La Place Bordeaux with the neighboring Catholic Church, Église Saint Vincent, visible in the photograph. Private Andrew A. Capets told his son Victor, that the photo was taken by arranging the men in a semi-circle, or horseshoe, thus allowing the camera to pan the faces of the entire company.

Although drill continued for the men in the Le Mans area, it was limited to only about four hours in the morning, with the afternoons open for sports and recreation. There was no drill on the weekends. The procurement of a leave pass became quite important to the men in the Battalion. Travelling within the entire area then occupied by the Division was allowed without a pass. Trips to the town of Tours was quite popular in this part of France and the ability to visit Paris and England, while sought after by many, was limited to a small number of passes.

March 29, 1919 - HAMILTON
[Letter to his brother Kenneth Hamilton 1988-1969]

I'm in England now on leave. I managed to diddle them for two 14 day leaves. I left on my first night, right after the Armistice and just four months later, you can only go every 4 months, I went again. As no leaves could extend beyond March 30, on account of the Division sailing, I felt jolly lucky to squeeze in two leaves.

Very few people in the Division have been able to manage it. I am with Uncle James [James Hamilton 1841-19xx, Edinburgh] now and it's rather stupid. But I've a wonderful bed, and they have swell food and am getting on alright. Also, it's cheap, and God knows it cost a dollar a minute to stop in either Paris or London.

Archie [Archibald Hamilton] is here, still a Captain, and about to go to the Rhine Army, and Kathleen is now 21 and nice. I can't imagine what sort of a cuss it is that marries an English girl. They are all bright, you know, but they haven't, they simply haven't got it.

I'll be home directly, so get to work and line up about 16 regulation American girls. Tell them I am the hero of the Marne, and want above all things, feminine sympathy, spelled with a capital S. My parlor talk has dwindled to nothing, my face has grown old and hard, my teeth have all gone, but I would appreciate the conversation and consolation of an American girl more than I can say.

April 6, 1919 – THOMAS

We have finally left Sennevoy-le-Bas and are now at a little town called St. Vincent, about 15 miles south of Le Mans. Had a rather uneventful trip here. Men were well behaved and made it in about 24 hours. Trip very uncomfortable. We got off at 12 o'clock at night and hiked 15 miles, arriving at about 6:30 AM, rather tired, but everybody in good spirits. This is the best part of France we have struck I think.

We are supposed to leave here in anywhere from three to five weeks. I don't care how soon it is much, but have a nice billet and my Company is more comfortable than it has ever been before. The length of time here depends on whether the men have been freed of cooties and whether the records are straight. As we are in good shape in both respects, we are to have easy sailing.

Spring is just threatening and it was very pleasant. We don't have much work, but they don't seem to be able to help harassing the men with useless drills, etc. The men take it in good part, however, and thank God there is not much more of it.

❧

In order for the troops to leave the Embarkation Center they had to receive a good bill of health, or rather, free of lice, the famed "cootie." Delousing facilities were prepared by the Sanitary Train and the Battalion surgeon was required to make a physical examination of the men and report his findings. These examinations included identifying any men who contracted a venereal disease, a condition subject to Court Martial charges and the possibility of separating the soldier from his unit, thus delaying his return to the States.

April 12, 1919 – THOMAS

We received a notice last night that we would be leaving here from the 18th to the 25th, so in all probability June 1 should see us well out of it all, so it is a very short time really before we finish.

Right now we are busy as per the Army requirements. Getting vaccinated, making lists and rolls, then training them all up, and doing it over again. But we hope, in spite of all that, we will get away in short order. I'm damn tired of it all and will be very glad to quit.

We have the best place here we have had in France and the men are all well as can be hoped for. I had a clean bill of health for my Company yesterday.

April 20, 1919 – THOMAS

Easter Sunday. We have gone through the same thing here as at Camp Lee. Desperate rush to get everything started and then everything to be done all over again. It is the same old Army staff, and although you get used to it, finally it is pretty raw.

You have no idea of the utter drudgery of everything now. We've been together so long that everybody is bored stiff with each. Easter seems to confine itself to a celebration for the children in this neighborhood. They are all out in gala attire today, but that is about the only sign you see. The church is about 50 yards from me, Roman Catholic of course, and there has been much bell ringing of course.

All the men have been going fishing for the last few days without much success, I think. We drill and hike and are inspected and so it goes. The fruit trees are beginning to blossom now and it is supposed to be spring beginning tomorrow.

One of my lieutenants is going to stay over here, and I'm getting back one of my old Sergeants, now a Lieutenant to go home with us.

∞

The Division received its orders on May 6 to move to Brest for embarkation. The transfer of the entire Division took place between May 9 and May 16. The Battalion Headquarters Company, along with A and B Companies left from Mayet on May 15, while C and D Companies boarded the train on the final day. The trains travelled through the French towns of Laval, Vitré, Rennes, Saint-Brieuc, Guingamp, and Landerneau, with the last train reaching Brest on May 17. The troops were received into Camp Pontanezen, an encampment first established at the beginning of the war to receive troops that landed at the port in Brest. This camp was housing over 70,000 troops bound for the States when the Battalion arrived. When they reached the camp the men learned through a May 16 Division Bulletin, that the 80th Division was heading back to Newport News, Virginia for disembarkation.

The troops were subjected to continuous formations to complete their paperwork, medical examinations and a trip through the delousing station before they received a new outfit of clothing. While in camp, the General Headquarters of the A.E.F. announced that the men who arrived in France with the Division were now permitted to wear a second overseas service chevron marking an additional 6 months of service. Two chevrons on the sleeve represented one year of service for most of the men in the Battalion.

The regulations for issuance of the official A.E.F. War Service Medal, the Victory Medal, and battle clasps were also announced while the men were assembled at Camp Pontanezen. The majority of the men who remained with the Battalion throughout the war had the following notations entered on their service record for those who participated in the following engagements: Artois Sector July 29 to August 18, 1918; St. Mihiel

Offensive, Corps Reserves, September 12 to 16, 1918; and Meuse-Argonne September 26 to October 12, and November 1 to 11, 1918. The titles on the battle clasps for these dates of the engagements varied only slightly for the Battalion. They received the clasp titled "Defensive Sector" for their time in the Artois Sector, Picardy; "St. Mihiel" for September 12 to 16, 1918; and "Meuse-Argonne" for the dates September 26 to November 11, 1918. A small bronze star was permitted to be attached to the service ribbon for those who served during the Meuse-Argonne offensive.

The Battalion boarded the battleship *USS New Jersey* and left port on May 21, 1919, along with the 314th Machine Gun Battalion and casuals attached to the 318th Infantry. Their time on the seas did not require travelling without lights, or to maintain a regimen of sentinel watch as they did on their initial trip to France. Instead, while military discipline was still maintained, it was a more relaxed voyage back home and allowed the men to enjoy motion pictures, boxing competitions, and a theatrical performance by members of B Company called, the *Three Act Farce Comedy*. There was also a pie eating contest that took place during the trip.

The men were anxious to get back to Camp Lee for demobilization, but there were several unexpected occurrences that delayed their arrival home. The first incident occurred when the *USS New Jersey* had to make an unscheduled stop in the Azores Islands. On May 26, the ship encountered engine troubles and found it necessary to harbor at Ponta Delgada. As the crew tended to the ship, a few of the men were allowed shore passes, while local merchants were permitted to board the ship for those men unable to reach the docks. Despite this impromptu stop, the men were distracted from the delay when they discovered that the Curtiss NC-4 seaplane was at the island refueling. They learned the plane was in the midst of a transatlantic crossing, a first in aviation history. Major Huidekoper told the *Pittsburgh Post-Gazette*, "We put into Ponta Delgada, Azores, because of engine trouble, but few of us regretted it, because while we were there we had the opportunity to see Commander Read make his hop-off from there for Lisbon, with his NC-4. Three days of the trip were rough, but the boys were too happy to be on their way home to allow themselves to be troubled" ("US Seaplane NC4").

The next morning, the Battalion watched the Curtiss NC-4 seaplane takeoff for Lisbon. In the afternoon, a wireless message was sent back to the port reporting the plane had indeed reached Lisbon. The boats in the harbor blasted their whistles in a celebratory fashion.

Departing the Azores Islands, the Battalion encountered a second delay when the *USS New Jersey* was warned of severe weather off the southern coast of the United States and the ship was directed to head to Boston to avoid the strong gale storms. On June 7, the *New Jersey* reached the shores of the United States.

June 7, 1919 - JOSEPH MILLER

The happiest day of them all. We arrived at Boston at 7:00 AM. The ship dropped anchor about a mile from harbor and the Boston YMCA and Red Cross and several other organizations came out in boats to welcome us they put over a barrage of chocolate and donuts, and some of the boys were badly wounded.

At 10:00 AM barges came out to take us off our ship and put us into Boston where the YMCA, JWCSA people gave us eats, drinks and furnished us with telegrams free. We boarded trains for Camp Devens, about an hour and a half ride from Boston. Arrived at Camp and went through sanitary process.

&

Arriving at Boston the Battalion had yet another minor obstacle that stood in the way of the troops quickly disembarking from the ship. The ship was initially headed for a new base built in the port of South Boston. However, while approaching this port they were told to instead anchor at a port in East Boston. When they did arrive at the port, another ship was in their path, and so after some maneuvering, the *New Jersey* was finally put in place and the Battalion was finally ready to disembark. Unfortunately, to their chagrin, one final snag delayed their arrival when it was discovered that there were no gangplanks available to get the men off the ship. The *Pittsburgh Post-Gazette* reported, "Meantime a flimsy board, that apparently would not bear the weight of an average sized soldier, was offered as a gangplank. Later, two or three ladders were produced by firemen attached to the army base fire company, and the soldiers climbed these to the pier. It was the merriest kind of a scramble, every khaki clad youth too tickled to get foot on American soil" ("Two Machine Gun Battalions").

A party of citizens travelled from Erie, Pennsylvania, to welcome the men back home. Miles B. Kitts, the Mayor of Erie, was part of the welcoming party that travelled to Boston. He met with Second Lieutenant Alexander MacWilliam while in Boston and learned that the men had a few more stops on their journey before returning to Erie. Once all the men were off the ship, they were put aboard a train and sent to Camp Devens, a camp located in the towns of Ayer and Shirley, Massachusetts. With the Army's request to expedite the process of demobilization, the troops were split into groups and permitted to travel to a camp that was nearest to their home. Most of the men in the Battalion travelled to either Camp Lee or Camp Dix as their final destination.

Once the soldiers reached their last camp, the final paperwork was completed and the men were mustered out of the Army and returned back to their homes. Thousands of communities across the country were anxiously awaiting the return of their beloved Doughboys.

Lieutenant MacWilliam was at Camp Dix when he received a letter from Mayor Kitts that read in part, "We are making preparations for a short parade and reception. We will rope off West Perry Square Park. I desire to give the Service Club all the prominence possible, but will be obliged to leave the question of where you desire to go after the short words of welcome are given to you at the City Hall, entirely up to you and the boys. I have taken care of the request about your baggage. A large space will be roped off at the depot and a motor truck will be waiting to take the baggage to the City Hall and it will be kept under police guard every minute from the time it is deposited at the depot until each boy receives it. Hoping we may see you all in good old Erie soon" (Kitts).

On Thursday evening, June 12, a troop train filled with 183 men from the Battalion left Camp Dix bound for Erie. The train stopped in Kane, Pennsylvania, the morning of the June 13, where the men were provided with a quick bite to eat before proceeding onto Erie. *The Kane Republic* reported seeing this message scrawled in chalk on the side of one of the coaches, "From the banks of the Rhine to the banks of Lake Erie" ("Erie Machine Gun Battalion in Kane"). A short ride down the tracks and the men were home at last.

CHAPTER 14
POST WAR

T he weeks that followed the welcome home parades, the patriotic speeches and the generous receptions provided for the returning Battalion was a difficult time for the grieving families who lost family members during the war. Information often arrived late, or never at all, about how their son or husband died.

In the case of Private Wallace Ben Holland, it wasn't until February 27, 1920 that the Adjutant General of the Army requested that the record of Holland be corrected to properly report his death. The message read in part, "Upon investigation it has been ascertained by the War Department that Private First Class Wallace Ben Holland who was previously reported by the Commanding General, American Expeditionary Forces, as severely wounded in action about November 5, 1918 was killed in action November 3, 1918. A notation to that effect has been placed upon the official records" (Burial File).

Holland's body was disinterred from its isolated grave on April 15, 1919. Lieutenant H.E. Strong, Graves Registration Service, reported Holland's body was buried "very poor, in uniform, and normally decomposed" (Burial File). His body was then placed in a new wooden casket and reburied in grave No. 168, Section 19, Plot 4 of the Meuse-Argonne American Cemetery. This cemetery was established in Romagne-sous-Montfaucon, France and designated as the final resting place for the more than 26,000 Americans who were killed during the Meuse-Argonne Battle.

On July 3, 1919, Holland's mother, Alphoretta Holland (1871-1939), wrote a letter to the Adjutant General of the Army requesting, "I do most respectfully ask that you send me a proper blank to be filled out for the request of the body of my son to be brought home for burial" (Burial File). When the Adjutant General's office received Mrs. Holland's request, a letter was sent to the Quartermaster General's Office, Cemeteries Branch, requesting information on the location of Holland's burial. A response was sent back to the Adjutant General on August 2, 1919 stating that the place of burial was not yet received. It was not until October 20 that the Adjutant General's office contacted the Chief of Graves Registration Services for a report requesting the date and burial location of Holland. Over one year had elapsed from the date Holland was killed, and the details of his burial were finally provided to the Adjutant General on November 26, 1919.

On May 24, 1921, George W. Holland (1866-1944) signed a form requesting that the body of his son be returned to Union City, Pennsylvania. His request was sent to the Graves Registration Service in France and one month later the body of Wallace Ben Holland was disinterred from the Meuse-Argonne American Cemetery. Supervisor and embalmer E.J. Frank noted on his report that the body was wrapped in burlap when it was placed in the wooden box, buried in uniform, and the body badly decomposed. A new box was prepared and marked for shipment back to the United States. Holland's body left Antwerp, Belgium on August 6th and arrived at the port in Hoboken, New Jersey on August 20th, 1921. The remains of another soldier from Union City, Lynn Larue LeBaron (1887-1918), also arrived in port to be returned home to the family. LeBaron was killed on October 14th, 1918 while serving with the 188th Infantry Regiment.

Private First Class Alfred C. Harmon, 28th Infantry Division, escorted both bodies from Hoboken, New Jersey to Union City, Pennsylvania by way of the Erie railroad. The remains of the men reached their families on September 7, 1921. Mayor A.F. Young of Union City requested that all businesses display the American flag at half-mast and asked that businesses close as the funeral procession travelled through Main Street. Both men were interred in the Evergreen Cemetery in Union City, Pennsylvania.

The delays in returning the remains of an American soldier back home to the family, as experienced by the Holland and LeBaron families, was not uncommon following the war. It was nearly three years after the death of Lieutenant Joseph M. Duff that the family was finally able to receive the remains of their son and bury him in the Chartiers Cemetery in Carnegie, Pennsylvania on September 9, 1921.

⤝

While the majority of the men in the Battalion were fortunate to return home to their families, many soldiers came back with physical or psychological effects brought on by the war. Lieutenant Alexander MacWilliam suffered from the effects of the gas attacks that occurred in October 1918. When he returned to Erie, Pennsylvania, on the advice of his doctor, he was encouraged to relocate to Florida to avoid the harsh cold weather that played havoc on the lungs. MacWilliam relocated to Vero Beach, Florida, and started his new life where he continued to excel as a leader. MacWilliam married Jeannette O'Flaherty in 1920 and together they raised nine children. While living in Vero Beach, MacWilliam served on city council and became the Mayor of Vero Beach in 1927. MacWilliam later became a Florida State Representative for Indian River County and was instrumental in building a veterans memorial on seven acres of land along the Indian River dedicated to all who were killed in the service of their country.

⤝

Major Prescott Huidekoper, the leader of the Battalion, returned from the war and worked his way up to becoming president of the American Insulator Corporation, a plastics manufacturing company, in New Freedom, Pennsylvania. Despite the economic struggles faced during the Depression, business went well for his company. A local newspaper announced in 1937 that his 400 or so employees discovered, to their surprise, a 10 percent increase in their paycheck ("New Freedom Firm Announces Increase").

However, on March 31, 1939, Huidekoper sat behind the desk in his office and shortly before noon, as the sound of a train passed outside his office window, he raised a .32 caliber revolver to his right temple and fired ("Head of Insulator Co"). Whatever thoughts haunted him as he sat in that chair were left unspoken and would forever leave his family to wonder why he chose that final act.

His family submitted that he was not well, as suggested in letters

291

written by members of the family. Earlier that year, his family believed he needed a vacation and encouraged him to take some time off from work and visit his daughter Page, hoping it "would perk up his spirits" (Wilson 38).

Huidekoper took a trip to Europe to visit his daughter to join her in celebrating her twenty-first birthday. Huidekoper rented a car and driver to travel around the French countryside hoping to locate the battlefields on which he had fought some twenty years earlier. His daughter said, "He hoped to find a ravine, a hillside, or a forest that triggered a memory" (Wilson 41). However, during their search, she observed him to be "quiet and dispirited," recalling that "nowhere did my father find a spot that summoned up the twenty-year old ghost he had both wanted and feared, to see." Sensing his dismay, she convinced him to cut their excursion short, knowing they would continue to find "evidence of more American graveyards and not the jolting memory for which he was looking" (Wilson 42).

With the war nearly twenty years behind him, one could only speculate on the reason Huidekoper took his own life. It would be unfair to suggest that anyone could possibly begin to understand the reason for his decision, but at the very least, we can acknowledge that the experiences of World War I changed the lives of millions of Americans and had profound psychological effects on the returning veterans.

❧

Lieutenant Minard Hamilton stayed in Europe at the close of the war and went to work for the American Relief Administration, the predecessor to the United States Food Administration. His orders took him to Libau, Russia to assist in a food relief mission where thousands of people were starving during the Russian famine of 1919.

Hamilton returned home to Dobbs Ferry, New York in 1920 and went to work as a clerk for a local company. His interest in aviation continued beyond his waning desires expressed in the letters written home during the war. Through a family friendship, he was given an opportunity to work in the field of aviation. The American Aviation Exploration Company, then located in New York, was a subsidiary of the Curtiss-Wright Aeronautical Corporation. Hamilton had a personal relationship with Clement Melville

Keys (1876–1952), president of Curtiss-Wright, who gave Hamilton an opportunity in 1929 to oversee a new venture in commercial air service in China with the China National Aviation Corporation (CNAC), founded through a partnership between Curtiss-Wright and the Chinese government.

Hamilton returned to the United States in the early 1930s, shortly before Pan American Airways purchased the interests of the Chinese Airline. He married Elizabeth Ten Broeck Hyde (1900-1963), a recently divorced mother of two young boys whom Hamilton later adopted as his own sons. Minard and Elizabeth had two daughters of their own and settled down in Warren County, New Jersey where they operated the Hidden Valley Farm.

※

Captain John Kean returned to Ursino following the war and became director and assistant treasurer of the Elizabethtown Gas Light Company in Elizabeth, New Jersey. In 1925, Kean married Mary Alice Barney (1903-1995), the daughter of John Stewart Barney (1867-1924), an architect and partner in the well-known architectural firm of Barney and Chapman of New York City. By 1930, John Kean was vice president of the gas company and the father of two children, John Jr. and Mary Alice. In 1932, following the death of his uncle, Julian Halstead Kean (1854-1932), John Kean inherited the 50 room mansion in Union, New Jersey. Mary Alice Kean gave birth to their second son, Stewart in 1934.

John Kean eventually became the president of the Elizabethtown Company. Over the years, he and his wife took an interest in the history of the property and began to bring together a collection of family antiques to decorate their home. Following the premature death of Captain John Kean in 1949, Mary Alice began to envision the mansion as a museum. Her love of history and antiquities allowed her to cultivate the property in the years following her husband's death. In 1974, she revived the name of the property, referring to it once again as Liberty Hall, honoring the history of the property. The building was constructed in 1772, the home of William Livingston, the first Governor of New Jersey and was listed as a National Historic Landmark in 2009. The property is currently owned by Kean University.

❧

Captain William George Thomas returned to Charlotte, North Carolina after the war and became a manager of a local textile mill supply company. He married Kathleen Leathers of Louisville, Kentucky in 1920. The wedding took place in Louisville, where friends and family travelled to celebrate with the couple. His good friend Spig was one of the groomsman in the wedding and several officers of the Battalion attended the wedding, including John Kean, Robert Cox, Robert Bradley, Leland Garretson, Prescott Huidekoper and Oscar Foley. The couple moved to New York City, and in December 1921, the couple welcomed their only daughter, Florence.

Jordan Thomas, father of Captain Thomas, passed away two months before Florence was born. Thomas and his family moved back to Charlotte by 1930, where he remained working in the textile industry as a Cotton Yarn Broker.

❧

Lieutenant Otto P. Leinhauser returned from the war and rejoined his wife Elizabeth in Sharon Hill, Pennsylvania. He went back to work at the Sun Shipbuilding & Dry Dock Company and eventually became foreman. He and his wife raised four daughters and a son while living in Sharon Hill. He provide 34 years of service to his employer, working alongside his father Christian, his brother Frank and also his son Otto Jr.

Leinhauser continued to impress those around him with his leadership abilities. He served as a commander of the Catholic War Veterans Association Post 1234, the American Legion Post 193, president of the Sharon Hill Fire Company and was a former Sharon Hill councilman. He also served as a National Commander of the 80th Division Veterans Association.

The 80th Division Veterans Association was organized to preserve the history of the Division and "foster and perpetuate the memories and incidents of the World War and to continue to strengthen the friendships among the officers and men which were formed during the months of service" (West Virginia).

The first reunion and business meeting of this association was held in Richmond, Virginia in September 1920. The group elected Brigadier

General Lloyd M. Brett (1856-1927) to be their President and made Major General Cronkite the Honorary President. A few of the Machine Gun Battalion members are recorded as Charter Members of the 80th Division Veterans Association, including Otto Leinhauser, John Fred Brei Jr. (1891-1947), Charles Vermeire (1894-1978), Luigi Agostini (1896-1987), and Emmet Edwin Chesley (1892-1978).

It was at this first meeting in 1920 that Sergeant Russell Lee Stultz of the 318th Infantry Regiment became part of the association's executive committee and was made the Division's Historian. He is credited with compiling the vast amount of records detailing the movement of troops and personnel who served in the Division. His efforts ultimately led to the publishing of the *History of the Eightieth Division A.E.F. in World War I* by Lee S. Anthony. Dr. Lee's publication was instrumental in building the framework for compiling this history of the 313th Machine Gun Battalion.

Following the Second World War, Emmet Chesley was elected as Commander of the 80th Division Veterans Association. He had the rules of the organization amended to allow veterans of World War II the opportunity to be nominated as future officers.

∽

While the Division had a veterans association organized for maintaining a long-term relationship for the larger group, the men of the Battalion also wanted their own association. Building upon their camaraderie and shared experiences, the men formed the 313th Machine Gun Battalion Club which operated on Peach Street in Erie, Pennsylvania for many years.

At their third annual reunion in 1923, the men gatherer at Eagle Point in Erie, Pennsylvania, where Mayor Kitts welcomed 130 members of the Battalion. The afternoon was devoted to "games and amusement, and for the most part, to relation of experiences of those other days of five years ago" ("313th M. G. Battalion has reunion at Erie").

It was at this meeting that the members elected their officers, naming Milton Neuroh (1887-1965) as president, John Growley (1892-1962) as vice president, and Russell Heth Duncombe (1894-1984) as secretary. The officers and organizers of the reunions were generally selected from the men living near Erie who could take on the responsibilities of organizing the annual reunions and running the matters related to the club. Later reunion organizers included Erie residents Leroy Welk, Arthur W. Young (1895-1983), John Brie, and John W. Kilmore (1894-1956).

The reunions were well attended as evidenced by the number of men that appeared in many of the group photos taken during the occasion. At the twentieth reunion, held at the Sunset Inn on East Lake Road in Erie, as many as 200 members of the Battalion were in attendance. However, as the years went on, the reunion numbers slowly began to dwindle. By the late 1970s, as the men of the Battalion were approaching their later years, the total members in attendance were minimal. At the 55th annual reunion, held at the Peach Street club in 1975, Andrew A. Capets joined just twelve of his fellow Battalion members for what would be his last reunion. He appears in the back row of this photograph under the number 55.

REUNION 1975 – 313th Machine Gun Battalion, Erie, PA.

Capets was proud of his service during the war and honored to have been associated with his Battalion. His wife, Mary, was also proud of him and she too attended many of the reunions as a member of the Battalion's Ladies Auxiliary.

After returning from the war, Capets found a new job working at the Westinghouse Manufacturing Company in Trafford, Pennsylvania. His job as a moulder was a dirty, labor intensive job, but the Westinghouse

Company was booming at the time and provided a decent wage for many of the returning veterans.

Within two years of his return, he met Mary E. Kuchta (1905-1981) and the couple eloped to Cumberland, Maryland where they were married in 1921. Capets donned his Army uniform while Kuchta wore a traditional Polish style wedding dress for their wedding picture. Their first three children were all born before the Great Depression; Albert B. Capets (1922-1987), Edward J. Capets Sr. (1924-2009), and Margaret Capets (1926-2015). The growing family needed their own home, and in 1927, they purchased a kit home from the pages of the *Sears, Roebuck & Company* catalog and built the *Manchester* model on Inwood Road in Trafford. The *Manchester* was advertised as a nine room home that could accommodate two families. Anna and Andrej Kapec (Anna and Andrew Capets Sr.), also lived in the home with the growing family.

CAPETS

Another six children were born to the couple over the years, including Vincent Capets (1930-1979), Irene, Victor, Veronica, John, and Madeline. Their Inwood home became the center of family activities for the multitude of grandchildren born into the family. Andrew Capets completed 40 years of service with the Westinghouse Corporation and retired on December 1, 1960. He spent the remaining years of his life in his Trafford home living a modest life with his wife Mary. He passed away on May 2, 1976 and was buried in the Monongahela Cemetery, Braddock Hills, Pennsylvania.

In 2013, a memorial tree and commemorative brick were placed in the Veterans Memorial Park in Trafford, Pennsylvania, to honor the service of Andrew A. Capets during World War I. The brick acknowledges his service as a member of the 313th Machine Gun Battalion. The tree symbolizes an appreciation to 'Andy' and the millions of Americans who pledged to protect this great Nation.

BATTALION ROSTER

The following pages provide a list of nearly 1,000 men who made up the ranks of the 313th Machine Gun Battalion. Due to the number of personnel changes that occurred throughout the war, this is not an all-inclusive list and apologize for any errors or name omissions.

The first column provides the soldier's name. The second and third columns provide Rank and Company assignment when the soldier left Newport News, Virginia in May 1918. The last two columns provide the Rank and Company assignment when the soldier left Brest, France in June 1919 (U.S., Army Transport Service). If no data is provided, the soldier did not travel on these ships as part of the 313th Machine Gun Battalion. Notes have been added for those known to have died while attached to the Battalion.

ABBREVIATIONS

1ST LT	First Lieutenant	MECH	Mechanic
1ST SGT	First Sergeant	MESSGT	Mess Sergeant
2ND LT	Second Lieutenant	PFC	First Class Private
BUGL	Bugler	PVT	Private
CAPT	Captain	SDLR	Saddler
CORP	Corporal	SGT	Sergeant
DA	Died of Accident	SGT MAJ	Sergeant Major
DD	Died of Disease	STBSGT	Stable Sergeant
DW	Died of Wounds	SUPSGT	Supply Sergeant
HRSR	Horseshoer	WAG	Wagoner
KIA	Killed in Action		

NAME	MAY 1918	CO	JUN 1919	CO
Abrams, George M			PVT	D
Ackers, Henning McPherson			PVT	B
Adams, Clabe			PVT	B
Adkins, Harry L	PVT	C	SGT	C
Adkins, James Clara			PFC	B
Adkins, Oscar Stephen	PVT	B	PVT	B
Affantranger, Alfred Charles	SGT MAJ	HQ	SGT MAJ	HQ
Ager, Carl			PVT	B
Alexander, Ora L			PVT	D
Alford, William R			PVT	D
Allen, Lafayette Hamilton	WAG	HQ	WAG	HQ
Allen, Neil J	PVT	A	PFC	A
Allen, William C			PVT	B
Allison, Robert D	PVT	D	PVT	D
Alves, Haywood			WAG	HQ
Amos, John Howard	PVT	B	PVT	B
Anderson, Chester I	PVT	C	PVT	C
Anderson, George S	PVT	C	PVT	C
Anderson, Henry Brown	WAG	HQ		
Anderson, Oliver Dee			PVT	C
Anderson, Ralph Wray	WAG	HQ	WAG	HQ
Anderson, Thomas N	PVT	D	CORP	D
Andre, Earl Laughton			PVT	D
Andrews, Lawson			PVT	B
Andrules, Stanley	PVT	B	PVT	B
Angelillo, Nicola	PVT	B		
Antonellis, Gaetano	PVT	A	PVT	A
Antonowicz, Joseph	COOK	D		
Apple, Philip G	PVT	D	PFC	D
Applegate, Edward Maskell	1ST LT	D		
Armour, Lee	CORP	A	CORP	A
Arnodt, John Henry Jacob	PFC	B	PFC	B

Ashton, Merton E			2ND LT	A
Atherholt, Frank E	PVT	A		
Aukerman, Harry	PVT	D		
Aungst, George M	PVT	D	PFC	D
Backus, Frank William	PVT	B	PVT	B
Bain, Dale F			PVT	B
Baird, Robert H	PVT	C	PVT	C
Baker, Allen	PVT	C	PFC	C
Baker, Alva E			PVT	D
Baker, Herman Lewis	PVT	HQ	SGT	HQ
Bald, Russell E			PVT	B
Bald, Russell Earl	PVT	B		
Bale, Harry Albert	PVT	B	PVT	B
Ball, Wilbur J	PVT	D	PVT	D
Ballinger, Norman D	PFC	D	PVT	D
Bancroft, Kohn C			PVT	C
Barbuzzi, Antonio			PVT	D
Barker, Leo L			PVT	B
Barnhart, Charles L	PVT	D	PVT	D
Bartholomew, Karl G	PVT	D	PVT	D
Bartolotta, Joseph			PVT	A
Basore, Carl I			PVT	B
Bath, James H			PVT	D
Baugher, Emil	PVT	HQ	PVT	HQ
Baumbach, William E			SUPSGT	D
Beabout, Howard P	PVT	C	PFC	C
Beach, Oscar H			PVT	D
Beadel, Andrew A			PVT	D
Beatty, Charles Albert	PVT	B		
Beck, Charles R	PVT	A	PVT	A
Beck, Christ James	MECH	B	MECH	B
Becker, John A			PVT	D
Bell, George F	PVT	MD	PVT	MD

Bender, Felix F	PVT	D	PFC	D
Bender, William J	PVT	D	SGT	D
Bengtson, Halge	PVT	B		
Bennett, George J	PVT	A	PVT	A
Bennett, John A	PVT	D	PFC	D
Benson, Roy L	PVT	C	PFC	C
Benson, Theodore Booton	1ST LT	B		
Berchtold, Fred A	PVT	C		
Bernard, Virgil E			PFC	HQ
Beu, Harry O	CORP	A		
Bevil, Robert Patrick	PVT	B	PVT	B
Bickford, Paul	PVT	D	CORP	D
Binion, Ora Lee			PVT	C
Birkbeck, John A			PVT	B
Black, Harvey Lester			PFC	B
Black, Walter Dean	PVT	B	PVT	B
Blackmer, Guy	WAG	HQ	WAG	HQ
Blakeley, Frank E	PVT	C	PFC	C
Blakeley, Roy E	PVT	D	PVT	D
Blazeski, Anthony E	PVT	B	PVT	B
Blessing, Homer			PFC	B
Blose, Walter R	PVT	C	PVT	C
Boase, Walter L			PVT	B
Boderick, Thomas J	PVT	A	PVT	A
Bogart, John E	PVT	MD	PFC	MD
Boggs, Ora			PVT	C
Bohimann, Fred H			PVT	D
Bohlen, John E.S.			PVT	D
Bohrer, Herman Joseph	PVT	B	PFC	B
Boland, Francis A	PVT	C	PVT	C
Bonin, Arthur Ralph	PVT	B		
Borawski, Stanley	PVT	D	PVT	D
Boronda, Robert L			PVT	D
Bosch, Oscar A	PVT	MD	PVT	MD

Bowdon, William G			2ND LT	A
Bowman, Clarence			PVT	D
Boyle, James T	PVT	D	PVT	D
Boyle, Ralph Jonas	PVT	B		
Bradley, Robert Ballantine	1ST LT	HQ	CAPT	HQ
Bradley, Thomas Frederick			PVT	B
Brakke, Peder Elias Martin	PVT	HQ	PVT	HQ
Branowicki, Constant			SDLR	B
Brassell, Harry E	PVT	A	PVT	A
Breene, Adolphus Francis	CORP	B	SGT	B
Brei, John Fred	WAG	HQ	WAG	HQ
Brendel, Leo J			PVT	B
Brewer, Norman M	PVT	A	PVT	A
Brooks, John	PVT	B	PFC	B
Brooks, Walter John	PVT	B	PVT	B
Broomall, Charles J			PVT	B
Brown, Walter	PVT	B	PVT	B
Browne, Hugh	PFC	MD		
Brownlee, Robert J	PVT	C		
Brumbaugh, Lewis A	PVT	D	PVT	D
Brunner, Anthony	PVT	B	PVT	B
Brunner, Jacob J	PVT	B	PVT	B
Brunner, Lawrence Frank	MECH	B	MECH	B
Brunner, Sebastian	PVT	A	PFC	A
Brunot, Edward L	PFC	A	PFC	A
Buchmeyer, Anthony B	CORP	C	SGT	C
Buckels, Earnest			PVT	C
Bullock, William H	PVT	B	PVT	B
Burgit, George Thomas	PVT	B	CORP	B
Burgman, Carl E	CORP	A		
Burgman, William E	PVT	B	PVT	B
Burk, Charles J	PVT	D	PFC	D
Burkett, Arthur W	PFC	D	PFC	D

303

Name	Rank	Co	Rank	Co	
Burkhalter, Henry			1ST LT	C	
Burkhart, Earl Wayne	PVT	B			
Burnham, Pliny Leroy	SGT	B	SGT	B	
Burns, William Masson			PFC	A	
Burton, Everett Parker	PVT	B			
Bussard, Clark Erwin	PVT	B			
Byroad, Robert J			SGT	MD	
Cable, Raymond J	PVT	C	PVT	C	
Cain, Raymond	PVT	B	PVT	B	
Caldwell, Max M	PVT	C	KIA OCT 5, 1918		★
Calk, George W			PVT	D	
Callahan, Raymond J	SGT	A	SGT	A	
Cameron, Richard F	PVT	B	PFC	B	
Campbell, James J	PVT	C	PFC	C	
Capets, Andrew	PVT	C	PVT	C	
Cappucci, Louis	PVT	C			
Carl, John	PVT	D	PVT	D	
Carlisle, Raymond L	SGT	B	1ST SGT	B	
Carlson, Carl E	CORP	C	SGT	C	
Carlson, Fred J	PVT	A	SGT	A	
Carothers, Coyle C	MECH	A	MECH	A	
Carr, William D	PVT	C	PFC	C	
Carroll, Harry O	PVT	A			
Carroll, William F	PVT	C	PVT	C	
Cashdollar, Murray S	PVT	B			
Casteel, Ralph M	PVT	A	PVT	A	
Catone, Joseph	PVT	A	PFC	A	
Chadwick, Harold E	PVT	D	PFC	D	
Chaffee, Tolstoi	PFC	D			
Chalupa, William P			PFC	A	
Chambers, Binford			PVT	A	
Charles, John W	PVT	A	DW NOV 13, 1918		★
Chase, Harry Deforrest	PVT	B	PFC	B	
Check, Earnest E	PVT	D	CORP	D	

Chesley, Emmet E	CORP	C	SGT	C	
Chevalier, Dudley			PVT	A	
Chrapowicz, Joseph F	PVT	D	CORP	D	
Christenson, John E	SGT	C	KIA OCT 6, 1918		★
Christie, Hewitt G	PVT	D	PVT	D	
Christoph, Frederick Joseph	WAG	HQ	WAG	HQ	
Christopher, John A	PVT	A	PFC	A	
Christopher, Wilbur T	PVT	B	PFC	B	
Chudzicki, Frank	PVT	D	PVT	D	
Churchill, Blair B	PFC	D			
Ciminaro, Tony			PVT	HQ	
Clair, Albert M	PVT	A	PVT	A	
Clark, Elmo O			PVT	A	
Clark, Frederick R	PFC	A			
Clark, Jerry			PVT	B	
Clark, Joseph T	PVT	MD	aka Friel, Edward J		
Clarkson, Ralph	PVT	B	CORP	B	
Clayton, Fowler O			PVT	C	
Clement, Aubrey B	PVT	A	COOK	A	
Clemmons, James T			PVT	D	
Cline, Wilmer H	HRSR	C	HRSR	C	
Coakley, John F	PVT	A	KIA OCT 4, 1918		★
Collins, John William			PVT	B	
Comerford, Earl	PVT	A	PVT	A	
Condon, Daniel M	PVT	C			
Conlan, John J			PFC	D	
Connell, John L	MECH	A	MECH	A	
Conroy, Bartley	CORP	A	SGT	A	
Conway, Arthur J	PFC	A	PFC	A	
Conway, John Eliason	PVT	B	KIA OCT 6, 1918		★
Cooke, George V	PVT	A	KIA OCT 4, 1918		★
Cooke, Wesley M			PVT	A	

305

Cooper, Charles F	PVT	C	PVT	C
Copeland, Hudy L			COOK	D
Copeland, Stewart	PVT	B		
Corman, Raymond B			PVT	A
Cottrell, Roy F	PFC	C	PFC	C
Cox, James	PVT	B	PFC	B
Cox, Leo Thomas			PFC	B
Cox, Robert Hill	CAPT	A		
Craig, William J	PVT	C	PFC	C
Crawford, Guy E	CORP	A	CORP	A
Cray, Clayton			SGT	B
Cray, Clayton Raphael	PFC	B		
Crook, John Bernard	PFC	D	DD JAN 4, 1918 ★	
Cross, Reid Melancthon	WAG	HQ	PVT	B
Crotty, Bernard	CORP	C	PVT	C
Crow, Archie F			PVT	C
Cummings, Edward P	SGT	D	SGT	D
Cummings, Edward P			SGT	D
Cunningham, John P	PVT	D	PVT	D
Curran, Bernard	PFC	D	PFC	D
Curtis, William Steward	PVT	B		
Cusic, Joseph Francis	PVT	B	DW OCT 6, 1918 ★	
Da Valle, Jacob J	PVT	C	PVT	C
Dalke, Carl August			PVT	B
Daly, Charles Francis	SGT	B	SGT	B
Daminski, Frank	PVT	D		
Daschbach, Herbert Louis	PVT	B	CORP	B
Dauenhauer, Thomas L			PVT	C
Davenport, Rex J			PFC	A
Davidson, Russell V			PVT	D
Davis, Dewitt T			PVT	B
Davis, Emery Amos	PVT	B	PVT	B
Davis, Walter			PVT	D
Dawley, Perry Andrew	SGT MAJ	HQ		

DeMauri, Augusta	PVT	C		
Deasey, John Wallace	PVT	B	PVT	B
Deeter, William B	PVT	D		
Delong. George			PVT	D
Deluca, Nick	PVT	C	PVT	C
Demarte, Ralph	PFC	C	PFC	C
Denmark, Howard E	PVT	C		
Densmore, James E	PVT	D	PVT	D
Derbin, Antoni	PVT	D		
Deutsch, Jacob John	PFC	B	SGT	B
Devir, Joseph R	PVT	A	PVT	A
Devore, Fred C	MECH	A	MECH	A
Dey, Harry S	PVT	A	PVT	A
Di Scipio, Joseph	PVT	C		
Dias, William M	PVT	A	PFC	A
Dickson, Joseph Wade			PVT	B
Digello, Anthony L	PVT	C		
Dillon, Saymon	PVT	B	PVT	B
Dimnitt, Clarence Robert	PVT	B	PVT	B
Dinkel, Fred Andrew	PVT	B	PVT	B
Dixon, Clyde Everett	PVT	B	PVT	B
Dixon, Vance			PVT	A
Dobbs, William J			PVT	D
Dodds, John Joseph	PVT	B	PVT	B
Donley, Joseph	WAG	HQ	WAG	HQ
Donovan, James	PVT	C	PVT	C
Dooley, Michael L	PVT	C	PFC	C
Dougherty, Neil Joseph	PVT	B	PVT	B
Douglass, Timothy E	PFC	A		
Downs, James Armour	PVT	B	PFC	B
Dransart, Jules	PVT	D		
Driscoll, Gerald A	PVT	C	PVT	HQ
Drott, Leo			PVT	C

Battalion Roster

Name					
Dudenhoefer, Herbert B	PVT	B			
Dudenhoefer, Herbert B			PVT	B	
Duff, Joseph M	PVT	D	KIA OCT 10, 1918		★
Duke, Clarence	PVT	D	PFC	D	
Dulisse, Antonio	PVT	A	PVT	A	
Duncombe, Russell H	CORP	A			
Dunham, Eben Emil	PFC	B	PFC	B	
Dunn, Haram			PVT	D	
Dunn, Thomas P	PVT	D			
Dye, Curtis Alexander	PVT	B	DW OCT 6, 1918		★
Eagen, Francis J	PVT	D	PVT	D	
Eaglehouse, Frank P	PVT	D	PVT	D	
Earls, Sid			PVT	D	
Early, Joseph H			PFC	A	
Easha, Albert	PVT	A	PVT	A	
Ebisch, Ernest	COOK	B			
Eblen Charles C			PVT	D	
Echels, Joseph	MECH	D	MECH	D	
Edwards, Robert R	PVT	C	CORP	C	
Elber, Carl Christian	PVT	HQ	CORP	HQ	
Eldred, Herman Deleslie	PVT	HQ	PVT	ORD	
Eldridge, Raymond L	PVT	A	PFC	A	
Eliason, Oscar Alfred	PVT	B	PFC	B	
Elig, Henry A	PVT	C	PFC	C	
Eller, Peter Christ	PVT	B	PFC	B	
Enlow, John J	PVT	A	PVT	A	
Erickson, Gustaf	PVT	C	PVT	C	
Erra, Samuel K	PVT	C			
Erwin, Shirley W	PVT	A	CORP	A	
Espey, Eugene S	PFC	A	PFC	A	
Esposito, Angelo	PVT	A	PVT	A	
Evans, Charles W	PFC	D			
Evans, Daniel H	PVT	A	CORP	A	
Evans, Frazier Lowell			PVT	D	

Evans, John	PVT	C	PVT	C
Evans, Robert			WAG	HQ
Evans, William T	PVT	A	PFC	A
Everhart, Robert L	PVT	C	PVT	C
Everitt, Clarence J	PVT	C	PVT	C
Ewing, Charles R	COOK	A	COOK	A
Fadely, Joseph H	PVT	D		
Fairbanks, Robert L			PVT	D
Fales, Oscar A	PVT	D	PVT	D
Fee, Frank	1ST SGT	C	1ST SGT	C
Fegley, James W	PVT	C	PFC	C
Felix, Joseph Carl	COOK	B	COOK	B
Ferguson, George Sindorf	PVT	B	PVT	B
Ferraro, Jimy	PVT	D	PVT	D
Ferraro, Joe	PVT	D	PVT	D
Ferrell, Andrew J			PVT	D
Fetterman, Arnold E	CORP	C	PVT	C
Fetting, Henry A			PVT	C
Field, Lawrence W	PVT	A		
Filicky, Steve F	PVT	D	PVT	D
Filippo, John R	PVT	D	PVT	D
Finocchio, Mauro	PVT	D	PVT	D
Fish, Joseph H	PVT	D	PFC	D
Fisher, Damon Robert	SGT	B	SGT	B
Flanagan, Patrick J	SUPSGT	D	MESSGT	D
Flaugh, Lee B	MESS SGT	D	CORP	D
Fletcher, John F			PVT	D
Flohr, Paul F	PVT	C		
Flood, Terence			PVT	A
Foley, Oscar	MAJOR	HQ		
Ford, Frank J	PVT	C	PVT	C
Foresman, Paul A	PVT	D	CORP	D
Forrest, David P			PVT	A

Forrester, Louis L	PVT	C	CORP	C
Foster, Alvin C			PVT	B
Foust, Arthur A	PFC	C	PFC	C
Franz, Matthew J	PVT	D	PFC	D
Freno, Daniel F	PVT	C	SUPSGT	C
Frese, Frederick W			PVT	D
Frese, Marcus L			PVT	D
Frey, Anthony Tony	PFC	B	PVT	B
Friel, Edward J	aka Clark, Joseph T		PVT	MD
Frost, Horace C	PFC	D	SGT	D
Fulton, Ellis Giles	PVT	HQ		
Fulton, Frank E	PFC	A	PVT	A
Fulton, Howard E	PVT	A	PFC	A
Furness, Clifford H	PVT	A	PVT	A
Gable, Ralph A	PFC	C		
Galbreath, Harry Lohr	PVT	B	PVT	B
Galladay, Samuel Wesley	COOK	HQ	COOK	HQ
Gallagher, John Joseph	PVT	B	PVT	B
Gallagher, Joseph M	SGT	D	SGT	D
Garber, Lewis W	PVT	D	PFC	D
Gardner, Miles Hammon	PVT	B	PFC	B
Garman, Frederic			PVT	C
Garry, Joseph	PVT	D	PVT	D
Gay, Clarence C	MECH	C	MECH	C
Gay, Oscar W	PVT	D	PFC	D
Gearhart, Earl Russell	PVT	B	PVT	B
Geis, Joseph A	PVT	D	CORP	D
Gentile, Agostino A	PVT	C	PFC	C
Gerbracht, William M	SUPSGT	C	PVT	C
Geser, Frank Anthony	SGT	B	SGT	B
Gibbes, Edwin Hasp			PVT	B
Gibbons, Edward	PVT	D	PVT	D
Gilbert, Robert J	PVT	A		
Gilliland, Carl C	PVT	A	PFC	A

Gilson, Don Rodger	WAG	HQ	WAG	HQ
Glaze, James Aylma			PVT	B
Glenn, David Blanton			PVT	B
Goldring, Abe			PVT	C
Goldsboro, James C	PVT	D	SGT	D
Goodwin, Wilfred O			COOK	B
Gorsuch, Roy			PVT	B
Graham, Donald M	PVT	C	PVT	C
Green, John A	PVT	C		
Green, Louis R			PVT	C
Gregor, Fred J	PVT	D	PFC	D
Gregor, John W	PVT	C	PVT	C
Gribben, Hugh			PVT	B
Grief, David A	PVT	C	PVT	C
Grover, Vern L	SGT	D		
Growley, John	SGT	A		
Grubbs, Miller	PVT	B	PFC	B
Guadagno, Charlie	PVT	D	PFC	D
Guirovich, John A			PVT	D
Gyder, Charles Anthony	PVT	B	PVT	B
Gzik, Wladslaw	PFC	B	PFC	B
Haas, Joseph A	PVT	D		
Haber, Henry	PVT	A		
Hadden, Leon	PVT	D	PFC	D
Hagmann, Joseph John	PVT	B	PFC	B
Hain, Albert Edward	PFC	B	CORP	B
Hale, William H			2ND LT	C
Hall, Howard P	PVT	D		
Hall, Leonard J	PVT	A	PVT	A
Halloran, Er C	PVT	C	PVT	C
Hamilton, Minard	1ST LT	C		
Hamilton, Paul Barnes	PVT	B	PVT	B
Hamlin, John Edward	PVT	B	KIA OCT 5, 1918	★

Hamm, Raymond O	PVT	C	PFC	C	
Hammann, John R	PVT	D			
Hammond, John Dallas	PVT	B	CORP	B	
Hanna, John Graff	PVT	B	PVT	B	
Hanson, Alfred W	PVT	A			
Harris, Robert Lee	PVT	B	PVT	B	
Hart, William H	PFC	D	PVT	D	
Havens, Jerrymyer			PVT	D	
Hawthorne, Leo G	CORP	D			
Hazen, Carle B	BUGL	C			
Hedderick, George Thomas	PVT	HQ			
Heidt, Martin	MECH	D	PFC	D	
Heinly, William Marcus	PVT	B	PVT	B	
Heinonen, John A	PVT	A			
Helt, Charles Edwin	PVT	B	PVT	B	
Henderson, Clint Virgil			PVT	B	
Henley, Robert L			PVT	B	
Henry, Joseph F	PVT	A	PVT	A	
Henshey, John H	PVT	D	PVT	D	
Herbst, Charles E	PVT	C	PVT	C	
Herrmann, Charles P	PVT	C			
Herzing, John J	PVT	A	DW OCT 14, 1918		★
Hespelein, Joseph G	PVT	B	CORP	B	
Heuing, Henry J			PFC	C	
Hickey, Joseph	CORP	A			
Higgins, John L	PVT	C	MECH	C	
Hightower, Floyd			PVT	D	
Hilliker, Mark W	PFC	A	CORP	A	
Hines, Charles	COOK	A	PVT	A	
Hoburn, Roy	PVT	A	DW NOV 4, 1918		★
Hodges, Robert T			PFC	B	
Hoffman, Gerhard P	PVT	D	PVT	D	
Hoffman, Morton			PVT	D	
Hoggarth, Sydney E	PFC	C	PVT	C	

Name	Rank	Co.	Rank	Co.	
Holden, Burton Franklin	PVT	B			
Holewinski, Bronislaw	PVT	D	PVT	D	
Holland, Wallace B	PVT	C	KIA NOV 3, 1918		★
Holler, George F	PVT	D	PVT	HQ	
Holt, Jessie L			COOK	D	
Hoover, Fred	PVT	A	PFC	A	
Hoover, James Steaves H			PVT	C	
Hopp, William A	PVT	D	PVT	D	
Hornick, Eli	PVT	B	DD OCT 19, 1918		★
House, George E			PVT	A	
Huber, Henry			PVT	A	
Huether, Charles William	PVT	B			
Huff, Kyle E			PFC	HQ	
Hughson, Norman H	PVT	C	PFC	C	
Huidekoper, Prescott			MAJOR	HQ	
Hume, Alfred B	PVT	A	CORP	A	
Hummell, Clyde P	PFC	A			
Humphrey, Kenneth M	SGT	C	SGT	C	
Hundley, John	SGT	A			
Hunter, Albert R	PVT	C	PFC	C	
Hunter, John E	PVT	C	PVT	C	
Hurd, Walter Francis	PVT	B	PFC	B	
Hutchinson, Harry K	SGT	D			
Iannell, Pasquale	PVT	A	PVT	A	
Idzikowski, Frank	PVT	D	PVT	D	
Italia, Domenico	SDLR	C	SDLR	C	
Jacobs, Albert E			PVT	D	
Jahraus, William G	PFC	MD	SGT	MD	
Jakuboski, Frank	PVT	B	PFC	B	
Jamison, Archibald J	PVT	D			
Jarman, Bernard L	1ST LT	MD			
Jay, Raymond	WAG	HQ	WAG	HQ	
Jelbart, James F	PFC	A	PVT	A	

Name	Rank	Co	Rank	Co	
Johnson, Adolph	PVT	D	PFC	D	
Johnson, Chester			PVT	A	
Johnson, Edward F	PVT	A	PVT	HQ	
Johnson, Frank F			PVT	D	
Johnston, James S	PVT	C	PVT	C	
Johnston, Jordan A			PVT	A	
Johnston, Robert Lee			PVT	A	
Johnston, Wilbert Leroy	PVT	B	PFC	B	
Johnston, William	1ST SGT	D	1ST SGT	D	
Johnstone, Robert T	CORP	A	SGT	A	
Jones, Clyde F	PFC	A	KIA OCT 5, 1918		★
Jones, Edward S			PVT	A	
Jones, Rolla W	PVT	A	PVT	A	
Kaiser, Eugene F	PVT	C	PVT	C	
Kakis, Guss	PVT	A	PVT	A	
Kaminski, Henry F	SDLR	D	SDLR	D	
Kaszlewicz, William	PVT	D			
Kean, John	CAPT	C			
Kearney, Francis Edward	PVT	B	KIA OCT 4, 1918		★
Keirn, Henry P	PVT	A			
Kelley, Harry			DA JAN 10, 1918		★
Kelley, James Joseph			PVT	D	
Kelley, John A	PVT	C			
Kelly, Albert C			PVT	C	
Kemp, Herbert Beeson Jr	PFC	HQ	WAG	HQ	
Kendig, John W	PVT	C	PVT	C	
Kennedy, Arthur R			PVT	MD	
Kerr, George Bently	PVT	A	PVT	A	
Kertcher, Ernest Elias	PVT	B	PVT	B	
Kevoian, Siragan	PFC	D	PFC	D	
Killheffer, Robert Leslie	STBSGT	B	STBSGT	B	
Kilmore, John W	HRSR	D	HRSR	D	
Kimmel, Samuel M	PVT	D	PVT	D	
Kinder, Stewart Manning	PVT	B			

Name				
King, John S			PVT	D
King, John T	PVT	A	PVT	A
King, William H			PVT	D
King, William V	PVT	D	PVT	D
Kirchner, Harold Chester	1ST LT	B	CAPT	B
Kister, Kemps	PVT	HQ	WAG	HQ
Kleckner, Walter S	PVT	C		
Klitz, Verner J	PVT	A	PVT	A
Knoll, Raymond Fred	WAG	HQ	WAG	HQ
Knotwell, Harry R	PVT	C	PVT	C
Kraft, Harry	PFC	D	PFC	D
Kreider, Elias Lindemuth	PVT	B	PVT	B
Kreider, Ralph Edward	PVT	B	PVT	B
Kudlovik, Hendry	PVT	D	PFC	D
Kuhn, John C	PVT	A	PVT	A
Lahare, John			PVT	A
Lakari, Matthew	PVT	C	PFC	C
Lambeth, Charles E			PVT	D
Lammons, Frank B			PVT	A
Lane, Joseph B	PVT	A	PVT	A
Lantz, Clark	PVT	A	PVT	A
Larue, Oren Wilford			PVT	B
Lassiter, David A	PVT	MD		
Latko, John	PVT	A	PVT	A
Lauer, Robert W	PVT	D		
Laurie, Walter	PVT	C	CORP	C
Lavery, William Philip	PVT	B		
Lavigna, Vincenzo	PVT	D		
Lee, Earl			PVT	B
Lee, Erney			PVT	D
Leinhauser, Otto Paul	2ND LT	C	CAPT	C
Lemon, Thomas Edward	PVT	B	PFC	B
Lenkner, Walter E	PVT	D	PVT	D

Lennon, Lawrence J	PVT	D	PFC	D
Lentz, Henry Peter			PVT	C
Leonard, Samuel Peter	WAG	HQ		
Leonhart, Rodney H	PVT	A	PVT	A
Leslie, Harry James	PVT	HQ	PVT	HQ
Levell, Foster R	PVT	A	PVT	A
Levendosky, Andrew	WAG	HQ	WAG	HQ
Lewis, Leland Lynn	WAG	HQ	WAG	HQ
Lezuhovsky, John	PVT	B	KIA OCT 4, 1918	
Licklider, William H	PVT	B	PFC	B
Lindquist, Carl G	CORP	D	CORP	D
Lindquist, Gustaf A.E.			PVT	D
Linn, Darrell Mart	WAG	HQ	WAG	HQ
Lisby, Albert M	PVT	A		
Lockett, Jesse W	PVT	C	PFC	C
Loesch, Peter P	SGT	A	SUPSGT	A
Loew, John W	PVT	C	PVT	C
Lonas, Edward R	PVT	C	PVT	C
Long, Harry Miller	1ST SGT	B		
Lowe, Dorsie A	PVT	D	PVT	D
Lowery, Elick Albert			PVT	D
Loxiey, William C			PVT	D
Lubejewski, Joseph	PVT	D	PVT	D
Lubowicki, John F	PVT	D	PVT	D
Ludwick, Paul	SGT	HQ	STBSGT	HQ
Lunden, Walter Carl	2ND LT	A	1ST LT	A
Lunn, Arthur	PVT	D	PVT	D
Lutman, Edwin R	PVT	C	PVT	C
Luton, Paul Edward	PVT	B		
Lutz, Charles	PVT	D	PFC	D
Lynch, James A	PFC	D	MECH	D
Mack, Earl G	SGT	A	MESSGT	A
Mackey, Sidney Augustus	1ST LT	A		
Mackey, William H	PVT	A	PFC	A

MacWilliam, Alexander	SGT	B	2ND LT	B	
Mahoney, Timothy James	SGT	B			
Maimgren, Clarence			PVT	D	
Mainzer, Peter G	PFC	MD	PFC	MD	
Malinoski, Stanley	PVT	B	PFC	B	
Maloney, William C	PVT	C	CORP	C	
Mando, Frank	PVT	B	PFC	B	
Mando, Joseph	PFC	B	PFC	B	
Manion, John	PVT	A	KIA NOV 3, 1918		★
Manning, Job Palmer	PVT	B			
Manson, Harry S	SGT	A			
Maral, Joseph L			PVT	A	
Maras, Stanley L	PVT	D	CORP	D	
Marek, Frank			PVT	B	
Markiewicz, Joseph	PFC	D	PFC	D	
Marks, John Henry			PVT	A	
Marr, William W			PVT	D	
Marshall, George W	PVT	C	KIA AUG 16, 1918		★
Martin, Alfred W	PVT	D	PFC	D	
Martin, Joseph F			BUGL	C	
Martin, Robert A	PVT	C			
Martin, Sloan	PVT	D	PVT	D	
Martindale, Edward B	PVT	A	PFC	A	
Marty, John A	PVT	B	PFC	B	
Mason, Randolph Fitzhugh			KIA JUL 20, 1918		★
Mason, Roy C			PVT	D	
Mathews, Harry C	PVT	A	PVT	A	
Matson, Ernest L	COOK	C	PVT	C	
Mattison, McClure Claire	WAG	HQ	WAG	HG	
May, Earl Cecil	WAG	HQ			
Maynard, Harry Lee Jr	CAPT	B	CAPT	B	
Mays, Arthur L	PVT	C	CORP	C	
McAndrew, Joseph Francis	SGT	B			

McArdle, Cliffton Dean	CORP	B	CORP	B
McCafferty, John Thomas	PVT	B		
McCann, Mark	PVT	C	DW OCT 6, 1918	
McCauley, Harry D	PVT	D	PVT	D
McCauley, Thomas W	CORP	C	SGT	C
McClimans, Elmer Ellsworth			PVT	D
McCreight, Joe Clarence			PVT	C
McCulley, William W	PFC	D	PVT	D
McDonald, Clarence Odelle			PFC	HQ
McDonald, Jim			PVT	B
McDonald, John J	PVT	A	PVT	A
McDonald, Roy			PVT	D
McEachern, Charles J	WAG	HQ	WAG	HQ
McGonnell, Joseph S	CORP	C	CORP	C
McGovern, John G	PVT	D		
McGrew, Thomas H			PVT	C
McHan, John R			PVT	A
McKee, George Roush	WAG	HQ	WAG	HQ
McKenzie, Alex W			PVT	D
McKinney, Oren B	PVT	B	PVT	B
McLaughlin, Edward J	PFC	C	COOK	C
McLaughlin, John F	MECH	C	PVT	C
McLaughlin, William J	PFC	C	PVT	C
McPherson, Clifford C	SGT	D	SGT	D
Meinhart, Eirven	PVT	B	PVT	B
Menzie, Lowman E	PVT	A		
Metz, Norman W	PVT	A	PVT	HQ
Mieczkowski, Walter	PVT	D	PVT	D
Millas, Athansios V	PVT	C	COOK	C
Miller Elmer J	PVT	C	2ND LT	C
Miller, Harry Adam	PVT	B	PVT	B
Miller, John C	PVT	A	PFC	A
Miller, John Ray	PVT	A	PFC	A
Miller, Joseph	SGT	A	SGT	A

Miller, Vincent A	PVT	B		
Miller, William C			PVT	C
Milton, Mike			PVT	C
Mischler, Karl O	SGT	C	SGT	C
Mix, Frank E			PVT	A
Mobley, George	PVT	C	PVT	C
Mobley, Sircey Edwin			PVT	A
Mohler, George W			PVT	A
Mohrhoff, John D	PVT	D		
Molenock, Andrew J	PVT	C	CORP	C
Monaco, Anthony J	PVT	A	PFC	A
Monahan, Frank J	MESSGT	C	PVT	HQ
Moore, Clyde Ray	PVT	B	PFC	B
Moore, Fred J	MECH	D		
Moore, James H			PVT	A
Moore, John Forest			PVT	D
Moore, John H			PVT	C
Morgan, George Elmer			PVT	D
Morgan, Robert W			PVT	C
Morris, Mathew	PVT	B	PVT	B
Morrison, Johnson G	CORP	A	PVT	A
Morrow, Joseph H	PVT	D	PFC	D
Moyers, Virgil	PVT	B	PFC	B
Muck, Lawrence A	PVT	A	PFC	A
Mularski, John	SGT	A	SGT	A
Muldowney, William			PFC	B
Mullen, Martin L	PVT	A	PVT	A
Mulvey, James Herbert	PVT	B		
Munson, John N	PVT	D	HRSR	D
Mura, Stephen T	PVT	A		
Murphey, Joseph W			PVT	D
Murphy, Alphonso Basil	PVT	B		
Murphy, Charles Dayton	PVT	B	CORP	B

Battalion Roster

Name	Rank	Co	Rank	Co
Murphy, Daley J	PVT	C	PVT	C
Murray, Adam	PVT	A	PFC	A
Murray, George F	PVT	A	CORP	A
Murray, Glen E	PVT	D	PVT	D
Musse, Paul John			PVT	C
Myers, Albert	WAG	HQ	WAG	HQ
Myers, Wilbur R	PVT	A	PVT	A
Myers, William			PVT	A
Nami, Penfilio	COOK	C	COOK	C
Nash, Stephen	PFC	D	PFC	D
Naul, Jesse F			PVT	D
Neilson, John	PVT	C	SGT	C
Nesbit, Edward B			PVT	C
Neuroh, Milton E	CORP	A	CORP	A
Newbrough, Carl D	PVT	A	PVT	A
Newsham, Arthur Edward	WAG	HQ	WAG	HQ
Newson, Robert C			PFC	D
Nick, Clarence			PVT	A
Niebauer, George	PFC	C	PFC	C
Nieman, Felix			PVT	B
Nornhold, Blaine B	PVT	D	PVT	D
Nowaczyk, Mieczyslaw	PVT	D	PFC	D
Nutter, Jasper E	PVT	D	PVT	D
O'Brein, William T	SGT	D	2ND LT	D
O'Brien, Joseph P	PFC	MD	PFC	MD
Ocamb, John	PFC	B	CORP	B
Ochs, Harold Wilfred	PVT	B	PVT	B
O'Donnell, Louis B	PVT	C	PFC	C
O'Donnell, Luke J	PVT	D	PVT	D
O'Hara, Pete	PFC	A	PFC	A
Oliver, William Joe			PVT	B
O'Malley, Hubert R	PVT	C	PVT	C
O'Toole, John A	PVT	A	CORP	A
Owen, Earl F	PVT	D	PVT	D

Painter, James L	PVT	C		
Palmer, Lewis V	PFC	MD		
Papathanassion, Athanasios	PVT	D	PFC	D
Parish, Burris B			PVT	A
Park, William A	PVT	D		
Parker, Avery D			PVT	D
Parker, Edward R	PVT	D	PVT	D
Parker, Jay A	PVT	A	CORP	A
Parker, Lynn C	PFC	C	PFC	C
Parsons, George	STBSGT	D	STBSGT	D
Parsons, Joseph H	1ST LT	MD	KIA OCT 4, 1918	
Pasterick, John	PVT	C	PVT	C
Pastorius, Lloyd D	PVT	C	CORP	C
Patrick, Calvin H			PVT	D
Patton, Charles H	PVT	A	PFC	A
Paull, Leo L	PVT	D	CORP	D
Payne, Norval	PVT	A	PVT	A
Payne, Wesley John	PVT	B	CORP	B
Peake, Leon			PVT	C
Pearce, James Newton	PFC	B	SGT	B
Pearlman, Morris B	PVT	A	PVT	A
Peden, Robert A			PVT	C
Pendenza, Oreste	PVT	D	PVT	D
Perkins, Clinton R	PVT	C	PVT	C
Perry, Ambrose			PVT	A
Peterson, Peter	PFC	D		
Phillips, August John			PVT	B
Phillips, Williams H Jr			PVT	D
Pierce, Clyde E	PVT	A	PFC	A
Pierce, Lewis Wesley	PVT	B	PFC	B
Plants, Harry E	PVT	C	PFC	C
Plummer, Arlie Lee	PVT	B	PFC	B
Pollard, Richard C	PVT	C	PVT	C

Porter, John P	PFC	MD	PFC	MD	
Porter, Walter H	PVT	A	PFC	A	
Potts, Harry	PVT	C	PVT	C	
Powers, Albert Joseph	PVT	B			
Powers, Raymond W	PVT	A	PVT	A	
Prasnitz, Rudolph J	PVT	C	PVT	C	
Prendiville, Garrett			PFC	D	
Preston, William	1ST LT	A	CAPT	A	
Prindle, Ralph			PVT	A	
Pritchard, James Arthur	PVT	B	PVT	B	
Proper, Ward E	PVT	A	CORP	A	
Puliti, Carlo	PVT	A	PVT	A	
Purdey, William H	1ST SGT	A	STBSGT	A	
Pyland, Pearlie			PVT	D	
Quick, Croy D	PVT	C	PFC	C	
Quigley, William J	PFC	A			
Quinn, Edward	PVT	D	DD NOV 2, 1918		★
Rader, Lora W	PVT	MD	DW OCT 4, 1918		★
Ragen, Arthur D	PFC	D	PVT	D	
Ragen, John F	PVT	C	PVT	C	
Ralston, Sumner L	PVT	A	PFC	A	
Ray, Anthony Joseph	PVT	B	PVT	B	
Ray, Charles E	SGT	C	SGT	C	
Reed, Harry	PVT	A	PVT	A	
Reed, Thomas	PVT	A	CORP	A	
Reetz, Anton Felix	PVT	HQ	SGTMAJ	HQ	
Reeves, Clarence J			PVT	C	
Reeves, Robert G			PVT	C	
Reiter, Sidney Howard	PVT	B	KIA OCT 5, 1918		★
Restivo, Dominic	PVT	D	PVT	D	
Revelis, George J			PVT	D	
Reynolds, Earl C	CAPT	MD	CAPT	MD	
Rice, Frank D	PVT	A	PFC	A	
Rich, Arnold Hoyer	2ND LT	C			

Richardson, William Emanuel	2ND LT	A	1ST LT	C
Richie, Frank P	PFC	C		
Rifley, Harry Ulysses	PVT	B	PFC	B
Ristife, Gaetano	PVT	B		
Ritzel, William T	PVT	A	PVT	A
Robb, Oscar J	CORP	A	SGT	A
Roberts, John H	PVT	A	PVT	A
Robinson, Neil C	SGT	C		
Roche, Lloyd E	COOK	A	PVT	A
Roche, Thomas B	1ST LT	HQ		
Roe, Hugh B	PVT	C	PVT	C
Rogers, Mattie E			PVT	D
Roller, Francis Oliver	2ND LT	B		
Rolls, Ben	CORP	D	DD OCT 23, 1918	
Rose, Joseph S	PVT	A	PFC	A
Rosencrans, Forrest Orville	SGT	B	SGT	B
Ross, Charles H			PFC	MD
Ross, Donald Wilson	PVT	B	PFC	B
Ross, Wilbur D	CORP	D	PFC	D
Ross, William J	PVT	A	PVT	A
Rote, Robert	PVT	A	PFC	A
Rucker, Claude L	PVT	D	CORP	D
Rusche, Ben			PVT	C
Rusche, John B			PVT	D
Sanders, Robert H			PVT	B
Sandifer, Ollie M			PVT	C
Sandom, Edwin	PVT	B	CORP	B
Saxton, Ray Herbert	HRSR	B	SGT	
Schall, Allen Bernard	2ND LT	D	2ND LT	D
Scharrer, Raymond F	CORP	A	CORP	A
Schauerman, Fred J	PVT	D	PVT	D
Schauerman, Henry Peter	PVT	B	PFC	B
Schemeck, Stephen J	SGT	D	SGT	D

Name	Rank	Co.	Rank	Co.	
Scherrer, Frank X	PFC	C	PVT	C	
Schillinger, Joseph George	SGT	B	MESSGT	B	
Schillinger, Raymond Fred	COOK	B	COOK	B	
Schlecht, Andrew	PVT	B	PFC	B	
Schmidt, Carl E	PVT	A	PVT	A	
Schmitt, William Roy	CORP	HQ			
Schneitter, Theodore F			1ST LT	D	
Schraeder, Karl Fred	BUGL	B	BUGL	B	
Schuda, Ernest Joseph	MECH	B	MECH	B	
Schultz, Louis	COOK	D	PVT	D	
Schwartz, Charles John	SUPSGT	B	SGT	B	
Seacrist, Lester Francis	BUGL	B	BUGL	B	
Sechler, George W	PVT	C	PVT	C	
Seeley, Floyd W	PVT	A	KIA OCT 5, 1918		★
Seelinger, George William	PVT	B	HRSR	B	
Seidel, Joseph	PVT	MD	PVT	MD	
Semuel, Milton	PFC	C	PFC	C	
Seubert, Joseph	PVT	D	PVT	D	
Seybert, Jesse	PFC	C	SUPSGT	C	
Shackelford, Richard S	SGT	MD			
Shade, George C	PVT	A	PFC	A	
Shannon, Clare A	PVT	D			
Shapira, Isidore	PVT	A	PVT	A	
Sharrer, Earl F	PFC	D	PFC	D	
Shaw, Walter B	PFC	A			
Shepherd, Albert	PVT	C			
Shepherd, James W			PVT	D	
Sherwood, Percy Heroy	1ST LT	HQ	1ST LT	HQ	
Shields, Gordon	PVT	C			
Shirey, Frederick, W	PVT	C	PFC	C	
Shirk, Lawrence G	PVT	D	COOK	D	
Shulgold, Jacob	PVT	C	2ND LT	C	
Shurm, Charles D	PVT	C	PVT	C	
Siefert, Louie E	PVT	C	KIA AUG 16, 1918		★

Silvaggi, Giacinto	PVT	C	PVT	C
Silverstein, Jack	PVT	D	PVT	D
Simpson, James			CORP	C
Skonieczka, Bronislaus K	SGT	D	SGT	D
Slizewski, Anthony S	PFC	B	CORP	B
Smith, Charles Edward	WAG	HQ	WAG	HQ
Smith, Clifford Allison	CORP	B		
Smith, Earl	PVT	C	PVT	C
Smith, Emanuel A	PVT	C	PVT	C
Smith, Frank C	PVT	A	PFC	A
Smith, John R	PVT	D	PFC	D
Smith, Leslie	PVT	C	PFC	C
Smith, Theodore William	WAG	HQ	WAG	HQ
Smith, William G	PVT	D		
Snyder, Bert Thayer	PVT	B	PFC	B
Snyder, Rufus E	PVT	D	PFC	D
Sokolove, Louis	PVT	B		
Spagnol, Jacob	PVT	A	PVT	A
Speacht, Eugene P	PVT	D	PVT	D
Spiro, Leon W	PVT	MD	DA DEC 15, 1918	
Spoon, Frank E	SGT	D	SGT	D
St. George, Fred A	PVT	D	PVT	D
Stanton, Emory			PVT	A
Steele, Wesley Cozzens	2ND LT	B	1ST LT	B
Steimer, James Patrick	PVT	B	PFC	B
Steimer, Leonard Roman	PVT	B	PFC	B
Steinford, Frank V	PVT	C	PVT	C
Stemplewski, Joseph	PVT	D		
Stenger, Frank E	PFC	D	SGT	D
Stevens, Paul E	PVT	C	PVT	C
Stewart, Edward H	PFC	D	CORP	D
Stewart, Floyd W	PVT	C	PVT	C
Stewart, Robert E	PVT	C	PVT	C

Stewart, Warren Trusdell	2ND LT	A	CAPT	A
Stillman, Paul W	SGT	A		
Stingle, Leroy H	PVT	A	PVT	A
Stitzlein, Gus H			PVT	A
Stoddart, Robert Stone	1ST LT	C	CAPT	C
Stolte, Wilfred Dingeldein	PVT	HQ		
Stough, Francis S	PVT	D	PVT	D
Strailman, Francis Orlando Jr	2ND LT	B	2ND LT	B
Stromer, Harry J	PVT	D	PFC	D
Stuhlfaut, Walter E	CORP	C	KIA OCT 5, 1918	★
Stump, Henry T	PVT	A	COOK	A
Sullivan, Leo John	PFC	B	PFC	B
Sumrall, Willie			PVT	C
Suriano, Saverio	PVT	D	PFC	D
Sutton, Lloyd L	PVT	A	HRSR	A
Swain, Homer L			PVT	C
Swanson, Edwin	COOK	C	MECH	C
Swanson, Ernest S	CORP	C	PVT	C
Swanson, Ralph B	PVT	A		
Swartz, George W	PFC	C	CORP	C
Swift, Leo Denyil	WAG	HQ	WAG	HQ
Szczutkowski, Bernard J	CORP	D	SGT	D
Taylor, Calvin J	PFC	A		
Terry, Lonnie L	PVT	C	PVT	C
Thixton, Homer A			PVT	B
Thomas, William George	CAPT	D	CAPT	D
Thorne, Gilbert George Jr	2ND LT	C	2ND LT	C
Thornhill, Thomas Murrell	2ND LT	D	1ST LT	D
Tibbs, Walter S			PVT	C
Titus, George Oliver	WAG	HQ	WAG	HQ
Titus, Ray	PVT	A	PVT	A
Tompkins, Frank McMurray	2ND LT	D		
Toohey, William L	PFC	C	PFC	C
Toussaint, Eugene	PVT	D		

Townsend, Ralph B	PVT	C	PFC	C	
Tucker, Owen C			PVT	B	
Turovich, Walter	CORP	C	SGT	C	
Tyczkowski, Alois	CORP	D			
Tysraczyk, Joseph C	PVT	A	PFC	A	
Ubinger, Fred Charles	PVT	B	PVT	B	
Vagiakos, John	PFC	C	PFC	C	
Valle, Sam	PVT	B	PVT	B	
Vamos, Andrew V	PVT	A	PVT	A	
Vance, George			PVT	C	
Vandervolt, Levi J	PVT	A	PFC	A	
Veazey, Harry H	PVT	A	PVT	A	
Veit, John G	PVT	A	PVT	A	
Vergilio, Joseph L	SGT	C	PFC	C	
Vermeire, Charles	PVT	A	PFC	A	
Vetrone, Fred	PFC	C	CORP	C	
Vincent, John Z	PVT	C			
Volkers, Robert J	PVT	C	PFC	C	
Wade, Francis J	CORP	D	PVT	D	
Wagner, Eugene Clarkson	PVT	B	PVT	B	
Walker, Byron J	PVT	C	PFC	C	
Ward, Bernard	PVT	D	PVT	D	
Ward, Jared	PVT	C	PVT	C	
Ward, William Frederick			PVT	B	
Warmbrodt, Frederick A	PVT	C	DW OCT 8, 1918		★
Warner, Moses C	PVT	A	PVT	A	
Wasielewski, John Anthony			DD APR 25, 1918		★
Wasko, Michael John	PVT	B			
Watkins, Evan	PVT	C	PVT	C	
Watkins, John Thomas			PVT	B	
Watson, James	PVT	D	PVT	D	
Weaver, Frederick E	PVT	A			
Weaver, Walter William	WAG	HQ	WAG	HQ	

Webber, Justin	PVT	A		
Weber, Henry	PVT	B	PFC	B
Weed, Lewis, M	PVT	D	PVT	D
Weeks, Benjamin R	SGT	A	1ST SGT	A
Welk, Leroy Edmond	PFC	HQ	PFC	HQ
Wentling, Manual C	PVT	C	PVT	C
Werling, Albert			PVT	B
Westman, Albert			PVT	B
Wetsel, James P			PVT	MD
Wheatly, Adlai S	PVT	C	PFC	C
Wheeling, Alfred A	PFC	A	SGT	A
Whetsell, Arthur G	PVT	D	PFC	D
White, Frank C			2ND LT	B
Whitehead, Dave Barness			PVT	A
Whitten, Harold E			2ND LT	A
Wike, Jesse R			PFC	MD
Wilcox, Robert Burns	PFC	B	DW OCT 31, 1918	★
Wilcox, Robert M	PVT	A	PFC	A
Wilkinson, Edgar McKinley	PVT	HQ		
Williams, Charles A	PVT	C	PVT	C
Williams, Sidney A	SGT	A	SGT	A
Wilson, Daniel	PVT	D	CORP	D
Wilson, Elmer J	PVT	C	CORP	C
Wilson, Herbert H	PVT	C	KIA OCT 5, 1918	★
Wilson, James A			PVT	B
Wilson, John Craig	PFC	HQ	CORP	HQ
Wilson, Walter P	PVT	C	PVT	C
Wiltcher, Burton			PVT	C
Wiltcher, Lee			PVT	C
Windham, William C			PVT	C
Winterbottom, Clifford R	PVT	A	PFC	A
Withem, George G			PVT	C
Wladyslaw, Krakowski	PVT	D	PVT	D
Wolfe, Olieander D	PVT	C	SGT	C

Woodard, Kersey Mendenhall	SGT	HQ		
Woods, Stephen			PVT	D
Woods, William	SGT	D	SGT	D
Wright, Jesse	PVT	D	PVT	D
Wurster, Charley	PVT	A	PVT	A
Wyatt, Antone R			PVT	A
Yanigan, Andrew Carl	PVT	B	PVT	B
Yaple, Claud E	PVT	A	PVT	A
Yarnell, William G	PVT	A		
Yartz, Henry F	CORP	D	SGT	D
Young, Arthur W	SGT	A	SGT	A
Young, George O			CORP	C
Youngman, Dee H			PVT	D
Younkins, Charles C	CORP	C	CORP	C
Yuengert, Martin A	CORP	D		
Zahner, Roy Gustave	CORP	B	CORP	B
Zahniser, Ralph N	PFC	A	PFC	A
Zaitsov, Alex	PFC	D		
Zierden, Ernest B	SGT	C	PVT	C
Zimmer, Arthur George	PFC	B	PFC	B
Zimmer, John	PVT	A	PFC	A
Zimmerman, Frederick W			PVT	D
Ziroli, Alfonso	BUGL	C	BUGL	C

BIBLIOGRAPHY

A list of all the sources pertaining to the research of the history of the 313th Machine Gun Battalion and their place in the Great War would be endless. The principal resources for this publication are listed here. I am greatly indebted to all those who shared their personal collections and material with me.

80th Division, Summary of Operations in the World War. Washington: U.S. G.P.O, 1944.

"313th M. G. Battalion has reunion at Erie." *The News-Herald* 21 Aug. 1923: p.6, *Newspapers.com* Web. 15 Aug. 2015.

Affantranger, Alfred C., *Overseas Record of the 313th Machine Gun Battalion, 80th Division.* Sennevoy le Bas, France, n.p., 1918.

"Another Warren Boy, Louie Siefert is Killed in Action in France a telegram states." *Warren Evening Times* 29 Aug 1919: p.4, *Newspapers.com* Web. *Warren Times Mirror* 19 Sep. 2017.

Burial File, Correspondence, Reports, Telegrams, Applications, and Other Papers Relating to Burials of Service Personnel, 1/1/1915 - 12/31/1939, Record Group 92: Records of the Office of the Quartermaster General, 1774 - 1985, National Archives at St. Louis, St. Louis, MO.

"Navy Official Statement On Results Of The Raid." *Chicago Daily Tribune* 4 Jun. 1918: p.1, *Newspapers.com* Web. 20 Sep. 2017.

"City Was Tensely Interested In The Draft Bulletins," *The Titusville Herald* 21 July 1917: p.1, *Newspapers.com* Web. 19 Sep. 2017.

Clarkson, Ralph. *Soldier's Diary*, Collection of Joyce Clarkson-Veilleux.

Craighill, Edley. *History of the 317th infantry.* Tours: Imprimerie Deslis frères et cie, 1919.

Company Records, Records of the 313th Machine Gun Battalion, Records of combat divisions, Record Group 120, Records of the American Expeditionary Forces (World War I), National Archives at College Park, College Park, MD.

Crowell, Thomas I. *History of the 313th Field Artillery U.S.A.* New York: Rand McNally & Company, 1920.

Devir, Joseph P. *War History of 313th M.G.Bn. Co A 80th DIV.* Paris : n.p., 1919.

"Draft Begun This Morning." *New Castle News* 20 Jul 1917: p.1. *Newspapers.com* Web. 19 Sep. 2017.

"Erie Machine Gun Battalion in Kane on Homeward Trip." *The Kane Republican* 13 Jun. 1919: p.1, *Newspapers.com* Web. 21 Feb. 2017.

Ferrell, Robert H. *America's Deadliest Battle: Meuse-Argonne, 1918.* Lawrence: University Pr Of Kansas, 2012.

Furr, Herman R, R A. Horner, W L. Lukens, and A R. Merritt. *314 Machine Gun Battalion History, Blue Ridge (80th) Division.* Published by the Officers and men of the battalion, 1919.

Grant, Amy G. *Letters from Armageddon: A Collection Made During the World War.* Boston: Houghton Mifflin Co, 1930.

Hamilton, *Minard. Papers 1913-1930,* Hoover Institution Archives: Stanford, CA.

"Harry Kelley Is Killed By Train At Richmond VA." *The Titusville Herald* 11 Jan. 1918: p.1, *Newspapers.com* Web. 6 Dec. 2015.

"Head of Insulator Co Ends His Life." *The Gazette and Daily* 1 Apr 1939: p.8, *Newspapers.com* Web. 6 Jul. 2015.

Headquarters Correspondence, Records of the 313th Machine Gun Battalion, Records of combat divisions, Record Group 120, Records of the American Expeditionary Forces (World War I), National Archives at College Park, College Park, MD.

Hemenway, Frederic V. *History of the Third Division, United States Army, in the World War: For the Period, December 1, 1917, to January 1, 1919*. Andernach-on-the-Rhine, Cologne: Printed by M. Dumont Schauberg, 1919.

History of the 318th Infantry Regiment of the 80th Division, 1917-1919. Richmond: The William Byrd Press Inc., 1919.

Holland, Wallace Ben, *Letters*, Collection of Jon Corklin.

Jarman, Bernard L., *Letter to James E. Jarman*, Collection of John H. Armstrong III.

"Joe Duff Chosen To Coach Pitt's Football Team." *The Pittsburgh Press* 10 Apr.1913: p.22, *Newspapers.com* Web. 31 Jan. 2016.

Kitts, Miles B., *Letter to Alexander MacWilliam*, Collection of Alexander MacWilliam Jr.

Kean, John, *Family Letters Collection at Liberty Hall Museum*, Union, New Jersey.

Lengel, Edward G. *To Conquer Hell: The Meuse-Argonne, 1918*. New York: Henry Holt and Company, 2013.

Leinhauser, Otto Paul, *Journal*, Collection of Otto Paul Leinhauser III.

"Leinhauser Quartet Gives 91 Work Years at Sun Ship." *Chester Times* 12 Nov 1942: p.19. *Newspapers.com* Web. *Delaware County Times*, 21 Feb. 2017.

"Lieutenant Mason Is Killed In France." *The Richmond Times Dispatch* 29 Aug. 1918: p.2, *Newspapers.com* Web. 23 Feb. 2017.

Lukens, Edward C., and E. McClure Rouzer. *A Blue Ridge Memoir and The Last Drive.* Baltimore: Sun Print. 1922.

Luxford, J. H., *With the machine gunners in France and Palestine: The official history of the New Zealand Machine Corps in the Great War 1914-1918.* Uckfield, UK: Naval and Military Press. 2003.

"Men Reported In Good Shape." *The Pittsburgh Press* 7 Sept 1913: p.17, *Newspapers.com* Web. 31 Jan. 2016.

Miller, Joseph M., *Soldiers Diary and Notebook,* Collection of Lewis McComb Jr.

"New Freedom Firm Announces Increase." *The Gazette and Daily* 1 May 1937: p.1, *Newspapers.com* Web. 20 Nov. 2015.

Pennsylvania, Death Certificates, 1906-1963. [Ancestry.com. database on-line]. Provo, UT, USA: Ancestry.com Operations, Inc. 2014.

Pennsylvania, WWI Veterans Service and Compensation Files, 1917-1919, 1934-1948 [Ancestry.com. database on-line]. Provo, UT, USA: Ancestry.com Operations, Inc., 2015.

Ray, Charles E., *A History of the Ray Family and the Mead Family,* 1974. Collection of Carol Porch.

Ryman, Herr Charles. *Company F History, 319th infantry.* Flemington, NJ. 1920.

Stultz, Russell L, and Lee S. Anthony. *History of the Eightieth Division, A.E.F. in World War I.* Roanoke, VA: Descendants of the 80th Division Veterans, 2004.

"Soldiers at Camp Lee Join in Celebration." *The Times Dispatch* 19 Oct. 1917: p.1, *Newspapers.com* Web. 23 Feb. 2017.

Thomas, William George, *William George Thomas Letters*, #1792-z, Southern Historical Collection, The Wilson Library, University of North Carolina at Chapel Hill.

"Two Machine Gun Battalions of 80th Landed at Boston." *The Gazette Times* 8 June 1919: p.1, *Newspapers.com* Web. *Pittsburgh-Post Gazette* 20 Nov. 2015.

"Union City Boy." *Union City Times-Enterprise* 16 Dec. 1918: p.1. microfiche Union City Public Library, Union City, PA.

U.S., World War I Draft Registration Cards, 1917-1918, [Ancestry.com. database on-line]. Provo, UT, USA: Ancestry.com Operations Inc., 2005.

U.S., Army Transport Service, Passenger Lists, 1910-1939 [Ancestry.com. database on-line]. Lehi, UT, USA: Ancestry.com Operations, Inc., 2016.

"US Seaplane NC4 Arriving at Azores Island." *The Gazette Times* 8 Jun. 1919: p.10, *Newspapers.com* Web. *Pittsburgh-Post Gazette* 3 May 2017.

West Virginia. *West Virginia blue book*. Charleston: publisher not identified. 1935

Wilson, Page. *Carnage & Courage: A Memoir of Fdr, the Kennedys, and World War II.*, Yucca Publishing: New York, 2015.

Wise, Jennings Cropper. *The Great Crusade. A chronicle of the late war.* Dial Press: New York. 1930

Young, Rush S. *Over the top with the 80th: 1917-1919*. Place of publication not identified: Rush S. Young, 1933.

PHOTOGRAPH SOURCES

BATTALION at Camp Lee VA, *Photograph* Front Cover, 1918. Collection of Lewis McComb Jr.

CAPETS, Andrew A. *Photograph* Back Cover, 1919. Collection of Victor Capets.

CAPETS, Andrew A. *Photograph* Interior, c. 1919. Collection of the author.

CLARKSON, Ralph, *Photograph*, c. 1918. Collection of Joyce Clarkson-Veilleux.

DUFF, Joseph Miller Jr., *Photograph*, 1914. *The Owl*, University of Pittsburgh, 1916. University of Pittsburgh Digital Research Library, Pittsburgh PA, 2006.

HAMILTON, Minard. *Passport Photograph*, 1919. National Archives and Records Administration (NARA); Washington D.C.; NARA Series: Special Passport Applications, 1914-1925; Box #: 4201; Volume #: Volume 14: Military, Civilian, Federal Employees and Dependents. Source: *U.S. Passport Applications, 1795-1925*, Ancestry.com Operations, Inc. Provo, UT, USA Published 2007.

HOLLAND, Wallace Ben. *Photograph*, c. 1917. Collection of Jon Corklin.

HUIDEKOPER, Prescott Foster. *Photograph*. Collection of Page Wilson. Courtesy Ariel Dougherty.

JARMAN, Bernard Lipscomb. *Photograph*, c. 1918. Collection of John H. Armstrong III.

KEAN, John. *Photograph*, c. 1919. Liberty Hall Museum at Kean University, Union, NJ. Image posted to @libertyhallmuseum on Facebook June 14, 2017.

LEINHAUSER, Otto P. *Photograph,* c. 1918. Camp Lee, VA. Collection of Otto P. Leinhauser III

MacWILLIAM, Alexander. *Photographs of Recipients of Allied Valor Awards, 1917 – 1919.* Record Group 120, Records of the American Expeditionary Forces (World War I), National Archives at College Park, College Park, MD.

MILLER, Joseph Mitchell. *Photograph,* c. 1918. Collection of Lewis McComb Jr.

PARSONS, Joseph Harold. *Photograph,* 1916. Senior Portrait University of Pennsylvania. Collection of Dr. Christopher Thomas.

RAY, Charles Earnest. *Photograph,* c. 1918. Collection of Carol Ray Porch.

REUNION. *Photograph,* 1975. 55th Reunion of the 313th Machine Gun Battalion, Erie, PA. Collection of the author.

SEIFERT, Louie Elisha. *Photograph,* c. 1918. *Warren County Boys Over There,* published by the Warren Historical Company, Warren, PA, 1918.

THOMAS, George William, *Senior Portrait,* 1909. *Yackety Yack,* University of North Carolina at Chapel Hill, Chapel Hill, NC. Internet Archive ID yacketyyackseria1909univ Site accessed: 26 Sep. 2017

68482324R00202

Made in the USA
Lexington, KY
12 October 2017